DARK AGES

D0690959

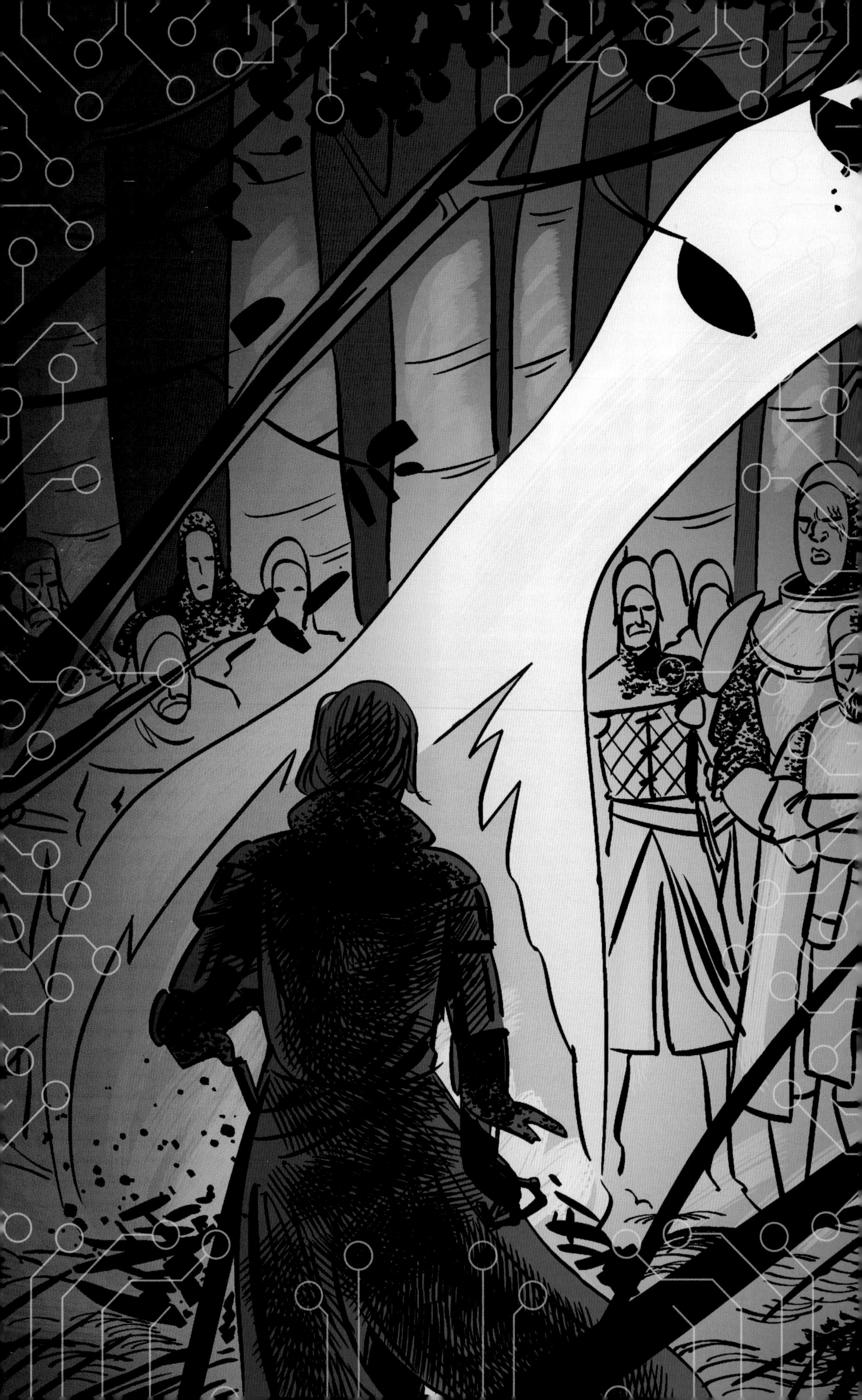

DARK AGES

SCRIPT
DAN ABNETT

ART, LETTERING, AND COVER ART
I. N. J. CULBARD

DARK HORSE BOOKS

PRESIDENT & PUBLISHER **MIKE RICHARDSON**
EDITOR **DANIEL CHABON**
ASSISTANT EDITOR **IAN TUCKER**
DESIGNER **BRENNAN THOME**
DIGITAL PRODUCTION **RYAN JORGENSEN**

NEIL HANKERSON EXECUTIVE VICE PRESIDENT **TOM WEDDLE** CHIEF
FINANCIAL OFFICER **RANDY STRADLEY** VICE PRESIDENT OF PUBLISHING
MICHAEL MARTENS VICE PRESIDENT OF BOOK TRADE SALES
SCOTT ALLIE EDITOR IN CHIEF **MATT PARKINSON** VICE PRESIDENT
OF MARKETING **DAVID SCROGGY** VICE PRESIDENT OF PRODUCT
DEVELOPMENT **DALE LaFOUNTAIN** VICE PRESIDENT OF INFORMATION
TECHNOLOGY **DARLENE VOGEL** SENIOR DIRECTOR OF PRINT, DESIGN,
AND PRODUCTION **KEN LIZZI** GENERAL COUNSEL **DAVEY ESTRADA**
EDITORIAL DIRECTOR **CHRIS WARNER** SENIOR BOOKS EDITOR **DIANA
SCHUTZ** EXECUTIVE EDITOR **CARY GRAZZINI** DIRECTOR OF PRINT AND
DEVELOPMENT **LIA RIBACCHI** ART DIRECTOR **CARA NIECE** DIRECTOR OF
SCHEDULING **MARK BERNARDI** DIRECTOR OF DIGITAL PUBLISHING

DARK AGES ™ & © 2014, 2015 DAN ABNETT AND I. N. J. CULBARD. ALL OTHER MATERIAL, UNLESS OTHERWISE SPECIFIED, ™ &
© 2015 DARK HORSE COMICS, INC. DARK HORSE BOOKS® AND THE DARK HORSE LOGO ARE REGISTERED TRADEMARKS OF
DARK HORSE COMICS, INC. ALL RIGHTS RESERVED. NO PORTION OF THIS PUBLICATION MAY BE REPRODUCED OR TRANSMIT-
TED, IN ANY FORM OR BY ANY MEANS, WITHOUT THE EXPRESS WRITTEN PERMISSION OF DARK HORSE COMICS, INC. NAMES,
CHARACTERS, PLACES, AND INCIDENTS FEATURED IN THIS PUBLICATION EITHER ARE THE PRODUCT OF THE AUTHOR'S IMAG-
INATION OR ARE USED FICTITIOUSLY. ANY RESEMBLANCE TO ACTUAL PERSONS (LIVING OR DEAD), EVENTS, INSTITUTIONS, OR
LOCALES, WITHOUT SATIRIC INTENT, IS COINCIDENTAL.

THIS VOLUME COLLECTS **DARK AGES** #1–#4.

PUBLISHED BY DARK HORSE BOOKS | A DIVISION OF DARK HORSE COMICS, INC. | 10956 SE MAIN STREET | MILWAUKIE, OR 97222

FIRST EDITION: MARCH 2015
ISBN 978-1-61655-602-0

1 3 5 7 9 10 8 6 4 2
PRINTED IN CHINA

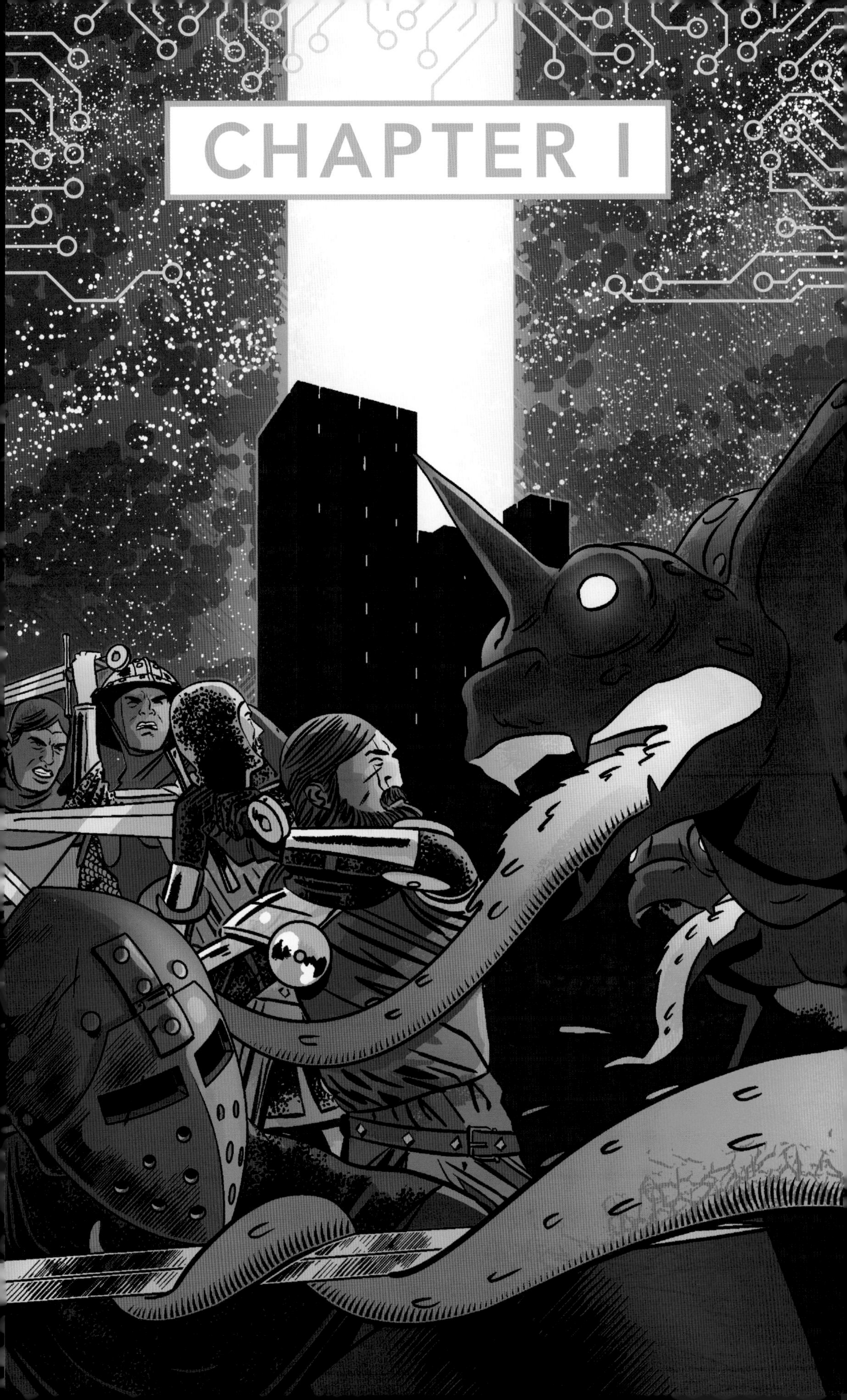
CHAPTER I

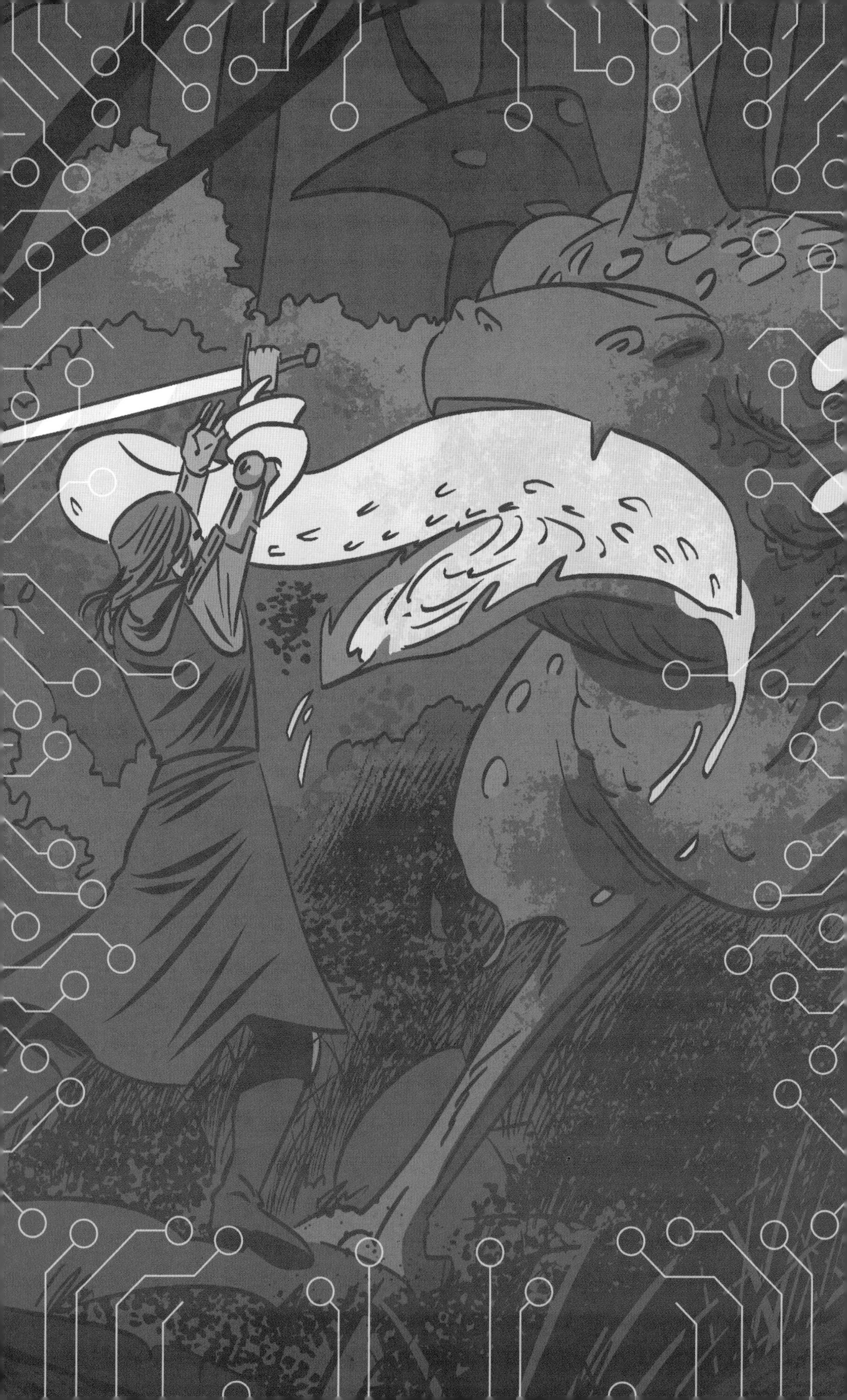

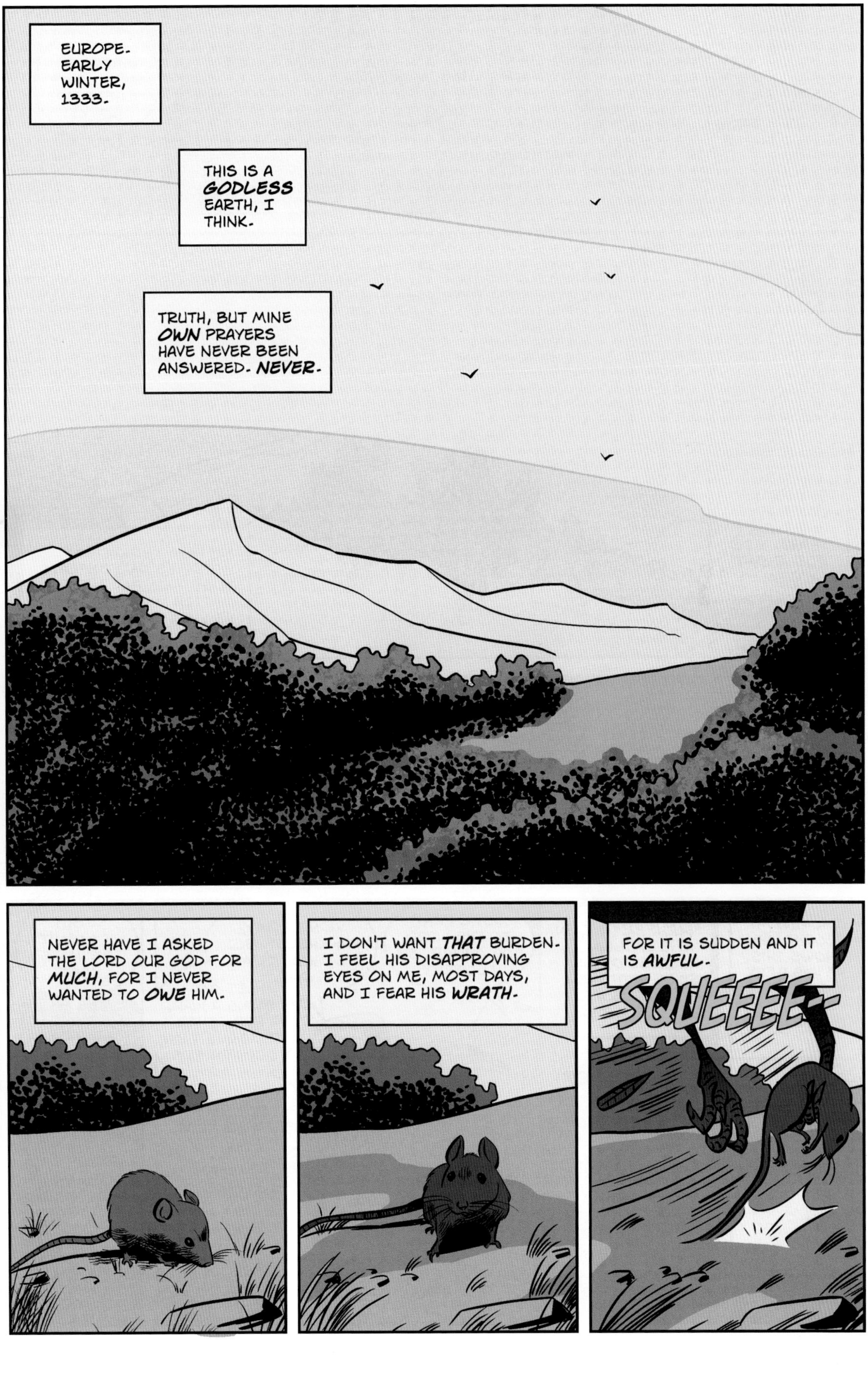
EUROPE. EARLY WINTER, 1333.
THIS IS A GODLESS EARTH, I THINK.
TRUTH, BUT MINE OWN PRAYERS HAVE NEVER BEEN ANSWERED. NEVER.
NEVER HAVE I ASKED THE LORD OUR GOD FOR MUCH, FOR I NEVER WANTED TO OWE HIM.
I DON'T WANT THAT BURDEN. I FEEL HIS DISAPPROVING EYES ON ME, MOST DAYS, AND I FEAR HIS WRATH.
FOR IT IS SUDDEN AND IT IS AWFUL.
SQUEEEEE

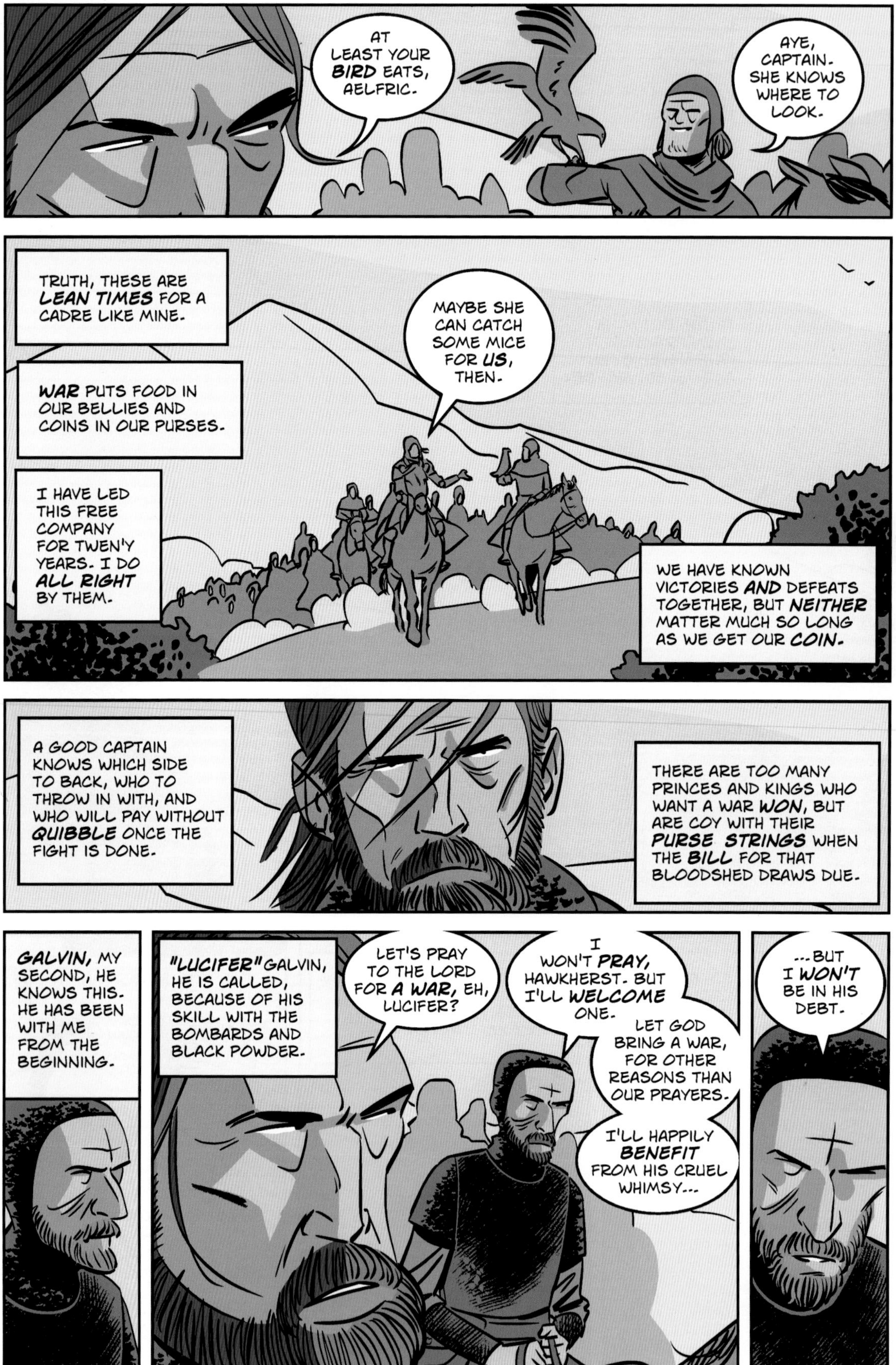

AT LEAST YOUR BIRD EATS, AELFRIC.
AYE, CAPTAIN. SHE KNOWS WHERE TO LOOK.
TRUTH, THESE ARE LEAN TIMES FOR A CADRE LIKE MINE.
WAR PUTS FOOD IN OUR BELLIES AND COINS IN OUR PURSES.
MAYBE SHE CAN CATCH SOME MICE FOR US, THEN.
I HAVE LED THIS FREE COMPANY FOR TWEN'Y YEARS. I DO ALL RIGHT BY THEM.
WE HAVE KNOWN VICTORIES AND DEFEATS TOGETHER, BUT NEITHER MATTER MUCH SO LONG AS WE GET OUR COIN.
A GOOD CAPTAIN KNOWS WHICH SIDE TO BACK, WHO TO THROW IN WITH, AND WHO WILL PAY WITHOUT QUIBBLE ONCE THE FIGHT IS DONE.
THERE ARE TOO MANY PRINCES AND KINGS WHO WANT A WAR WON, BUT ARE COY WITH THEIR PURSE STRINGS WHEN THE BILL FOR THAT BLOODSHED DRAWS DUE.
GALVIN, MY SECOND, HE KNOWS THIS. HE HAS BEEN WITH ME FROM THE BEGINNING.
"LUCIFER" GALVIN, HE IS CALLED, BECAUSE OF HIS SKILL WITH THE BOMBARDS AND BLACK POWDER.
LET'S PRAY TO THE LORD FOR A WAR, EH, LUCIFER?
I WON'T PRAY, HAWKHERST. BUT I'LL WELCOME ONE.
LET GOD BRING A WAR, FOR OTHER REASONS THAN OUR PRAYERS.
I'LL HAPPILY BENEFIT FROM HIS CRUEL WHIMSY...
...BUT I WON'T BE IN HIS DEBT.

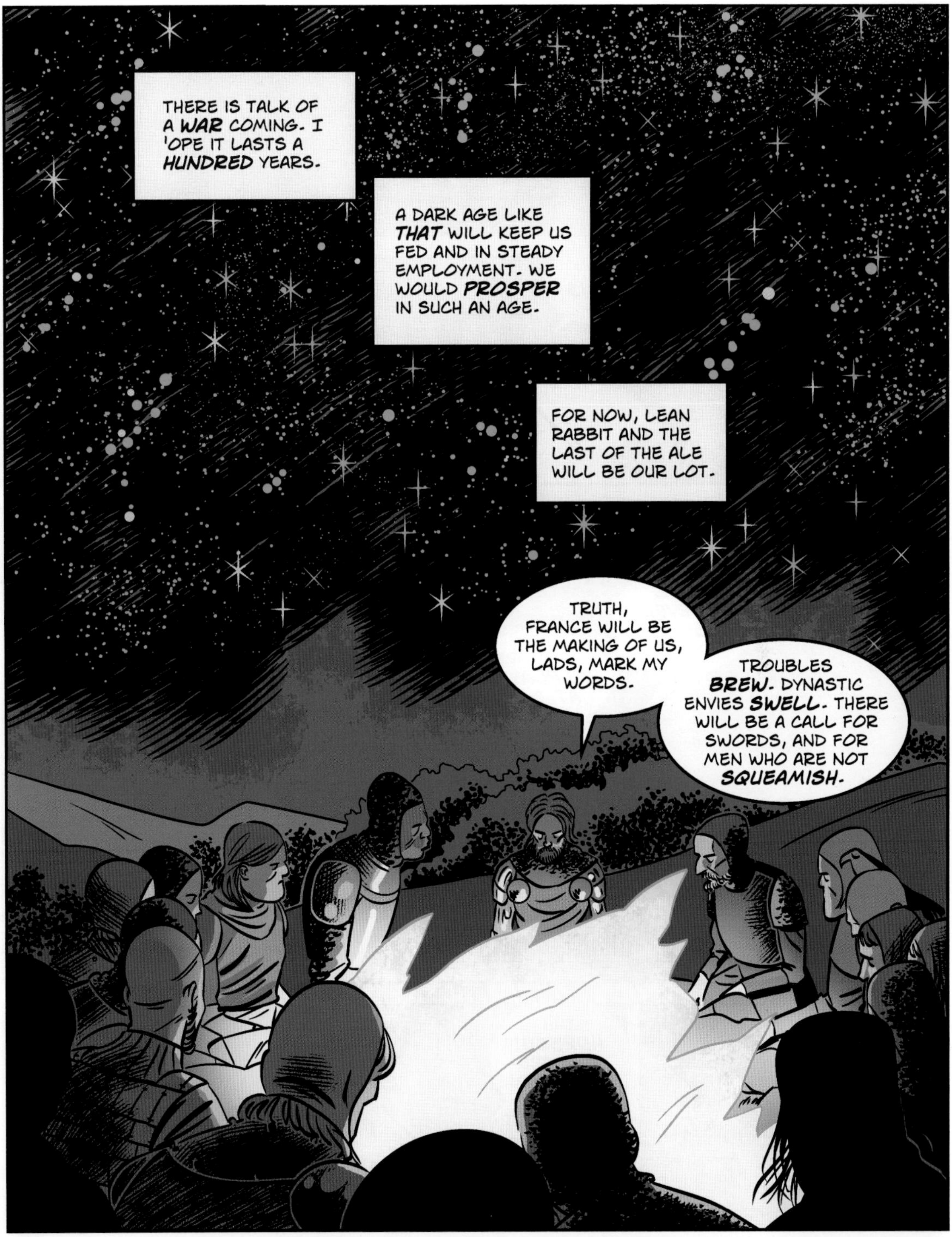
THERE IS TALK OF A WAR COMING. I 'OPE IT LASTS A HUNDRED YEARS.
A DARK AGE LIKE THAT WILL KEEP US FED AND IN STEADY EMPLOYMENT. WE WOULD PROSPER IN SUCH AN AGE.
FOR NOW, LEAN RABBIT AND THE LAST OF THE ALE WILL BE OUR LOT.
TRUTH, FRANCE WILL BE THE MAKING OF US, LADS, MARK MY WORDS.
TROUBLES BREW. DYNASTIC ENVIES SWELL. THERE WILL BE A CALL FOR SWORDS, AND FOR MEN WHO ARE NOT SQUEAMISH.

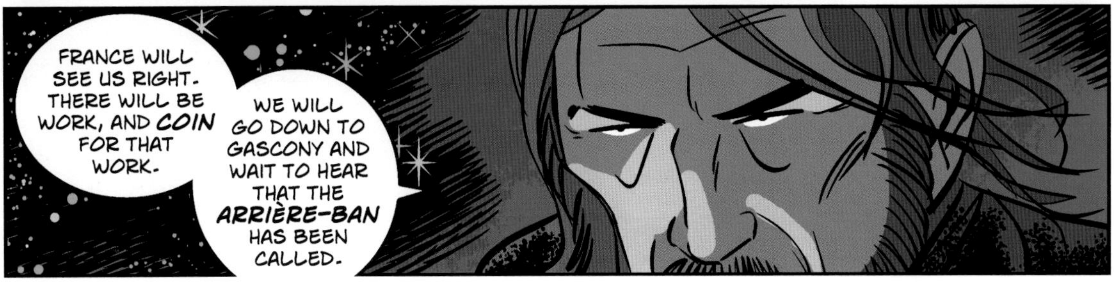
FRANCE WILL SEE US RIGHT. THERE WILL BE WORK, AND COIN FOR THAT WORK.
WE WILL GO DOWN TO GASCONY AND WAIT TO HEAR THAT THE ARRIÈRE-BAN HAS BEEN CALLED.

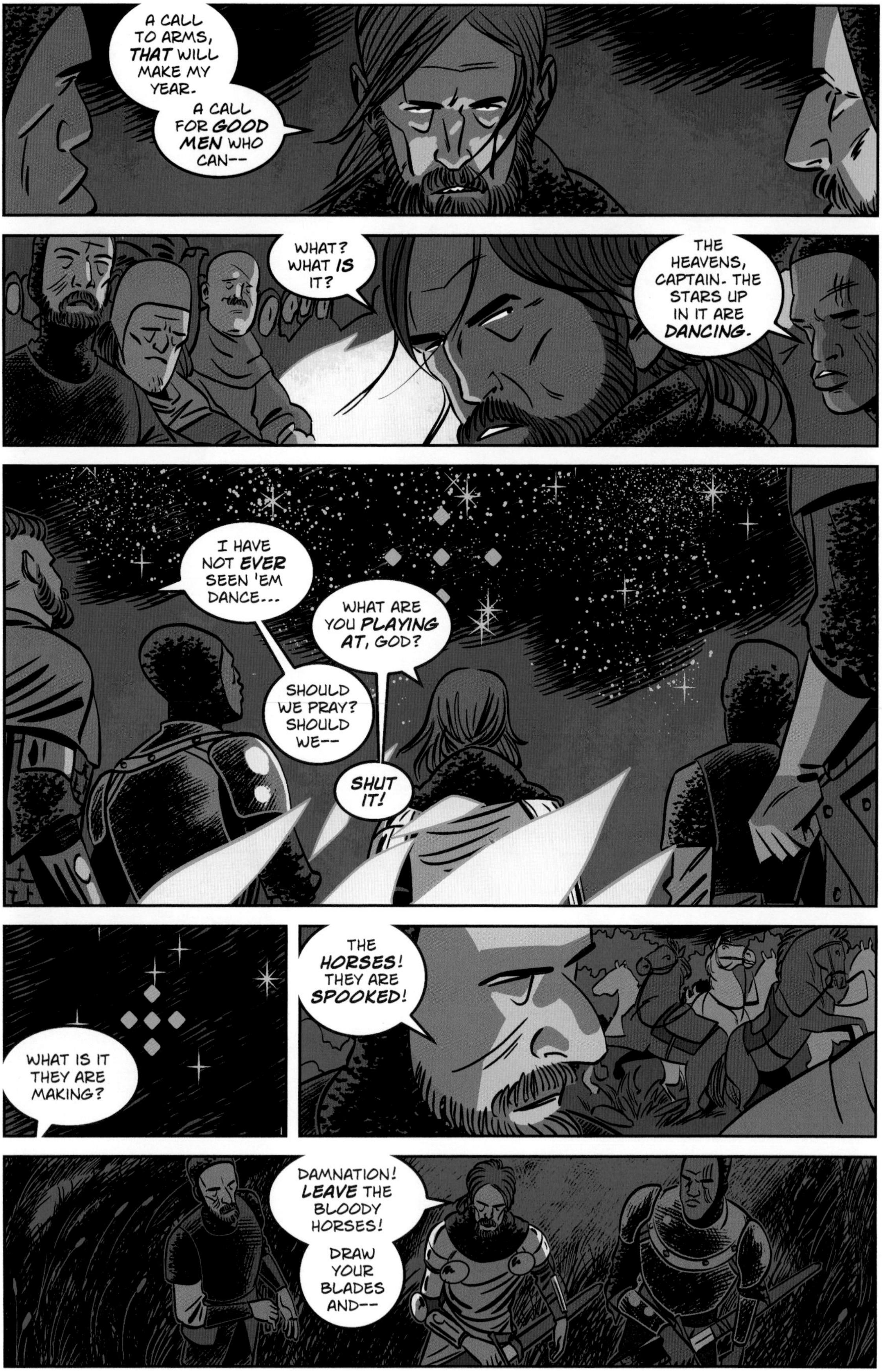
A CALL TO ARMS, THAT WILL MAKE MY YEAR.
A CALL FOR GOOD MEN WHO CAN--
WHAT? WHAT IS IT?
THE HEAVENS, CAPTAIN. THE STARS UP IN IT ARE DANCING.
I HAVE NOT EVER SEEN 'EM DANCE...
WHAT ARE YOU PLAYING AT, GOD?
SHOULD WE PRAY? SHOULD WE--
SHUT IT!
WHAT IS IT THEY ARE MAKING?
THE HORSES! THEY ARE SPOOKED!
DAMNATION! LEAVE THE BLOODY HORSES!
DRAW YOUR BLADES AND--

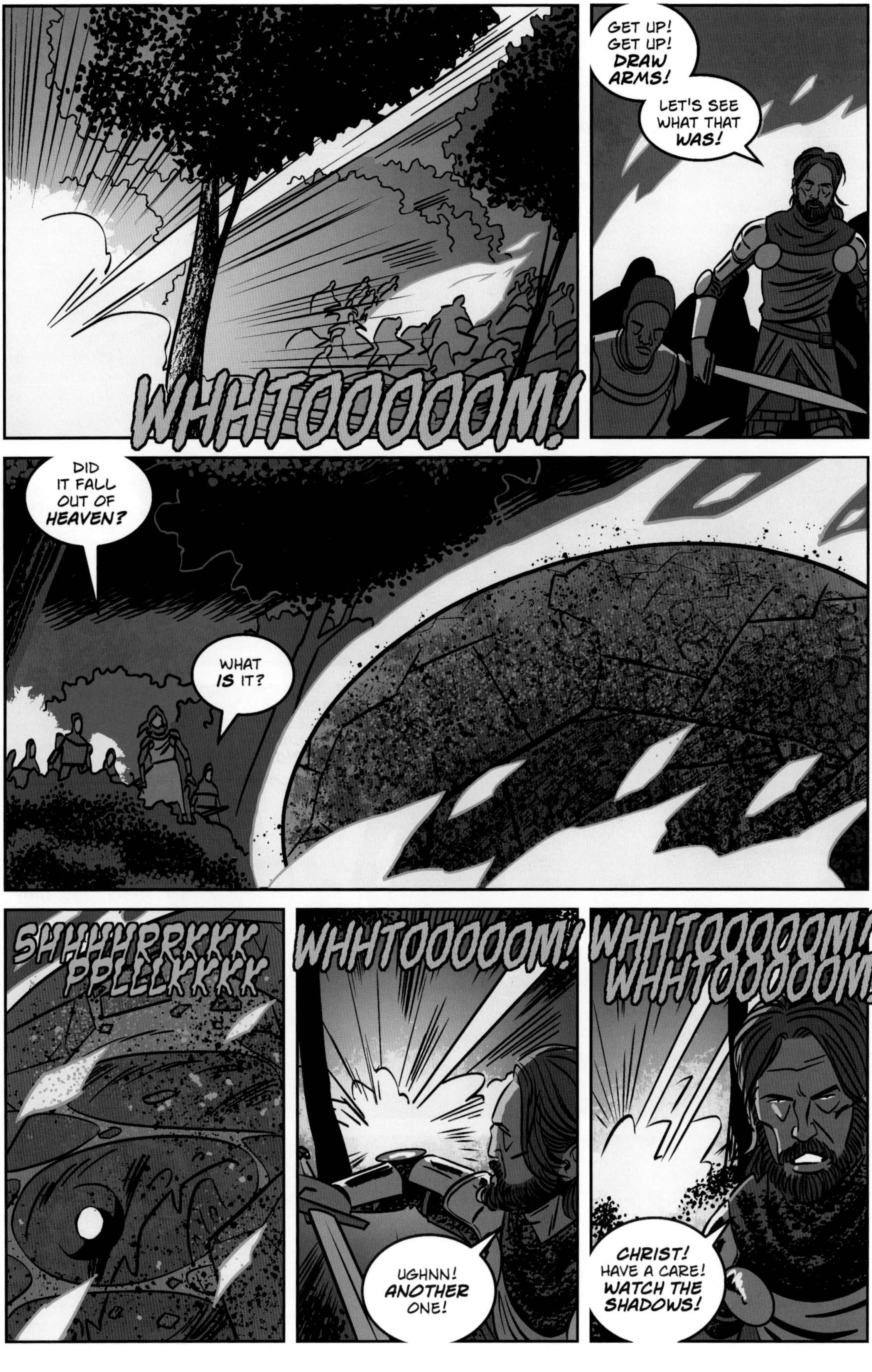
WHHTOOOOOM!
GET UP! GET UP! DRAW ARMS!
LET'S SEE WHAT THAT WAS!
DID IT FALL OUT OF HEAVEN?
WHAT IS IT?
SHHHHRRKKK PPLLLKKKK
WHHTOOOOOM!
UGHNN! ANOTHER ONE!
WHHTOOOOOM! WHHTOOOOOM!
CHRIST! HAVE A CARE! WATCH THE SHADOWS!

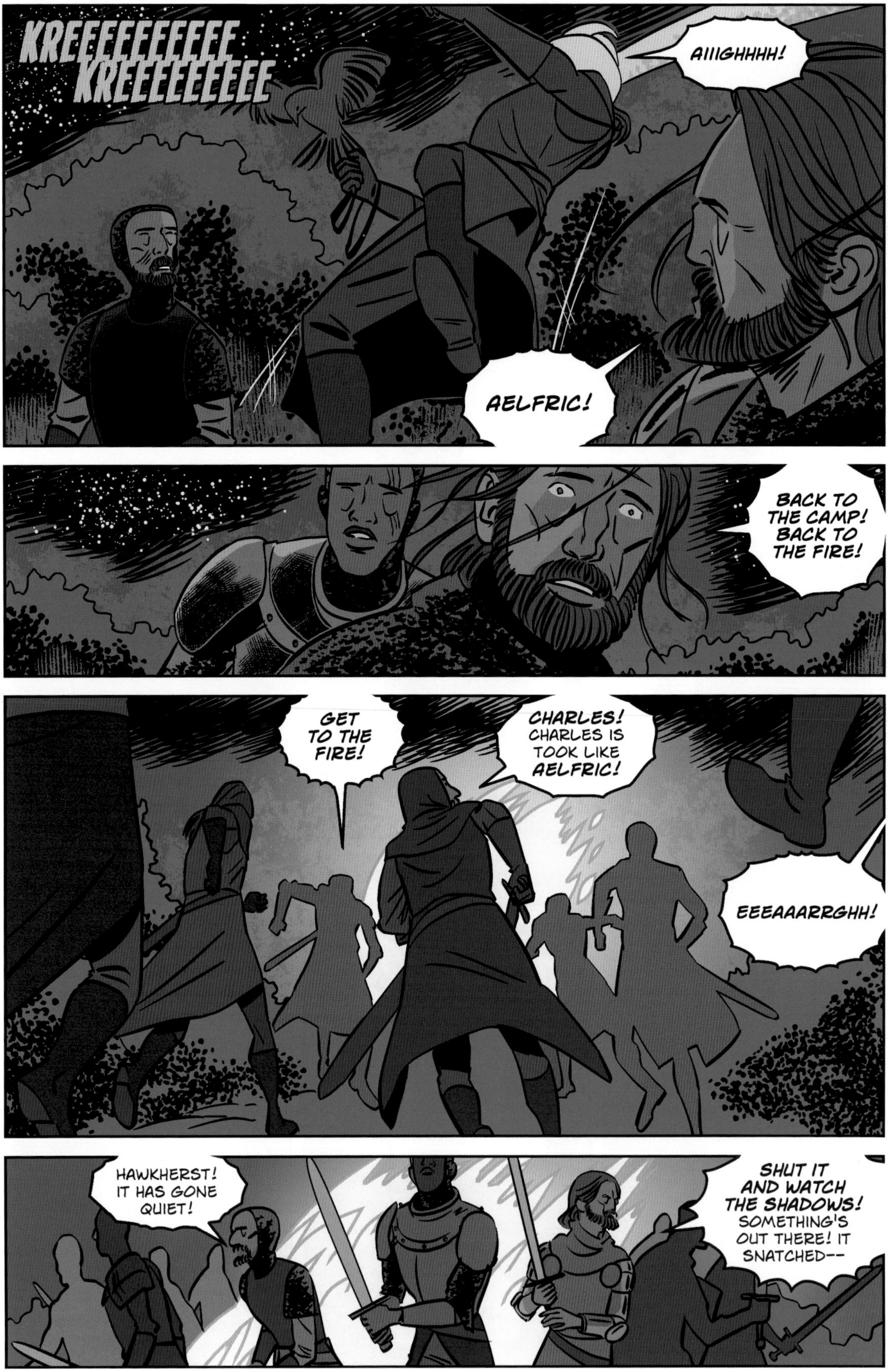
KREEEEEEEEEE
KREEEEEEEEE
AIIIGHHHH!
AELFRIC!
BACK TO THE CAMP! BACK TO THE FIRE!
GET TO THE FIRE!
CHARLES! CHARLES IS TOOK LIKE AELFRIC!
EEEAAARRGHH!
HAWKHERST! IT HAS GONE QUIET!
SHUT IT AND WATCH THE SHADOWS! SOMETHING'S OUT THERE! IT SNATCHED--

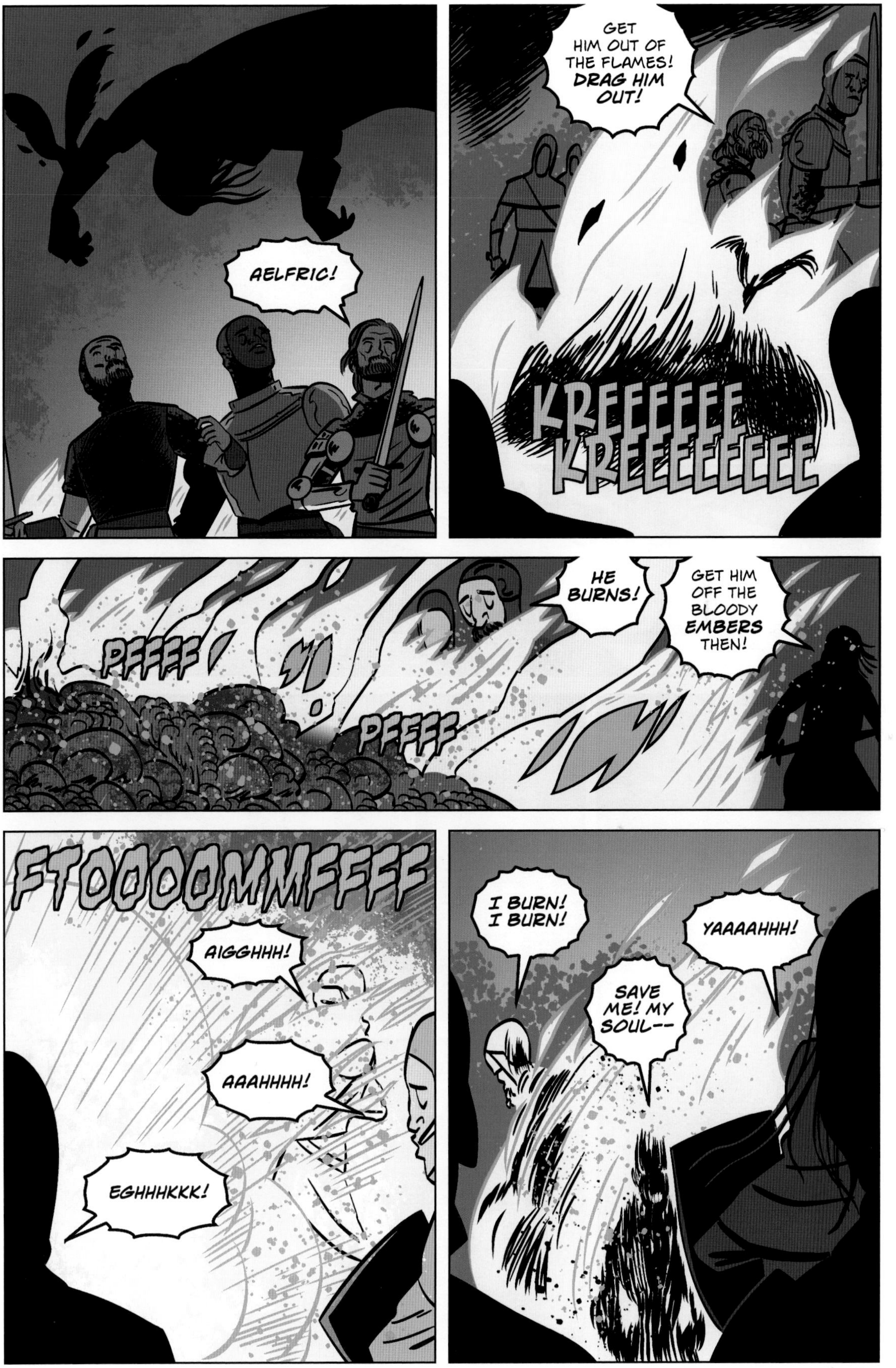
AELFRIC!
GET HIM OUT OF THE FLAMES! DRAG HIM OUT!
KREEEEEE KREEEEEEEE
PFFFF
PFFFF
HE BURNS!
GET HIM OFF THE BLOODY EMBERS THEN!
FTOOOOMMFFFF
AIGGHHH!
AAAHHHH!
EGHHHKKK!
I BURN! I BURN!
YAAAAHHH!
SAVE ME! MY SOUL--

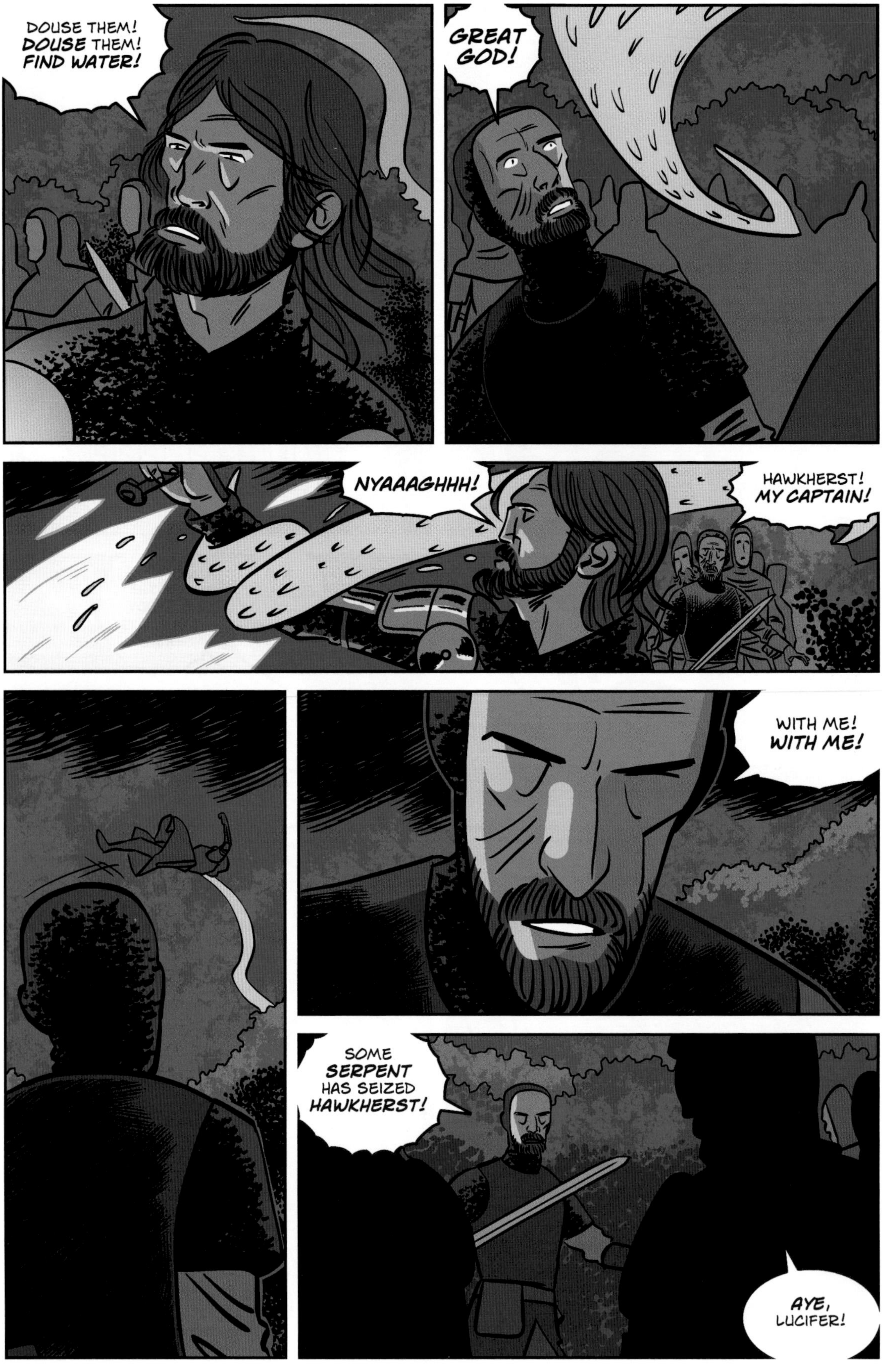
DOUSE THEM! DOUSE THEM! FIND WATER!
GREAT GOD!
NYAAAGHHH!
HAWKHERST! MY CAPTAIN!
WITH ME! WITH ME!
SOME SERPENT HAS SEIZED HAWKHERST!
AYE, LUCIFER!

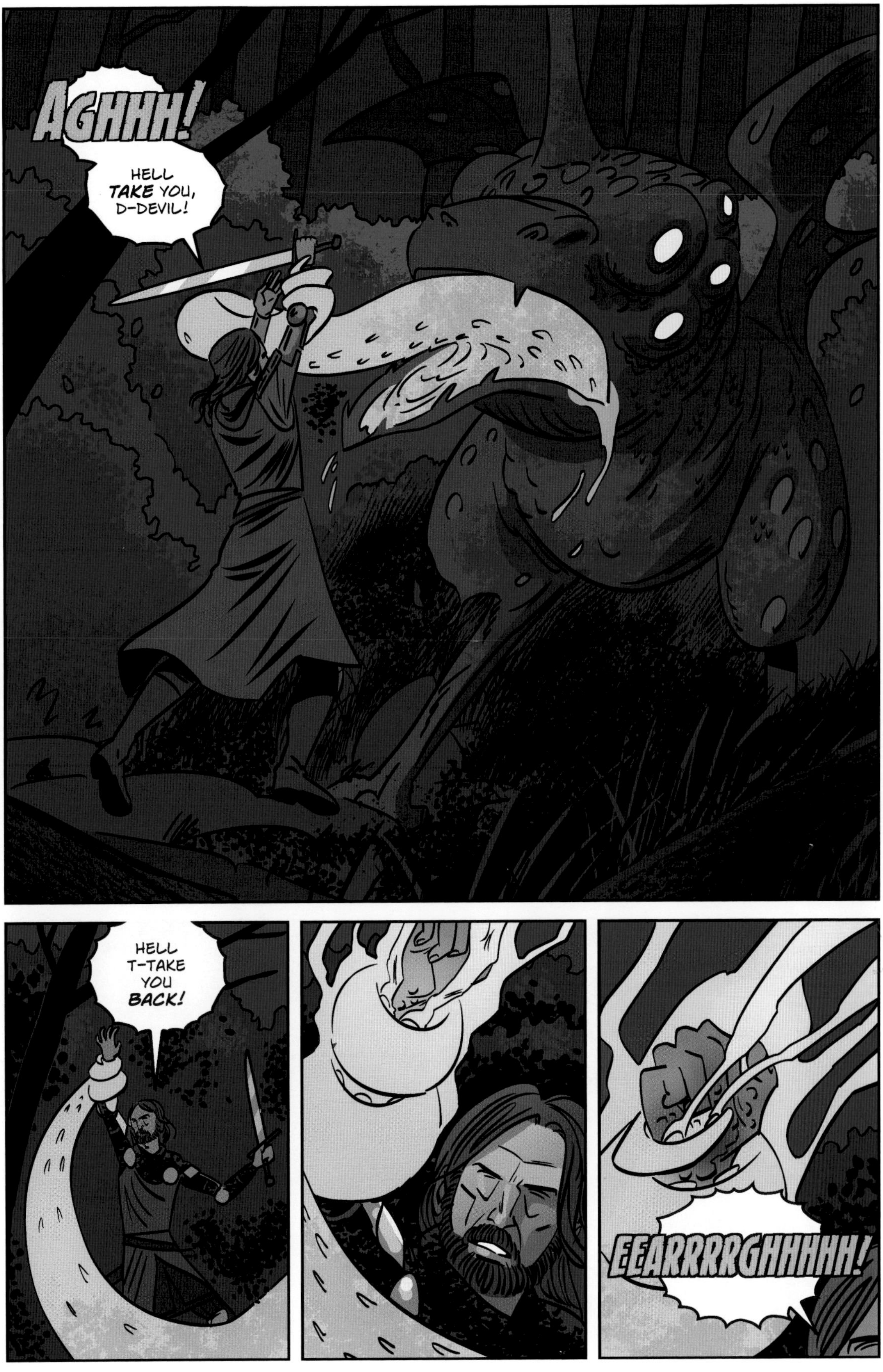
AGHHH!
HELL TAKE YOU, D-DEVIL!
HELL T-TAKE YOU BACK!
EEARRRRGHHHHH!

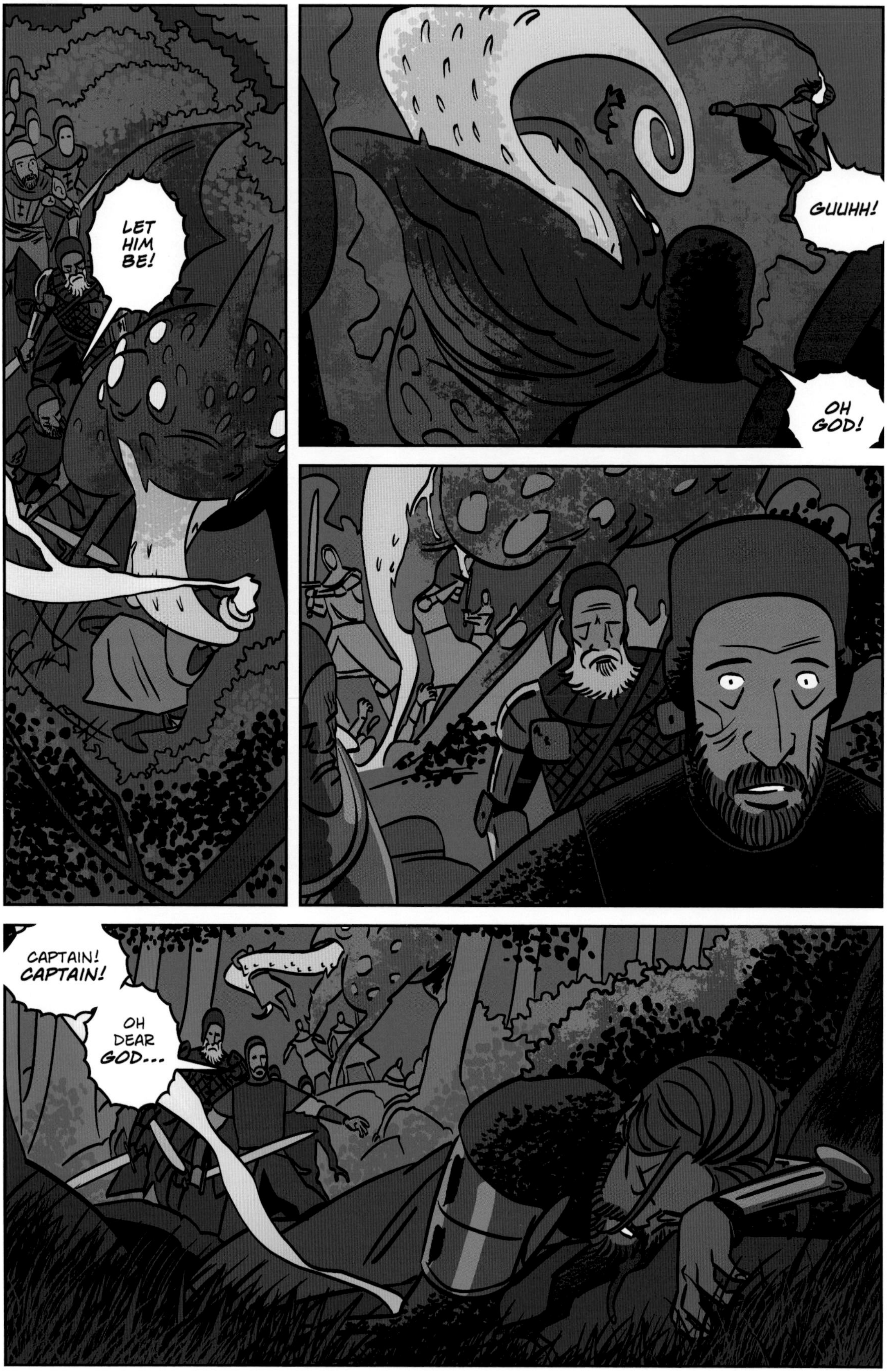
LET HIM BE!
GUUHH!
OH GOD!
CAPTAIN! CAPTAIN!
OH DEAR GOD...

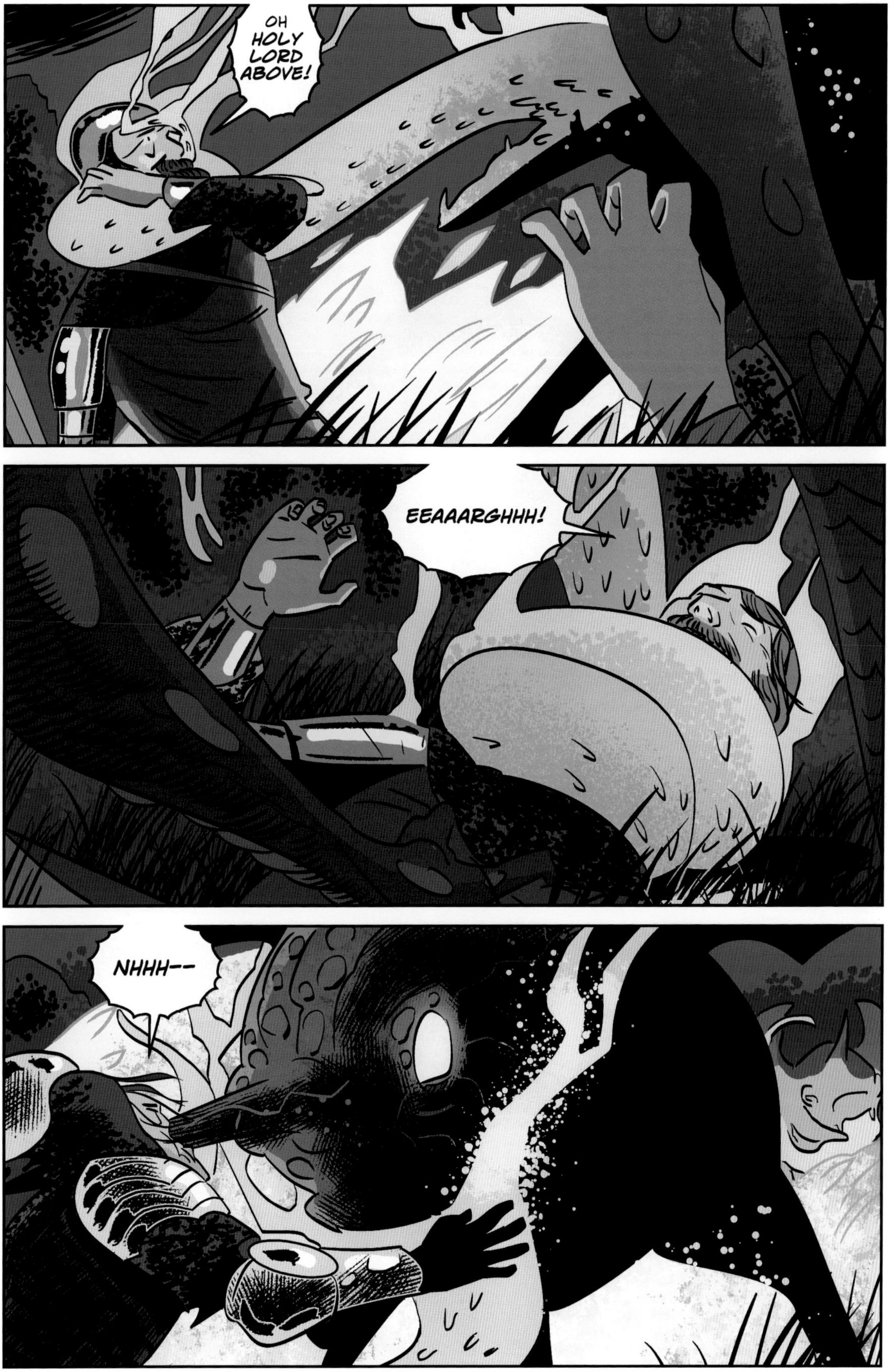
OH HOLY LORD ABOVE!
EEAAARGHHH!
NHHH--

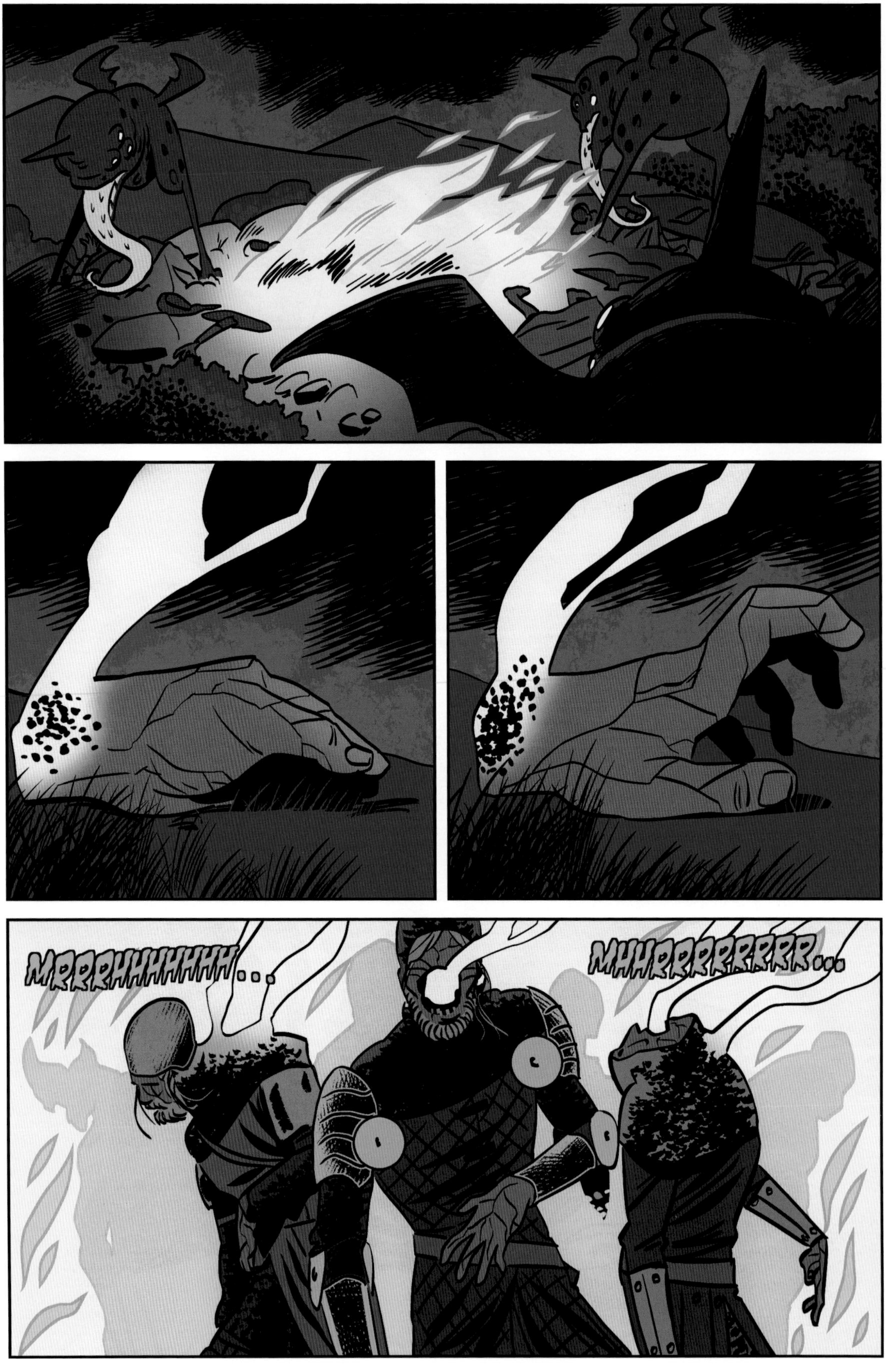
MRRRHHHHHHH...
MHHRRRRRRR...

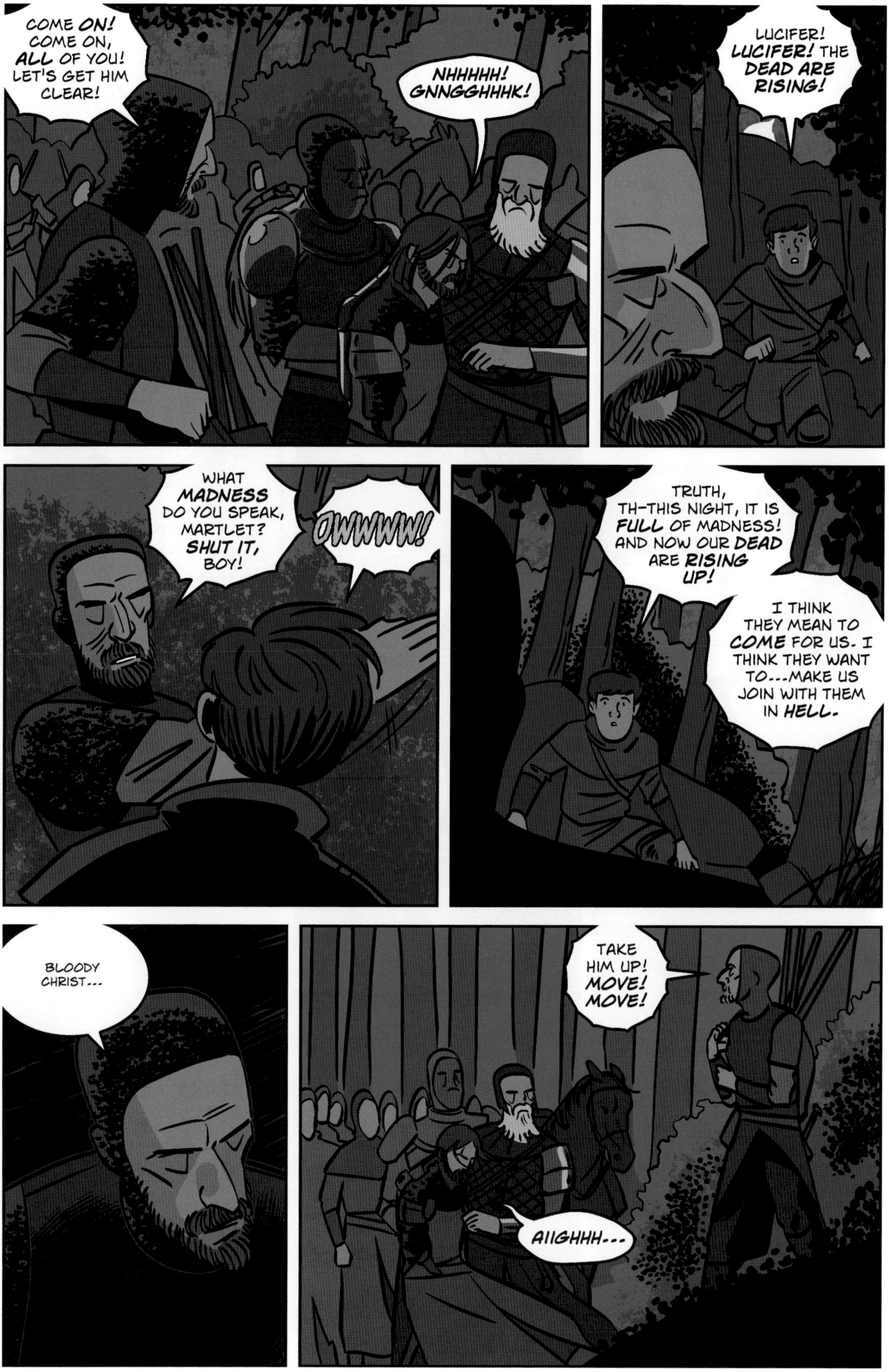
COME ON! COME ON, ALL OF YOU! LET'S GET HIM CLEAR!
NHHHHH! GNNGGHHHK!
LUCIFER! LUCIFER! THE DEAD ARE RISING!
WHAT MADNESS DO YOU SPEAK, MARTLET? SHUT IT, BOY!
OWWWW!
TRUTH, TH-THIS NIGHT, IT IS FULL OF MADNESS! AND NOW OUR DEAD ARE RISING UP!
I THINK THEY MEAN TO COME FOR US. I THINK THEY WANT TO...MAKE US JOIN WITH THEM IN HELL.
BLOODY CHRIST...
TAKE HIM UP! MOVE! MOVE!
AIIGHHH...

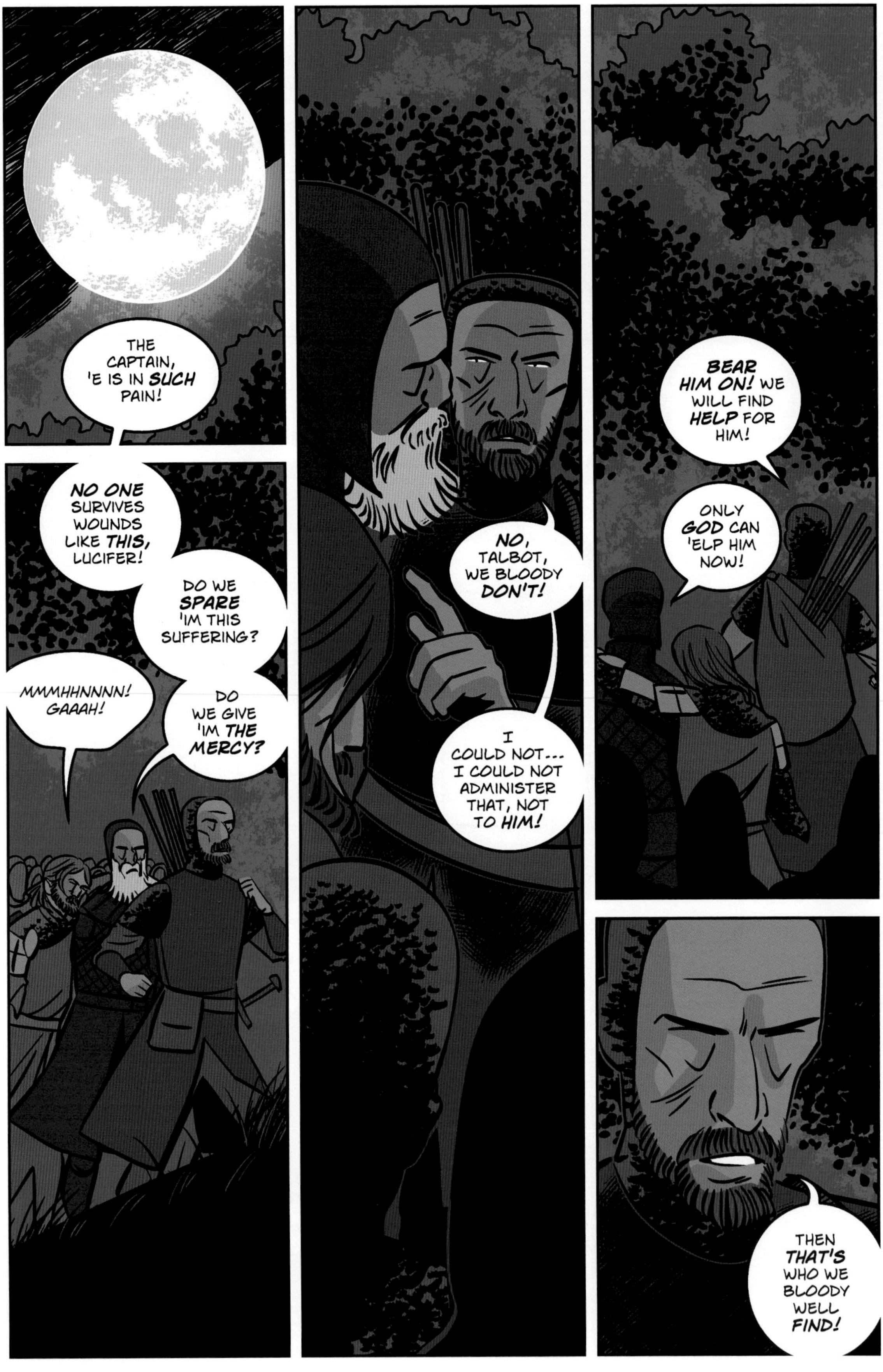
THE CAPTAIN, 'E IS IN SUCH PAIN!
NO ONE SURVIVES WOUNDS LIKE THIS, LUCIFER!
DO WE SPARE 'IM THIS SUFFERING?
MMMHHNNNN! GAAAH!
DO WE GIVE 'IM THE MERCY?
NO, TALBOT, WE BLOODY DON'T!
I COULD NOT... I COULD NOT ADMINISTER THAT, NOT TO HIM!
BEAR HIM ON! WE WILL FIND HELP FOR HIM!
ONLY GOD CAN 'ELP HIM NOW!
THEN THAT'S WHO WE BLOODY WELL FIND!

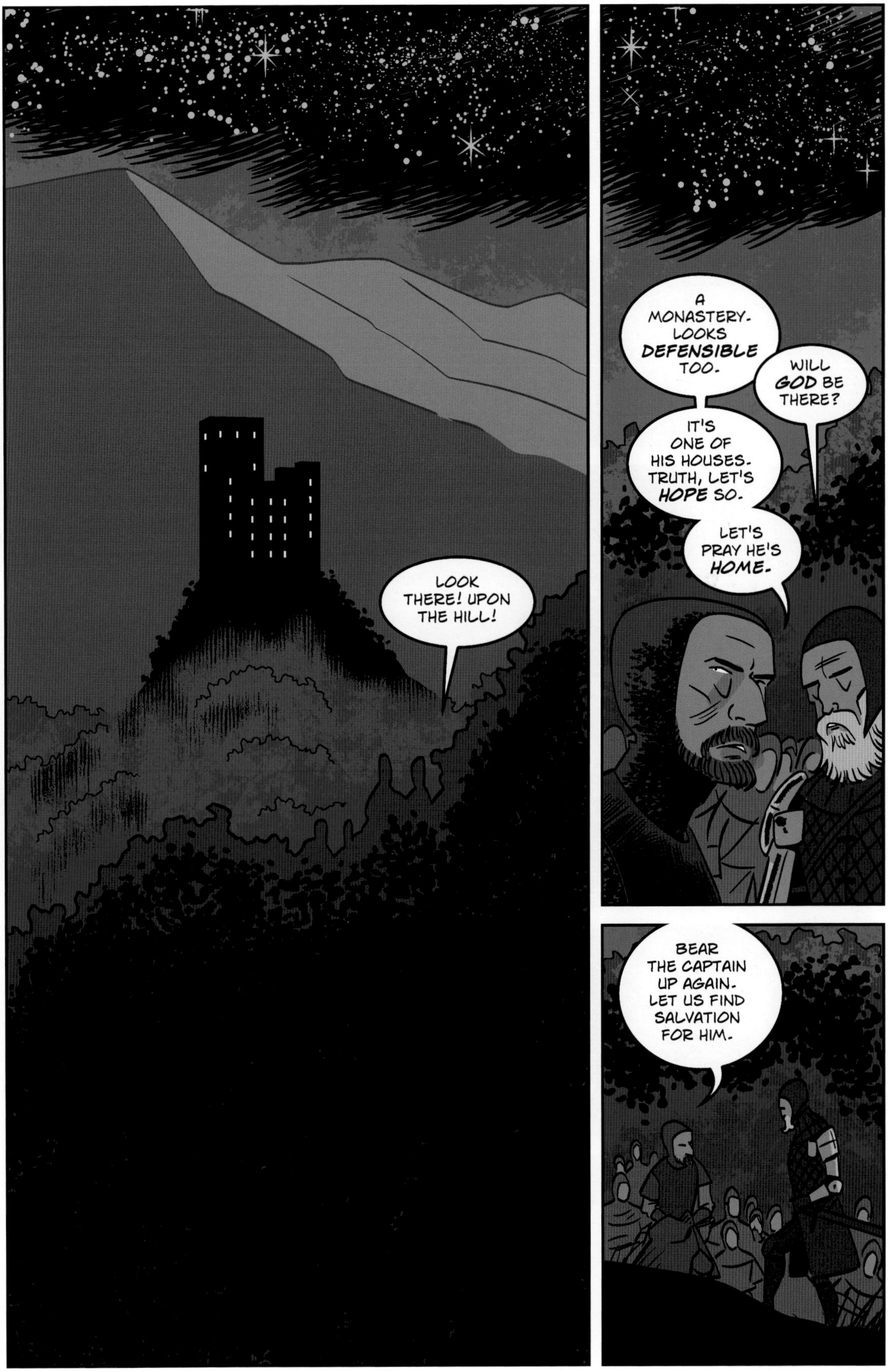
LOOK THERE! UPON THE HILL!
A MONASTERY. LOOKS DEFENSIBLE TOO.
WILL GOD BE THERE?
IT'S ONE OF HIS HOUSES. TRUTH, LET'S HOPE SO.
LET'S PRAY HE'S HOME.
BEAR THE CAPTAIN UP AGAIN. LET US FIND SALVATION FOR HIM.

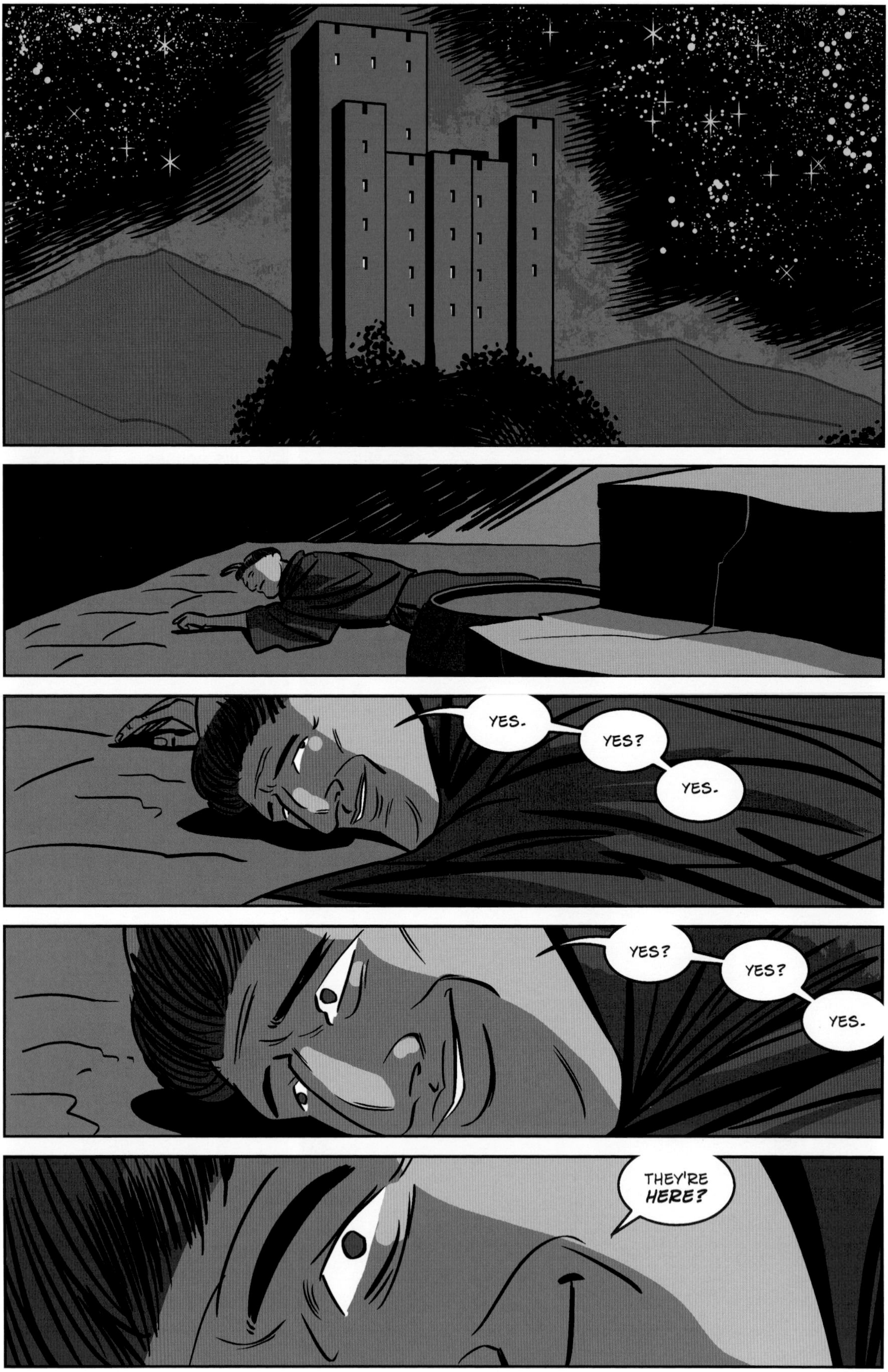
YES.
YES?
YES.
YES?
YES?
YES.
THEY'RE *HERE?*

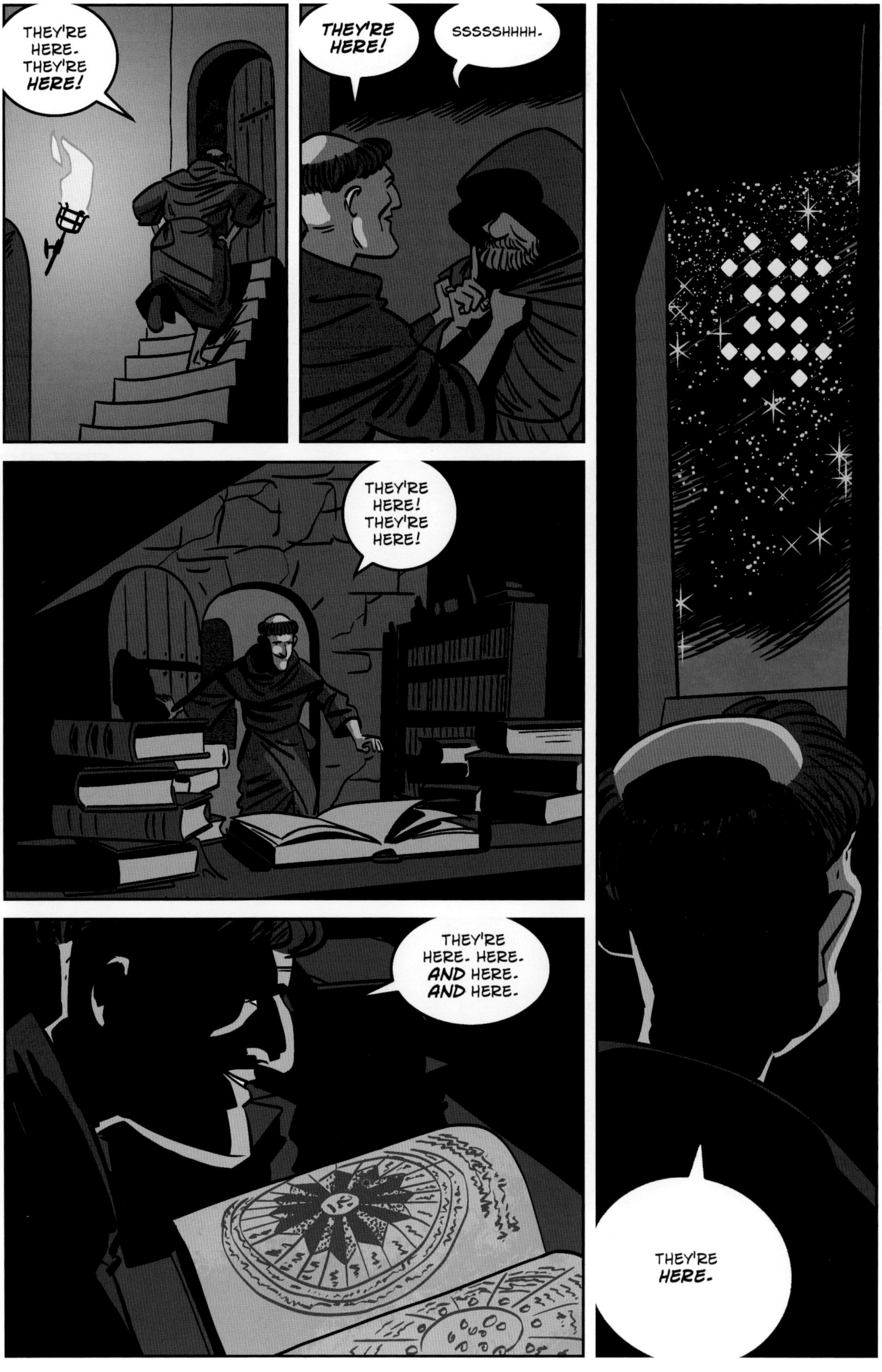
THEY'RE HERE. THEY'RE *HERE!*
THEY'RE HERE!
SSSSSHHHH.
THEY'RE HERE! THEY'RE HERE!
THEY'RE HERE. HERE. *AND* HERE. *AND* HERE.
THEY'RE *HERE.*

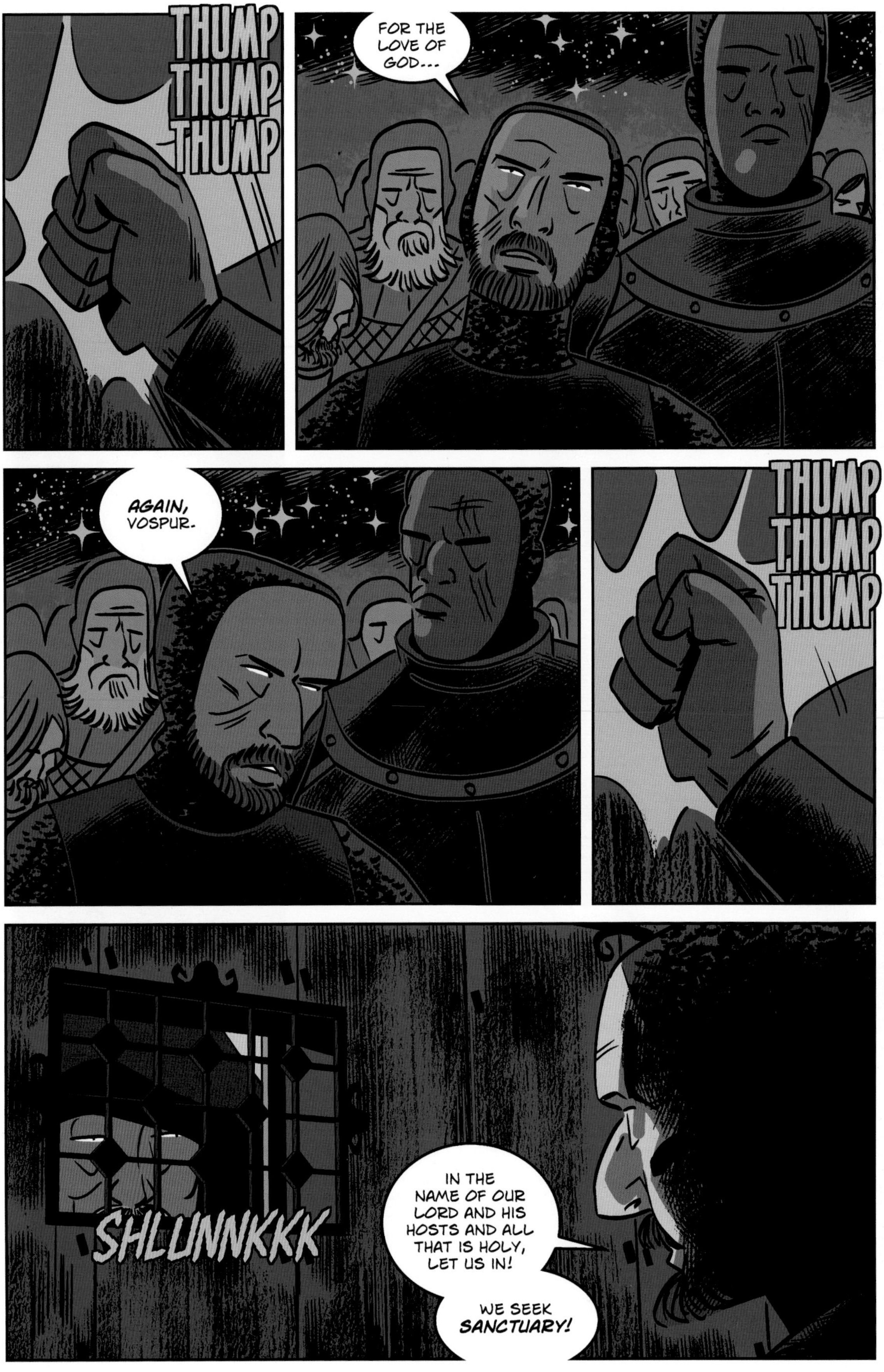
THUMP
THUMP
THUMP
FOR THE LOVE OF GOD...
AGAIN, VOSPUR.
THUMP
THUMP
THUMP
SHLUNNKKK
IN THE NAME OF OUR LORD AND HIS HOSTS AND ALL THAT IS HOLY, LET US IN!
WE SEEK SANCTUARY!

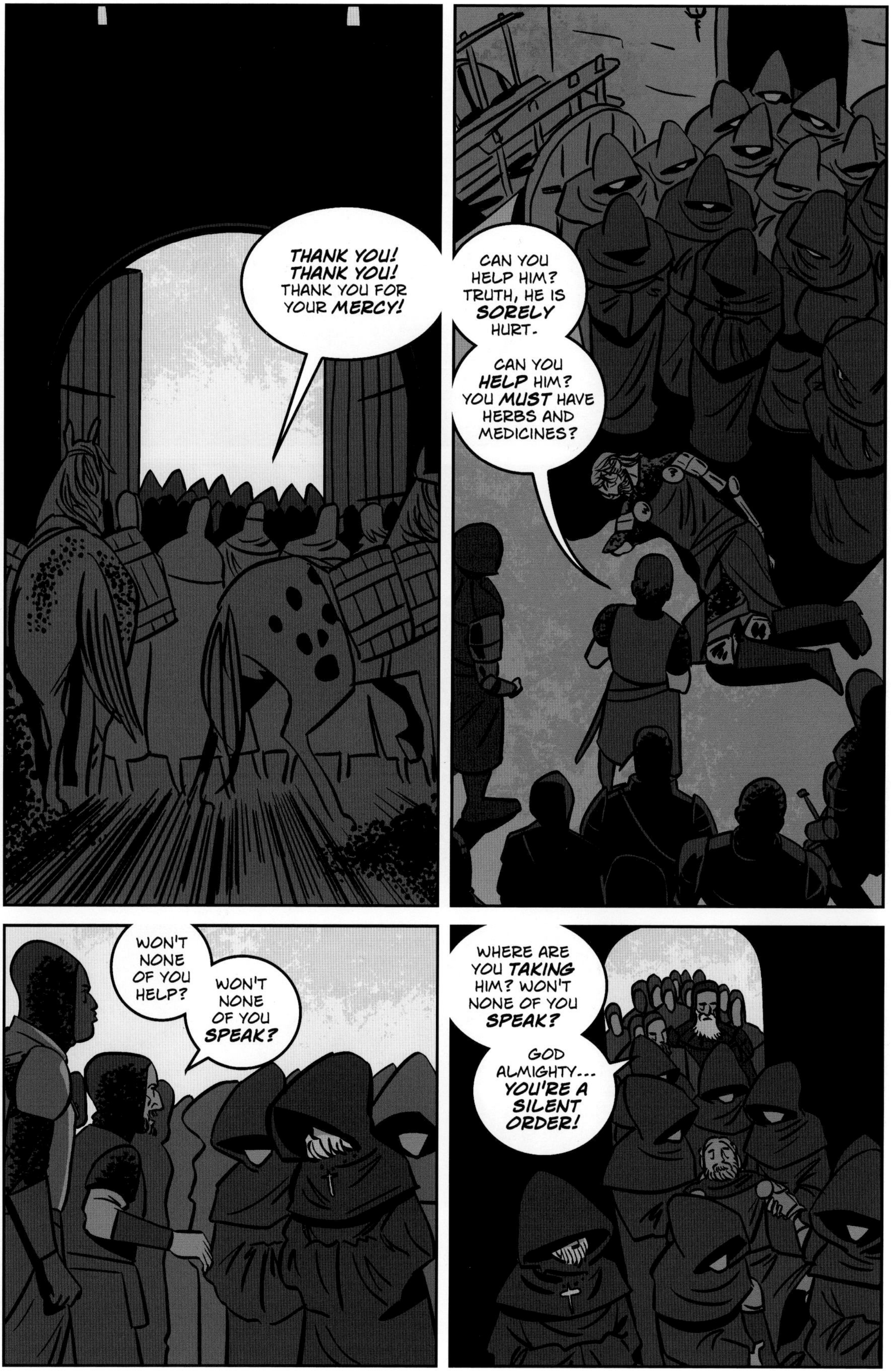
THANK YOU! THANK YOU! THANK YOU FOR YOUR MERCY!
CAN YOU HELP HIM? TRUTH, HE IS SORELY HURT.
CAN YOU HELP HIM? YOU MUST HAVE HERBS AND MEDICINES?
WON'T NONE OF YOU HELP?
WON'T NONE OF YOU SPEAK?
WHERE ARE YOU TAKING HIM? WON'T NONE OF YOU SPEAK?
GOD ALMIGHTY... YOU'RE A SILENT ORDER!

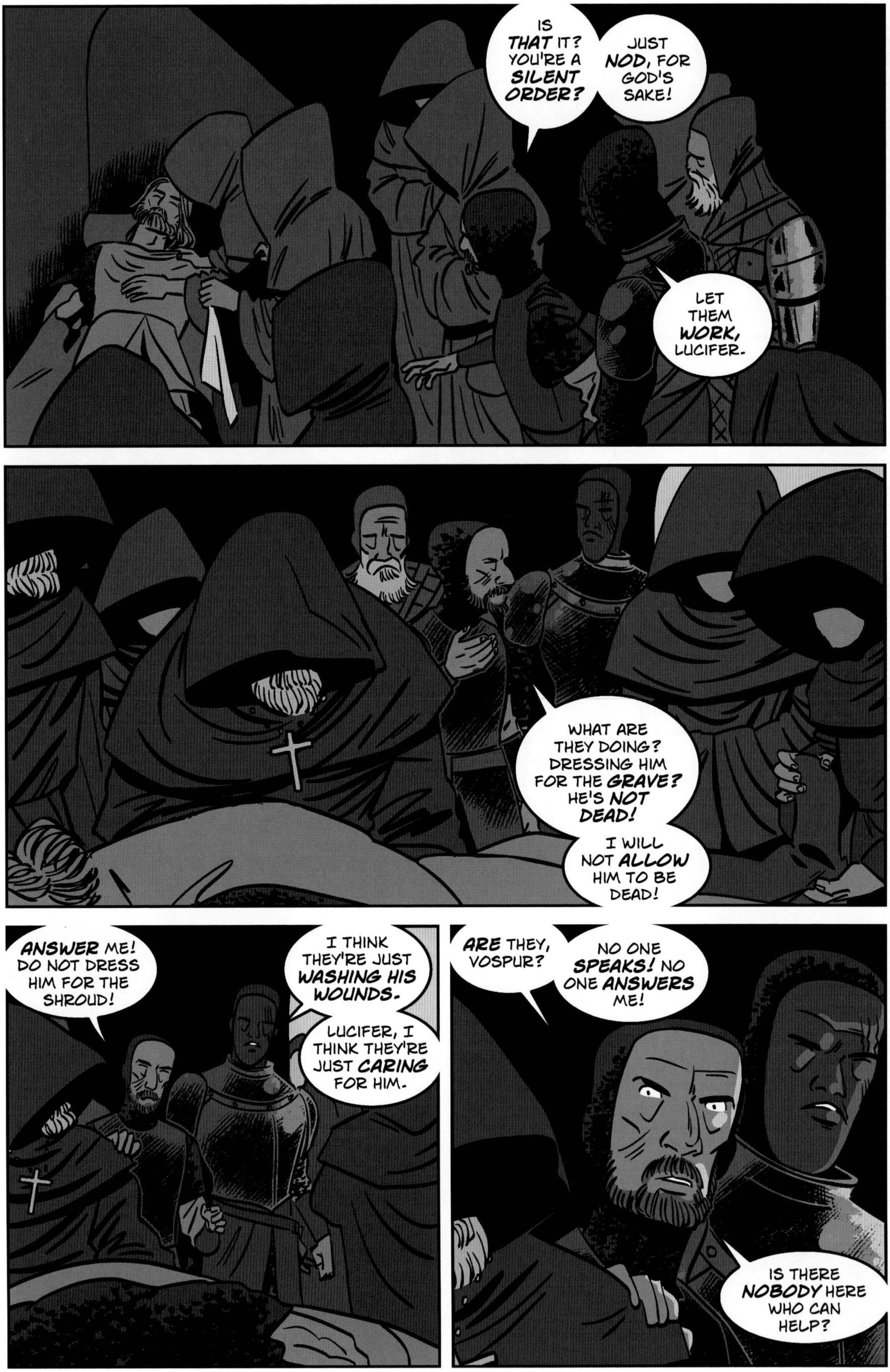
IS THAT IT? YOU'RE A SILENT ORDER?
JUST NOD, FOR GOD'S SAKE!
LET THEM WORK, LUCIFER.
WHAT ARE THEY DOING? DRESSING HIM FOR THE GRAVE? HE'S NOT DEAD!
I WILL NOT ALLOW HIM TO BE DEAD!
ANSWER ME! DO NOT DRESS HIM FOR THE SHROUD!
I THINK THEY'RE JUST WASHING HIS WOUNDS.
LUCIFER, I THINK THEY'RE JUST CARING FOR HIM.
ARE THEY, VOSPUR?
NO ONE SPEAKS! NO ONE ANSWERS ME!
IS THERE NOBODY HERE WHO CAN HELP?

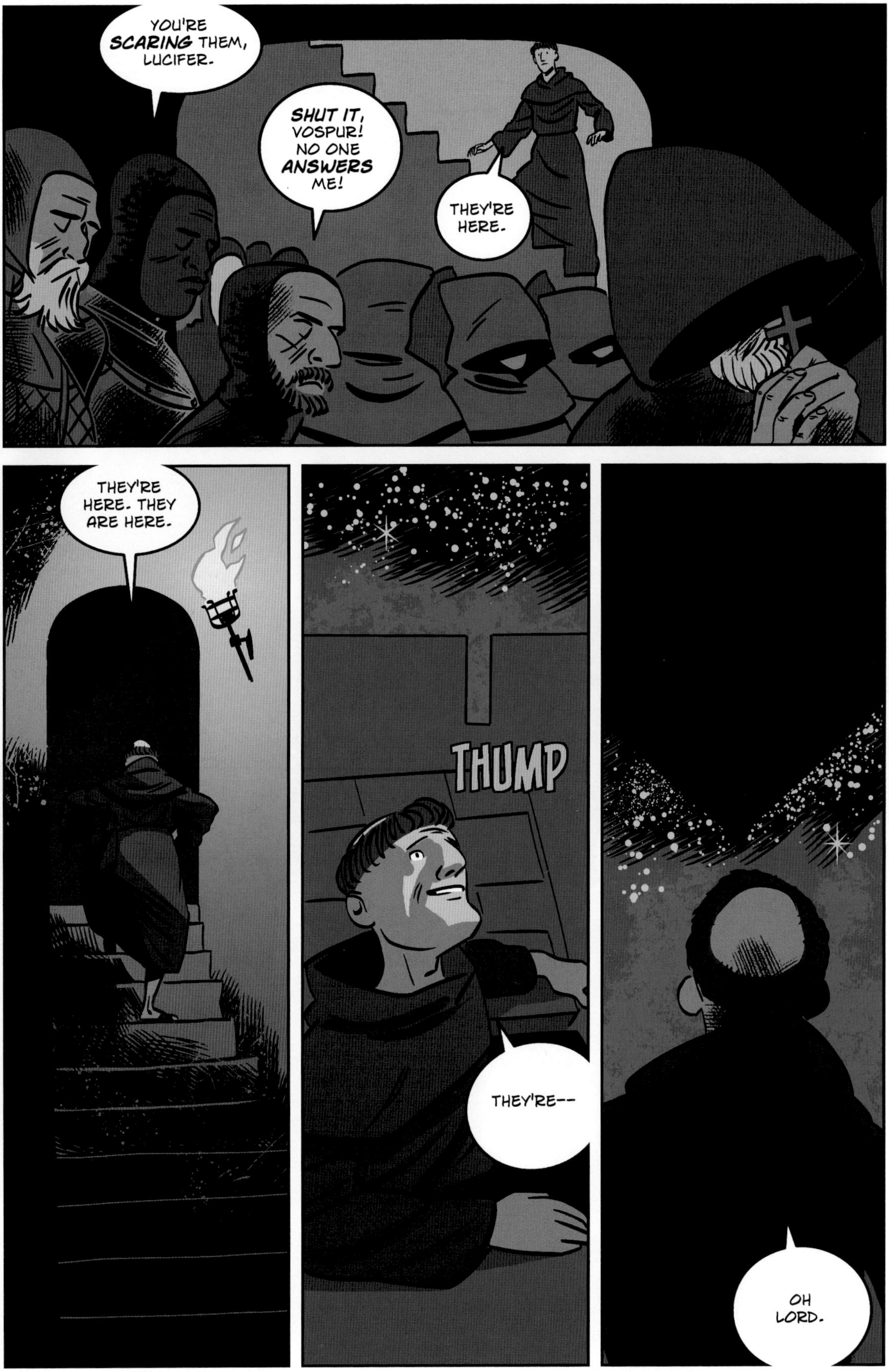
YOU'RE SCARING THEM, LUCIFER.
SHUT IT, VOSPUR! NO ONE ANSWERS ME!
THEY'RE HERE.
THEY'RE HERE. THEY ARE HERE.
THUMP
THEY'RE--
OH LORD.

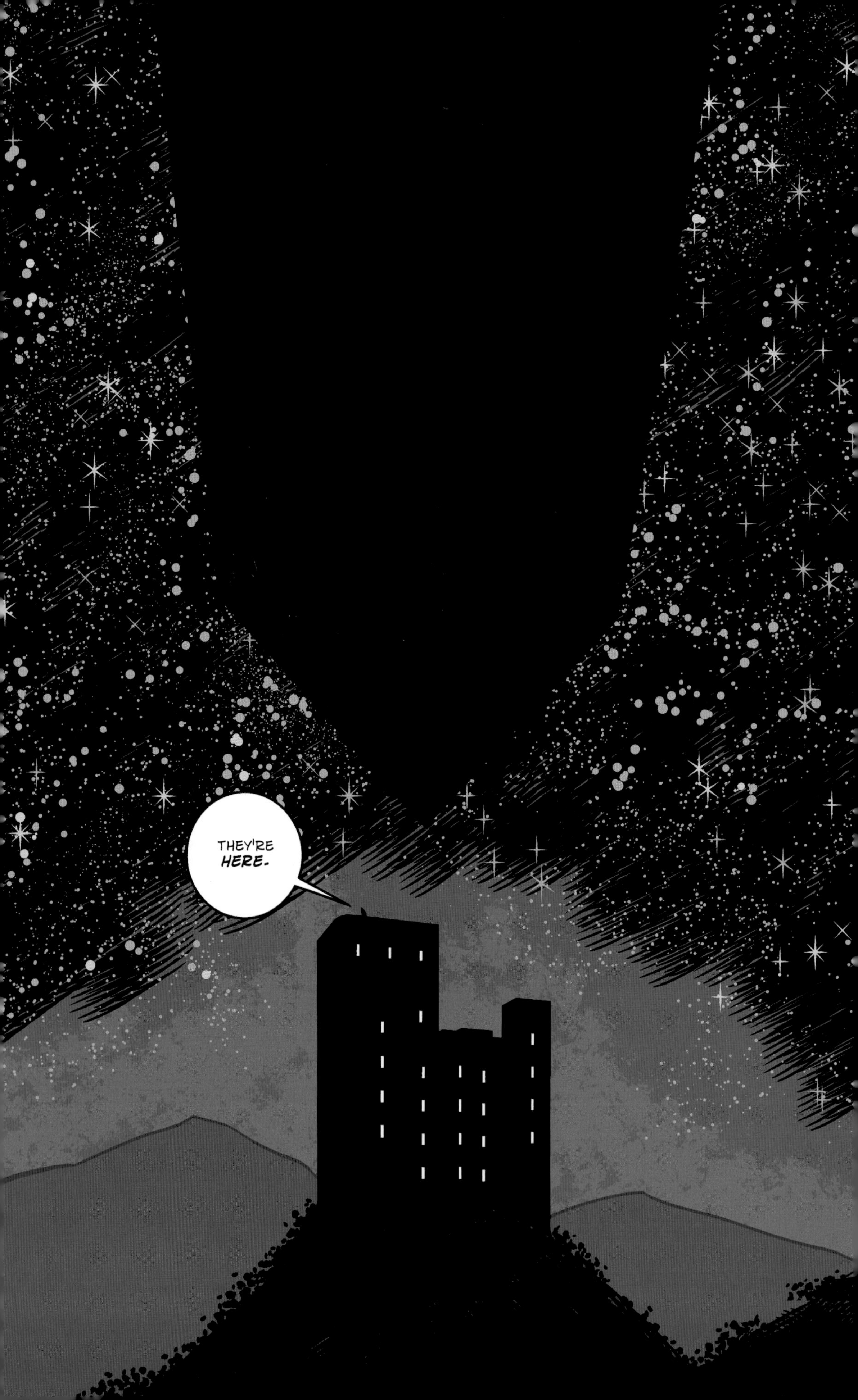
THEY'RE *HERE.*

CHAPTER II

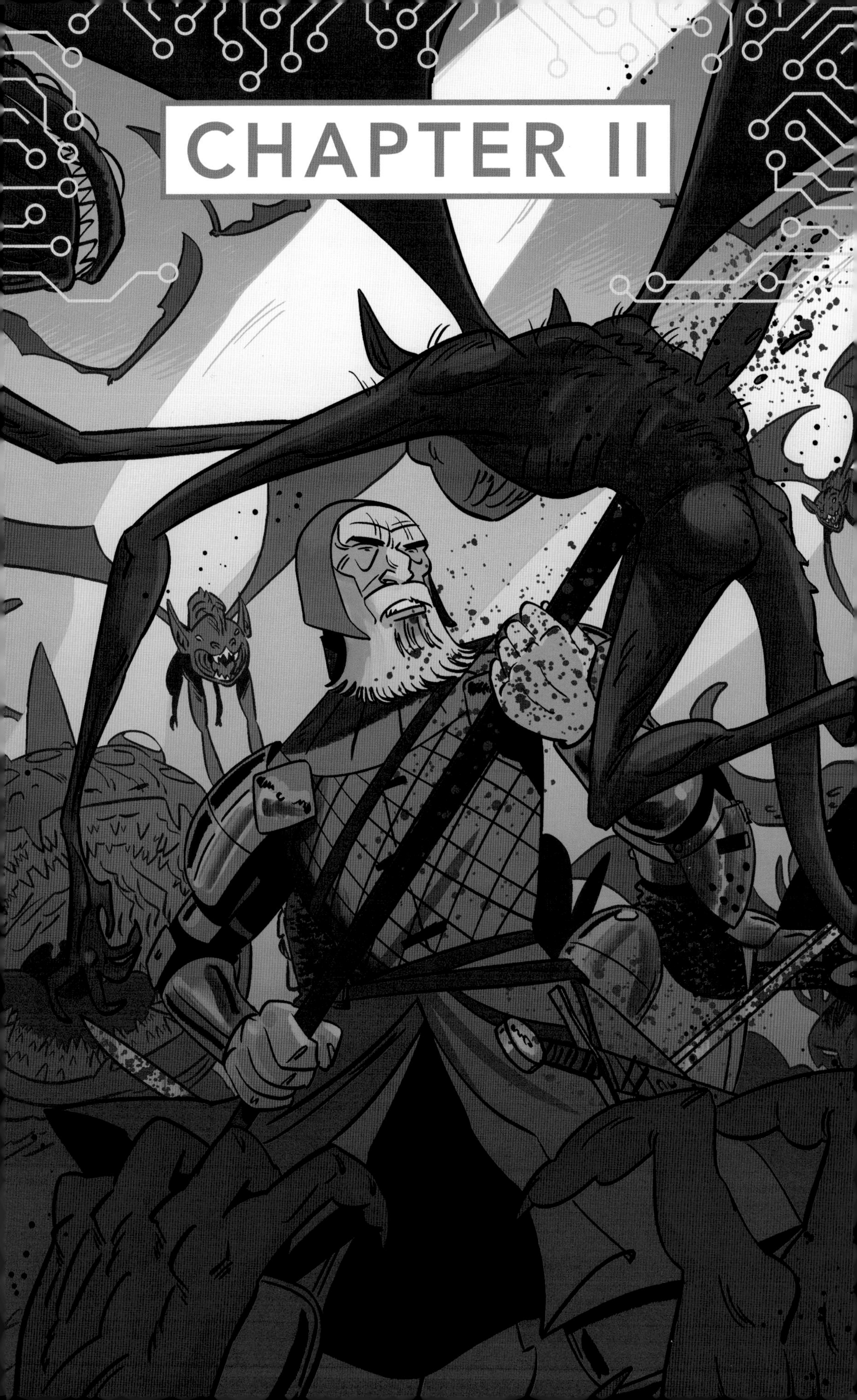

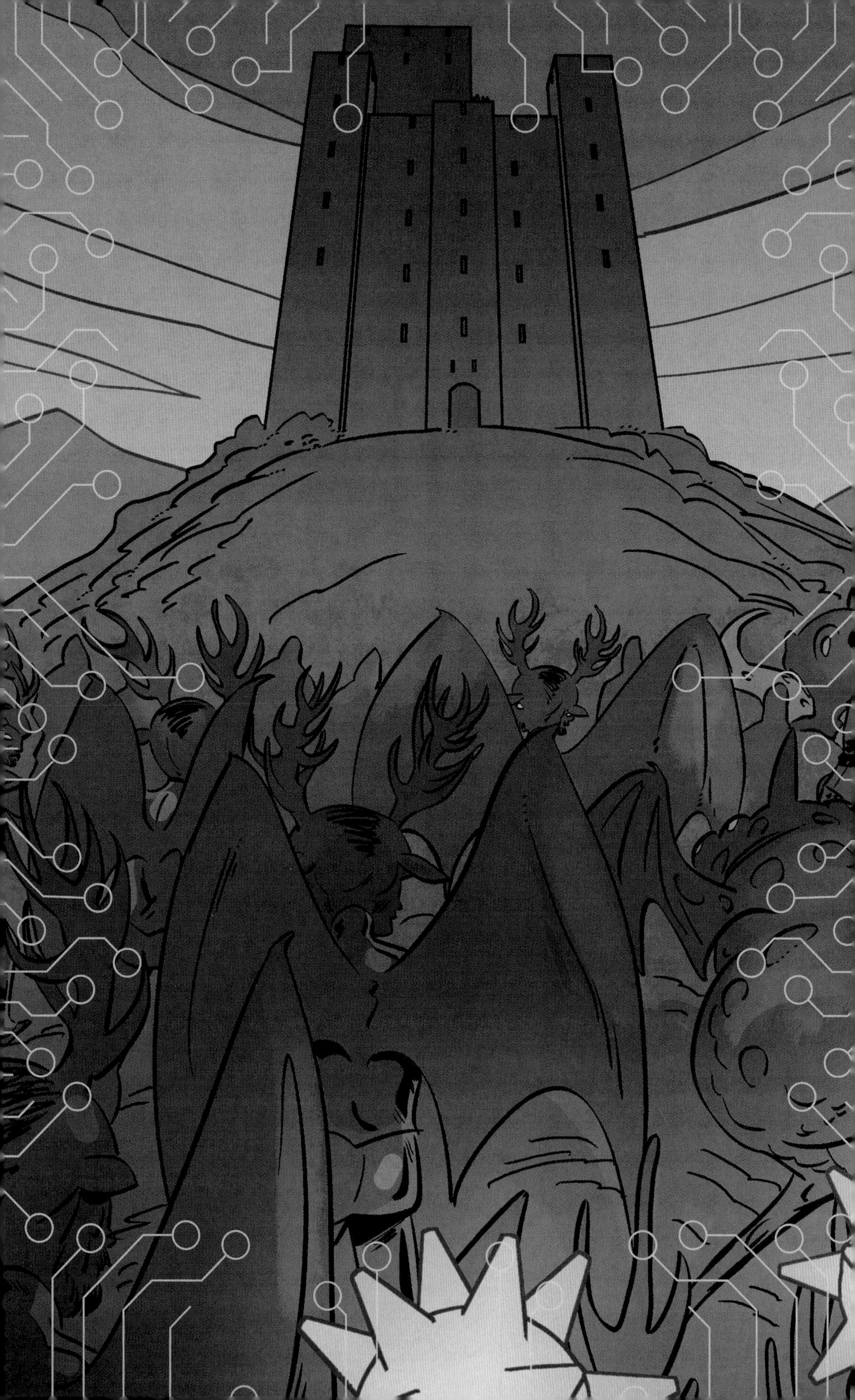

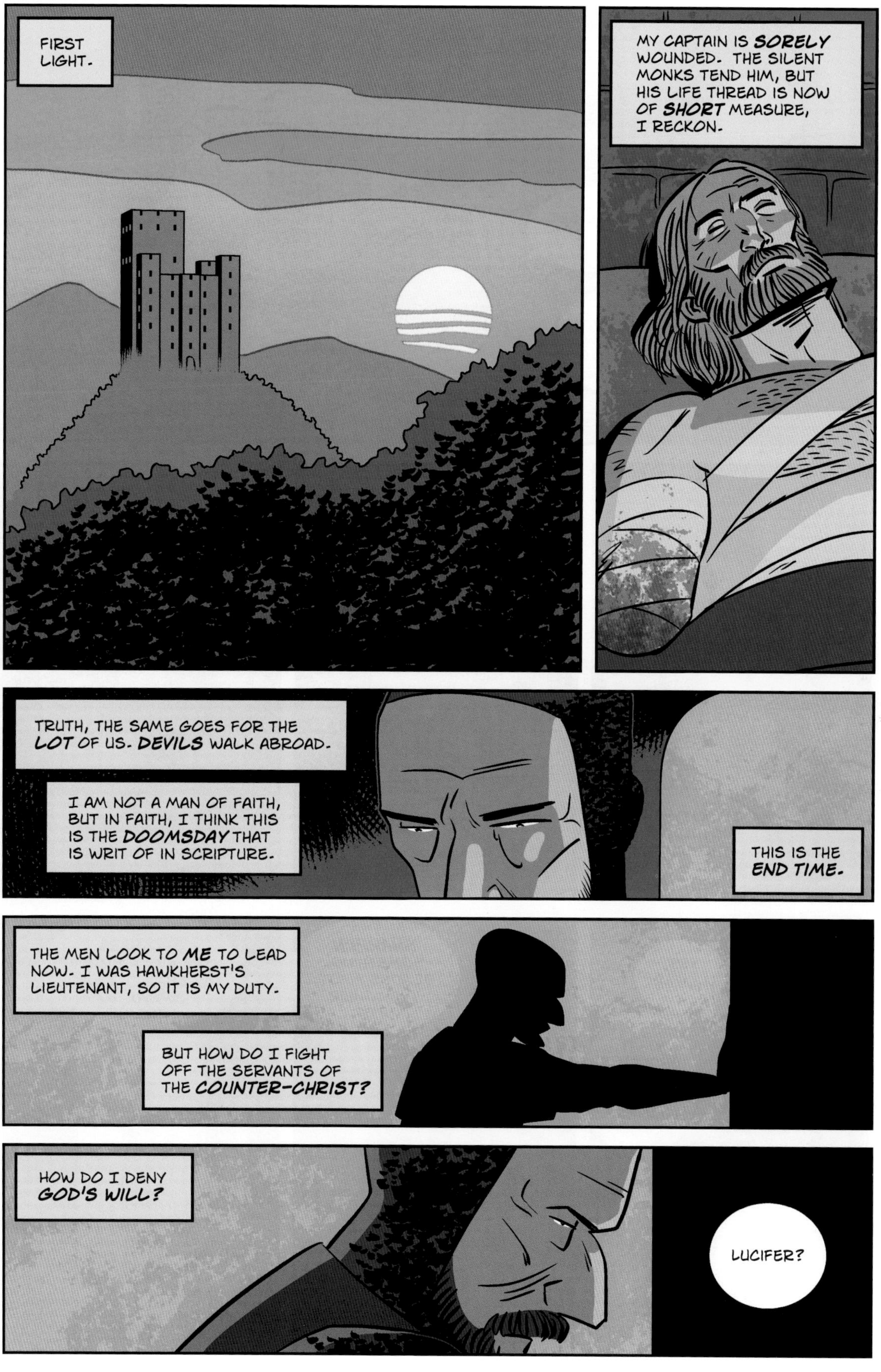
FIRST LIGHT.
MY CAPTAIN IS SORELY WOUNDED. THE SILENT MONKS TEND HIM, BUT HIS LIFE THREAD IS NOW OF SHORT MEASURE, I RECKON.
TRUTH, THE SAME GOES FOR THE LOT OF US. DEVILS WALK ABROAD.
I AM NOT A MAN OF FAITH, BUT IN FAITH, I THINK THIS IS THE DOOMSDAY THAT IS WRIT OF IN SCRIPTURE.
THIS IS THE END TIME.
THE MEN LOOK TO ME TO LEAD NOW. I WAS HAWKHERST'S LIEUTENANT, SO IT IS MY DUTY.
BUT HOW DO I FIGHT OFF THE SERVANTS OF THE COUNTER-CHRIST?
HOW DO I DENY GOD'S WILL?
LUCIFER?

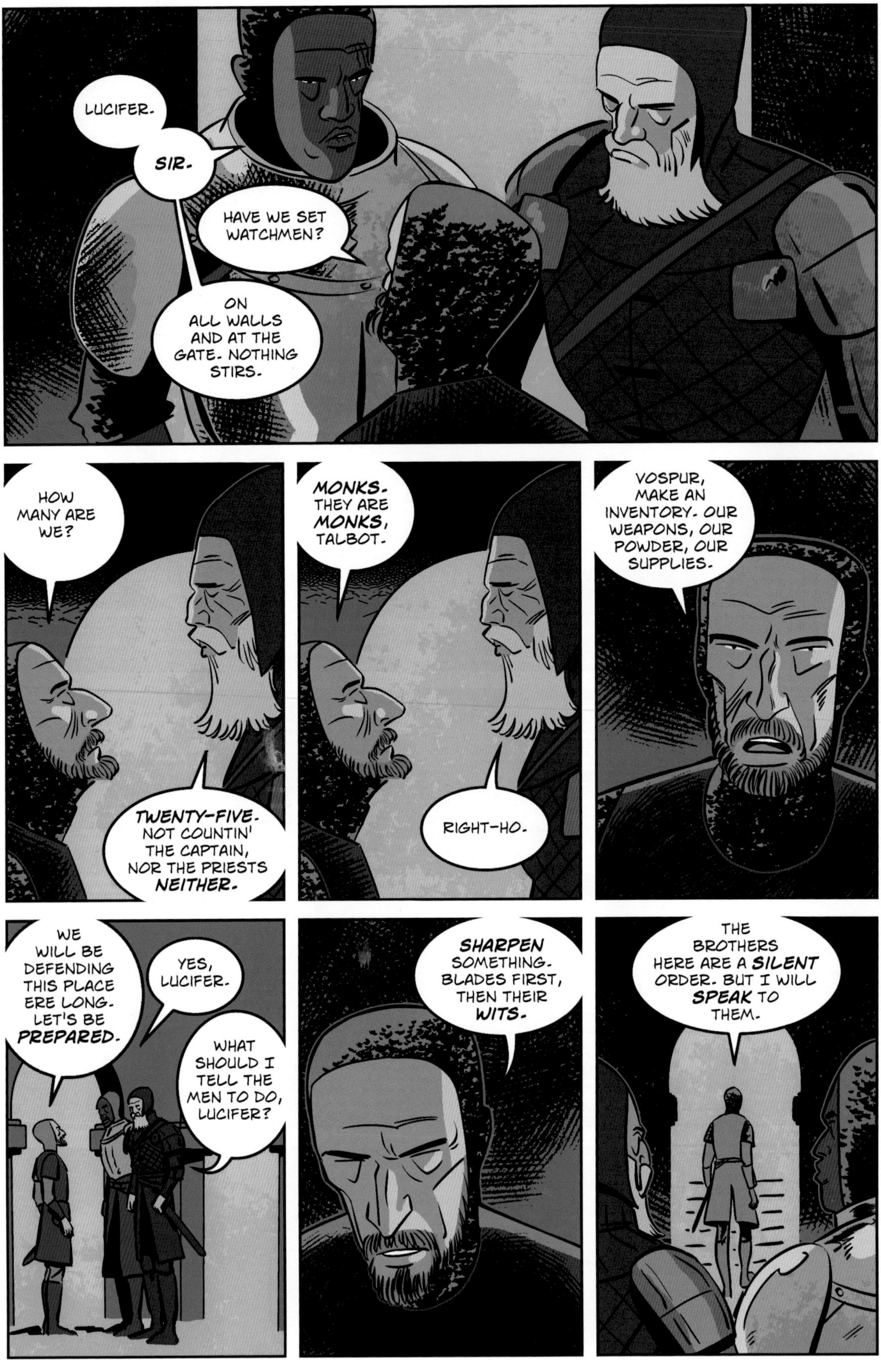
LUCIFER.
SIR.
HAVE WE SET WATCHMEN?
ON ALL WALLS AND AT THE GATE. NOTHING STIRS.
HOW MANY ARE WE?
TWENTY-FIVE. NOT COUNTIN' THE CAPTAIN, NOR THE PRIESTS NEITHER.
MONKS. THEY ARE MONKS, TALBOT.
RIGHT-HO.
VOSPUR, MAKE AN INVENTORY. OUR WEAPONS, OUR POWDER, OUR SUPPLIES.
WE WILL BE DEFENDING THIS PLACE ERE LONG. LET'S BE PREPARED.
YES, LUCIFER.
WHAT SHOULD I TELL THE MEN TO DO, LUCIFER?
SHARPEN SOMETHING. BLADES FIRST, THEN THEIR WITS.
THE BROTHERS HERE ARE A SILENT ORDER. BUT I WILL SPEAK TO THEM.

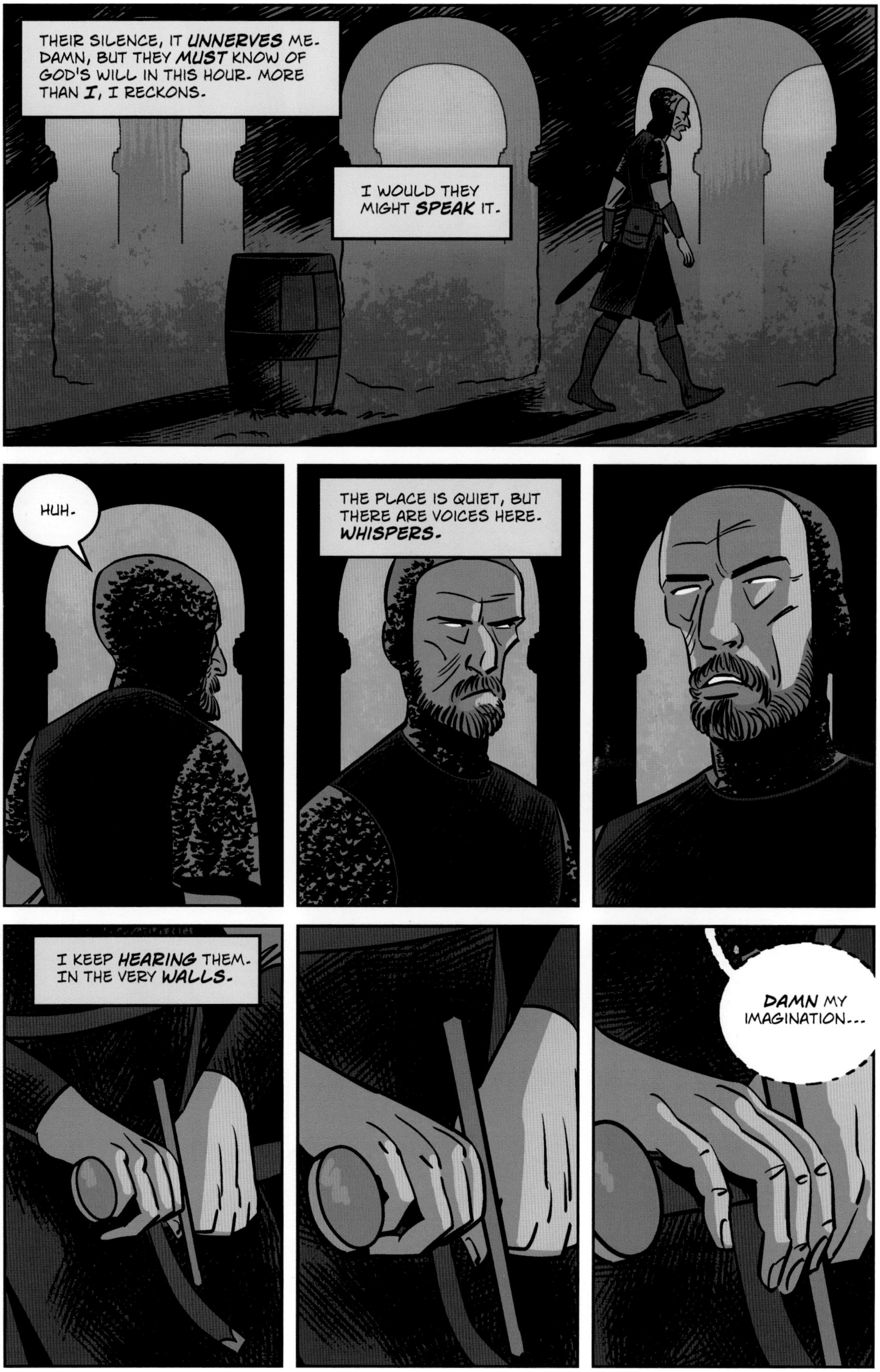
THEIR SILENCE, IT UNNERVES ME. DAMN, BUT THEY MUST KNOW OF GOD'S WILL IN THIS HOUR. MORE THAN I, I RECKONS.
I WOULD THEY MIGHT SPEAK IT.
HUH.
THE PLACE IS QUIET, BUT THERE ARE VOICES HERE. WHISPERS.
I KEEP HEARING THEM. IN THE VERY WALLS.
DAMN MY IMAGINATION...

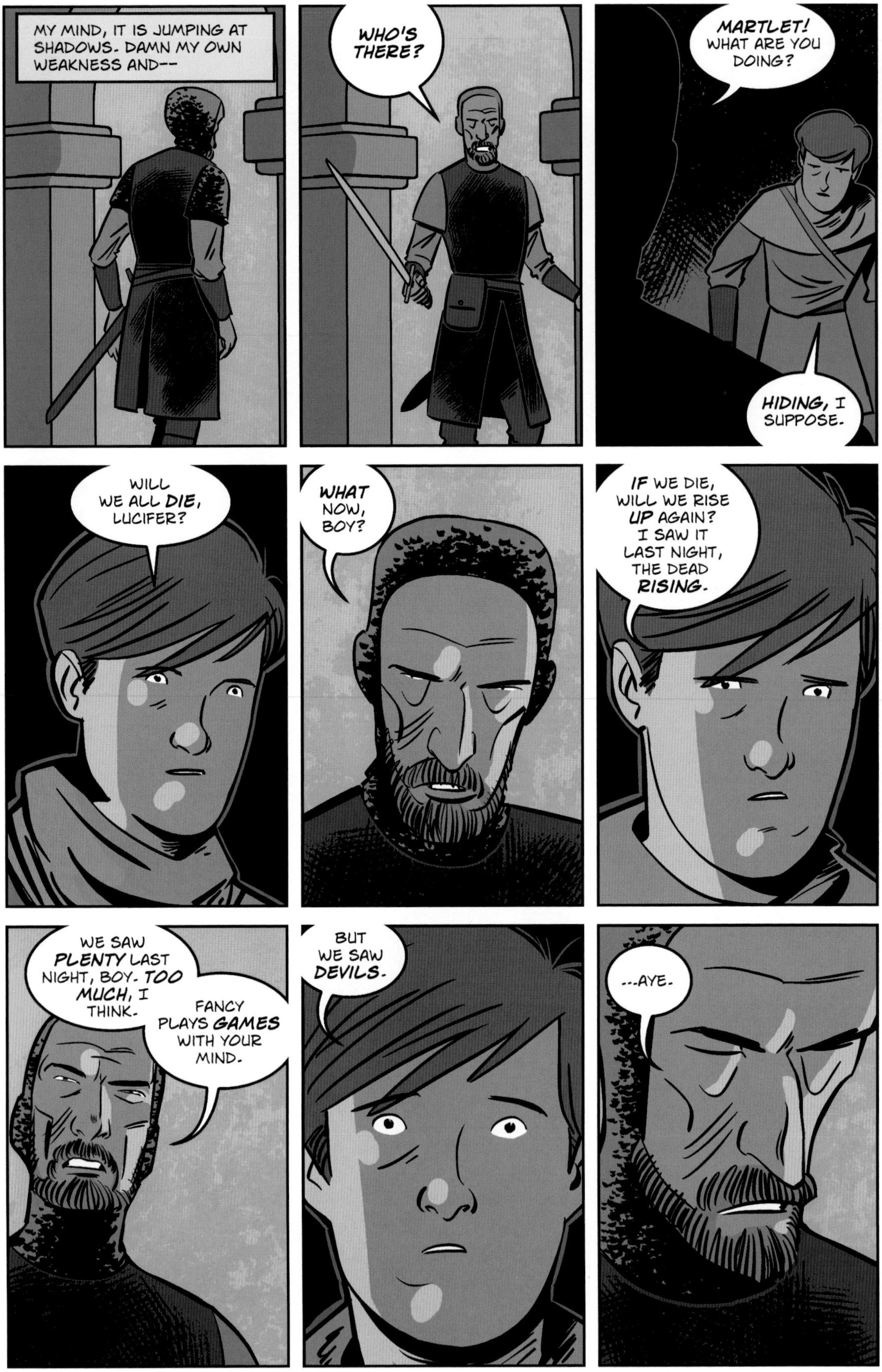
MY MIND, IT IS JUMPING AT SHADOWS. DAMN MY OWN WEAKNESS AND--
WHO'S THERE?
MARTLET! WHAT ARE YOU DOING?
HIDING, I SUPPOSE.
WILL WE ALL DIE, LUCIFER?
WHAT NOW, BOY?
IF WE DIE, WILL WE RISE UP AGAIN? I SAW IT LAST NIGHT, THE DEAD RISING.
WE SAW PLENTY LAST NIGHT, BOY. TOO MUCH, I THINK.
FANCY PLAYS GAMES WITH YOUR MIND.
BUT WE SAW DEVILS.
---AYE.

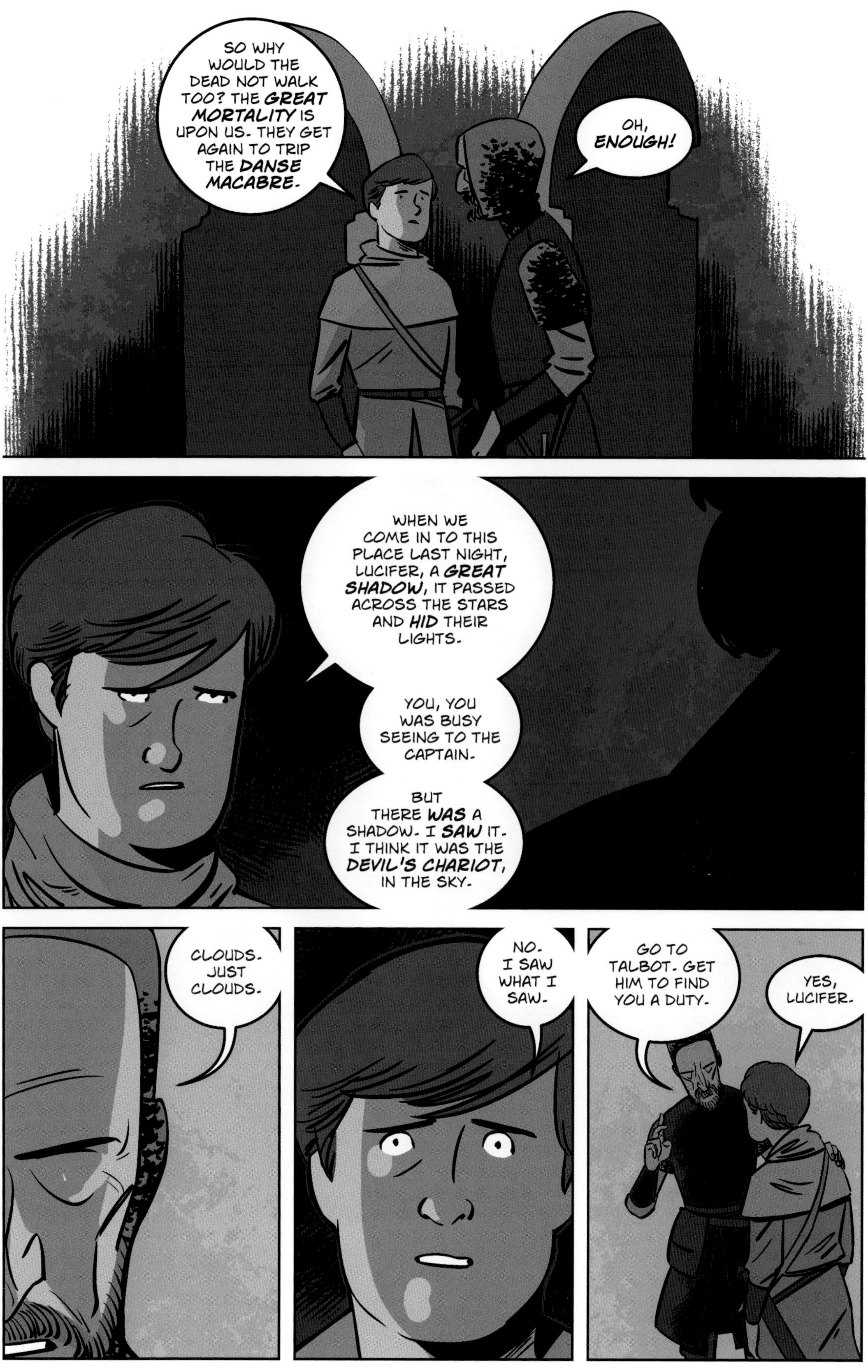
SO WHY WOULD THE DEAD NOT WALK TOO? THE GREAT MORTALITY IS UPON US. THEY GET AGAIN TO TRIP THE DANSE MACABRE.
OH, ENOUGH!
WHEN WE COME IN TO THIS PLACE LAST NIGHT, LUCIFER, A GREAT SHADOW, IT PASSED ACROSS THE STARS AND HID THEIR LIGHTS.
YOU, YOU WAS BUSY SEEING TO THE CAPTAIN.
BUT THERE WAS A SHADOW. I SAW IT. I THINK IT WAS THE DEVIL'S CHARIOT, IN THE SKY.
CLOUDS. JUST CLOUDS.
NO. I SAW WHAT I SAW.
GO TO TALBOT. GET HIM TO FIND YOU A DUTY.
YES, LUCIFER.

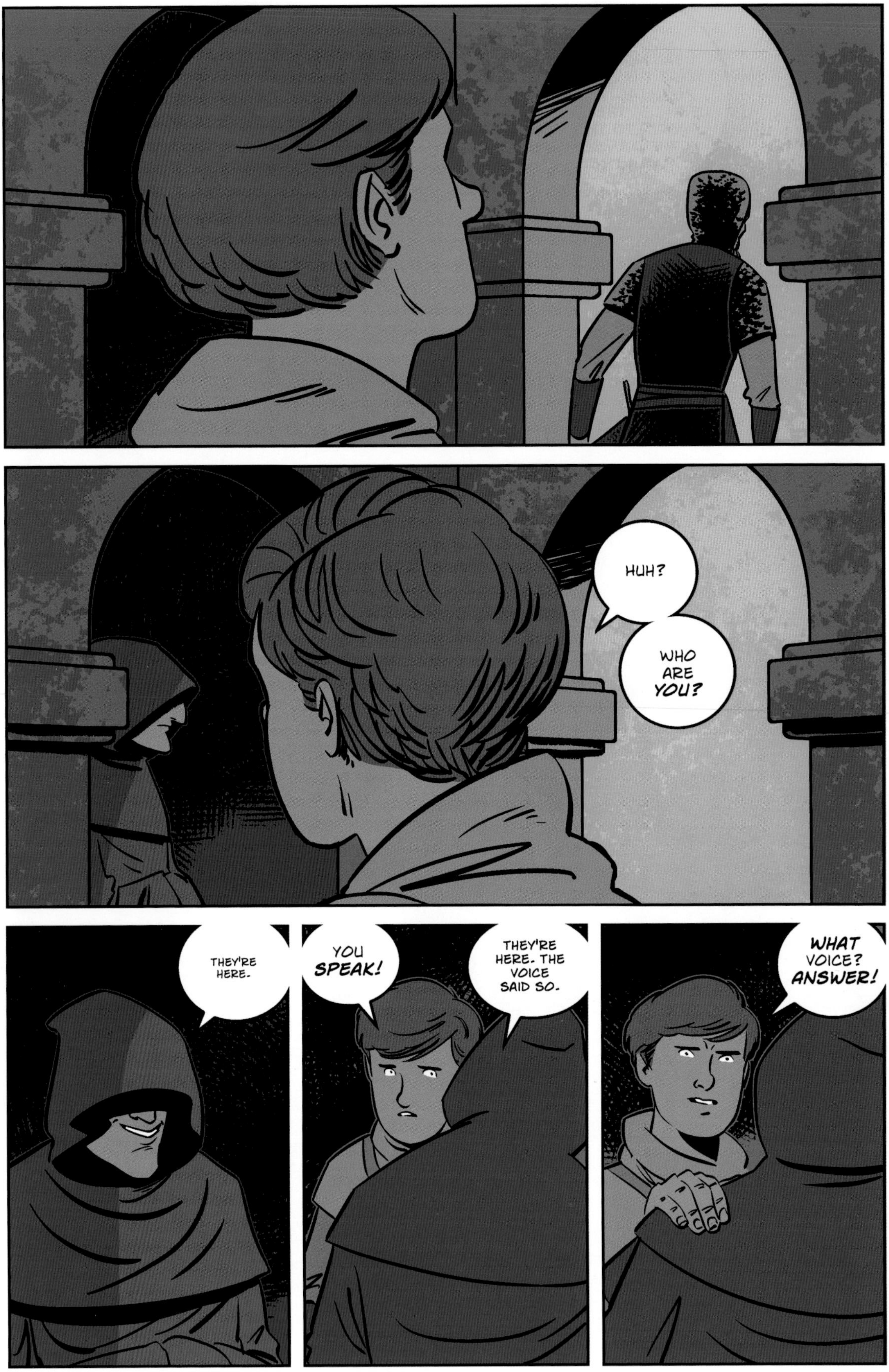
HUH?
WHO ARE YOU?
THEY'RE HERE.
YOU SPEAK!
THEY'RE HERE. THE VOICE SAID SO.
WHAT VOICE? ANSWER!

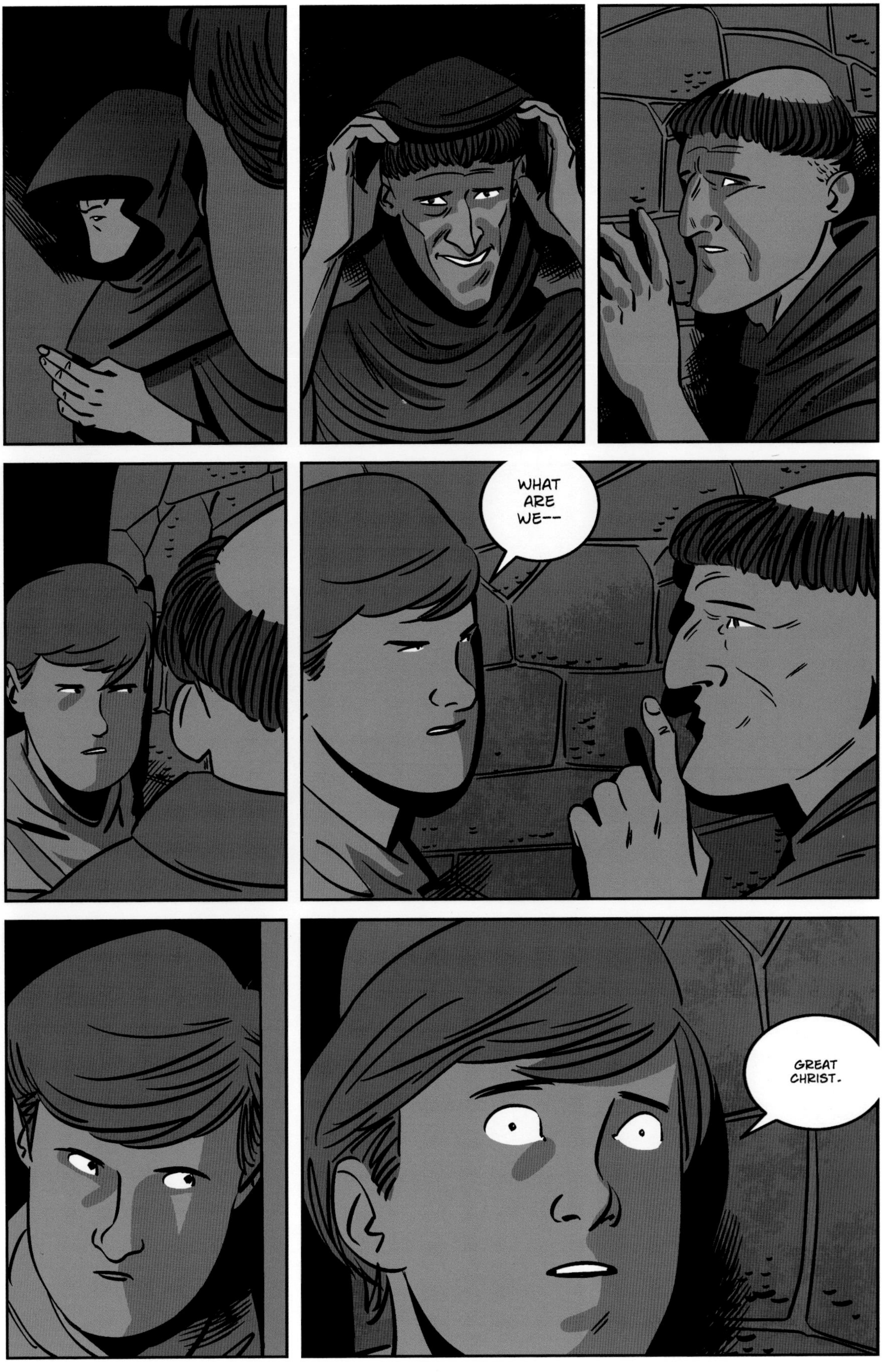
WHAT ARE WE--
GREAT CHRIST.

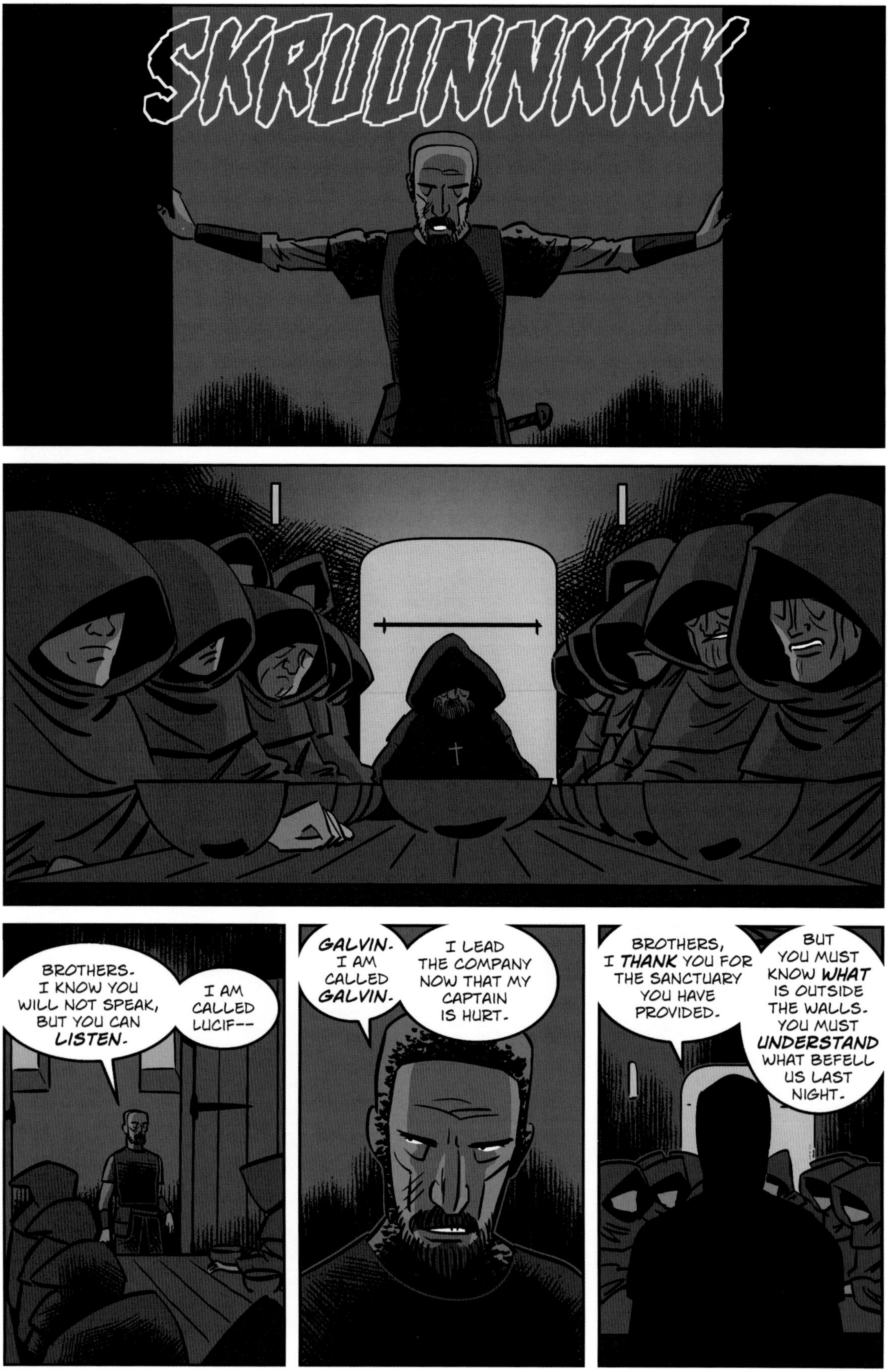
SKRUUNNKKK
BROTHERS. I KNOW YOU WILL NOT SPEAK, BUT YOU CAN LISTEN.
I AM CALLED LUCIF--
GALVIN. I AM CALLED GALVIN.
I LEAD THE COMPANY NOW THAT MY CAPTAIN IS HURT.
BROTHERS, I THANK YOU FOR THE SANCTUARY YOU HAVE PROVIDED.
BUT YOU MUST KNOW WHAT IS OUTSIDE THE WALLS. YOU MUST UNDERSTAND WHAT BEFELL US LAST NIGHT.

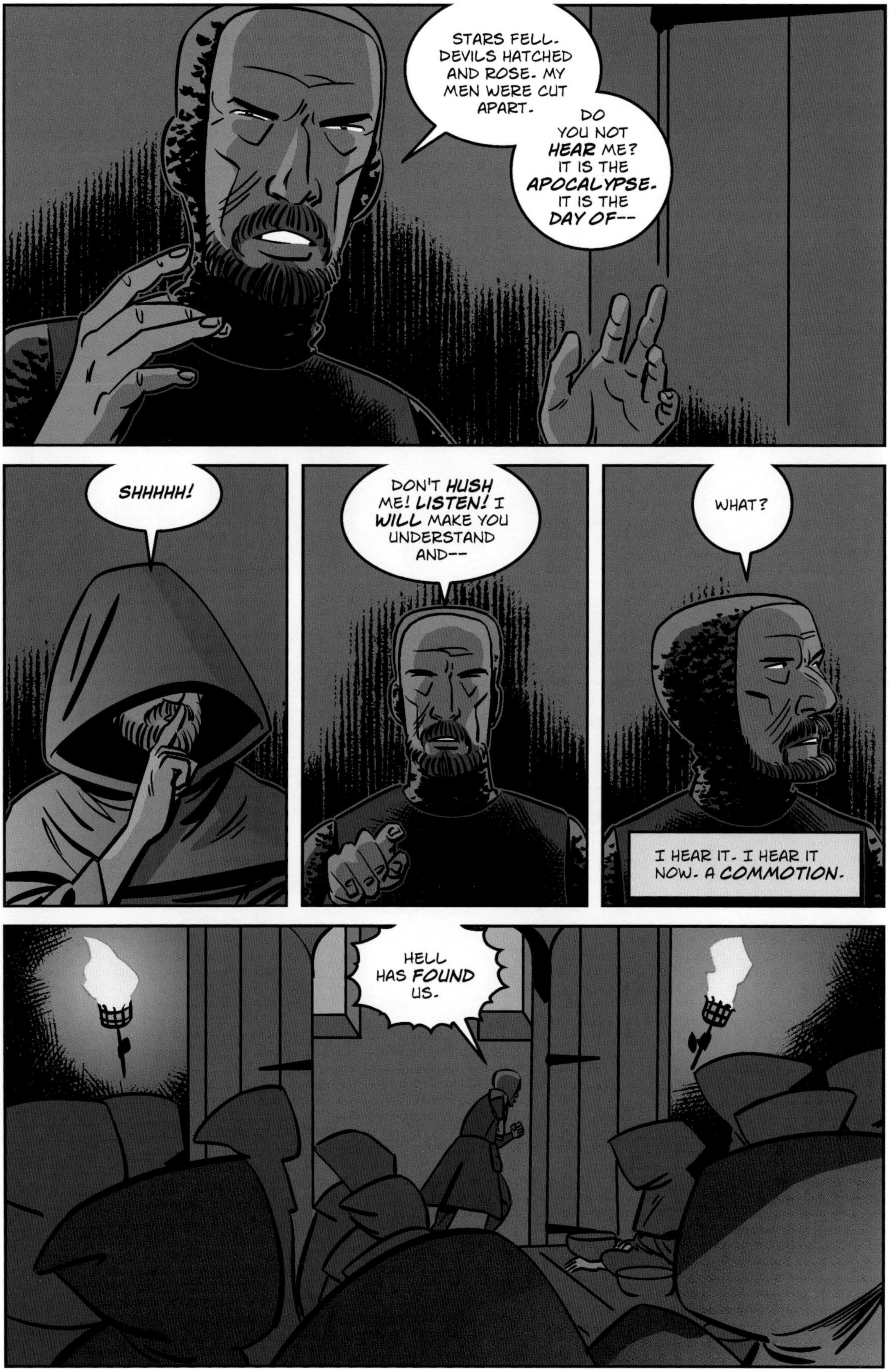
STARS FELL. DEVILS HATCHED AND ROSE. MY MEN WERE CUT APART.
DO YOU NOT HEAR ME? IT IS THE APOCALYPSE. IT IS THE DAY OF--
SHHHHH!
DON'T HUSH ME! LISTEN! I WILL MAKE YOU UNDERSTAND AND--
WHAT?
I HEAR IT. I HEAR IT NOW. A COMMOTION.
HELL HAS FOUND US.

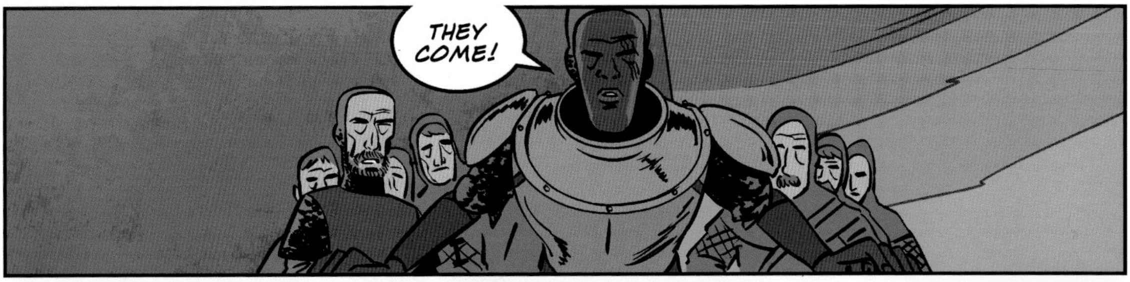
THEY COME!

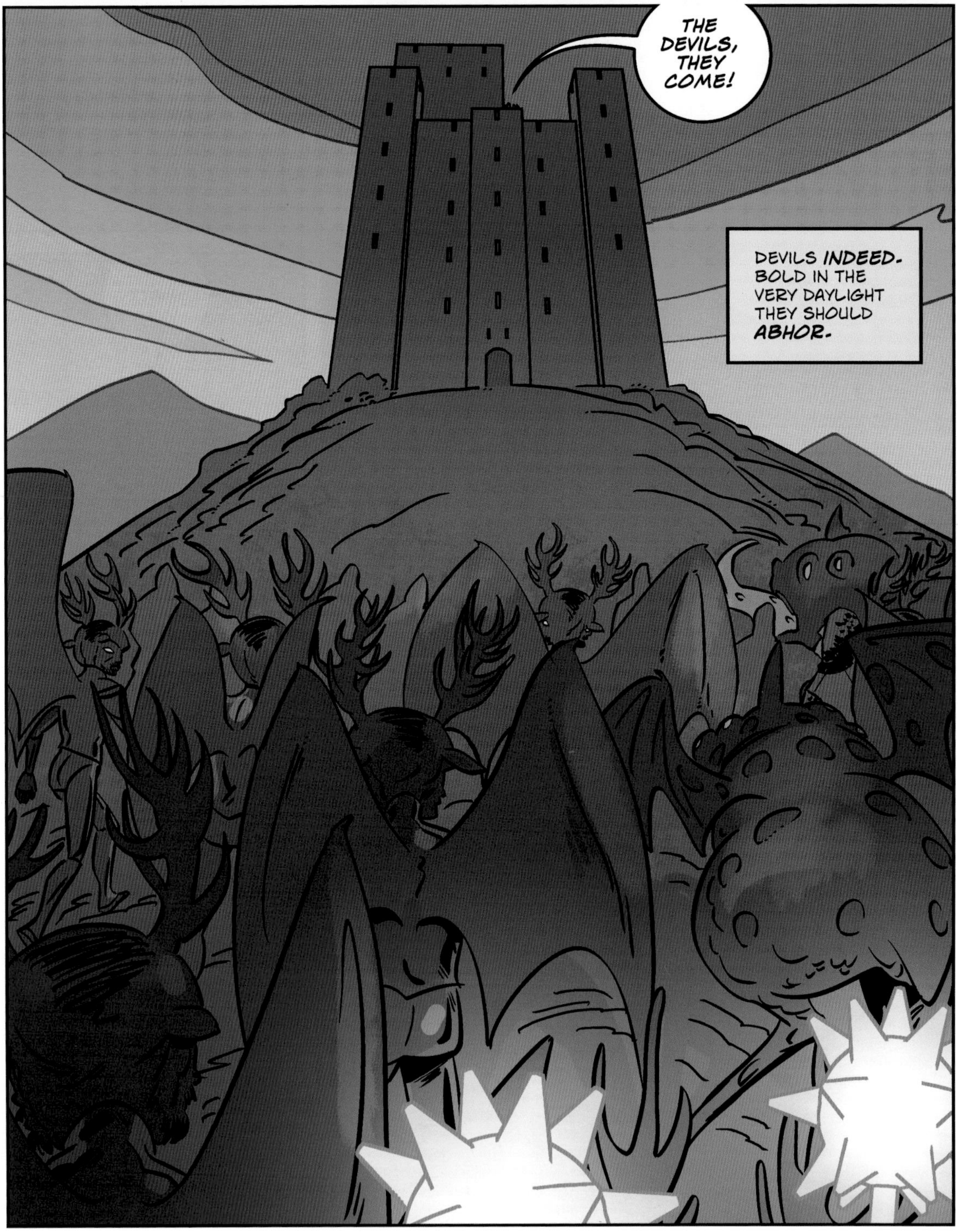
THE DEVILS, THEY COME!
DEVILS INDEED. BOLD IN THE VERY DAYLIGHT THEY SHOULD ABHOR.

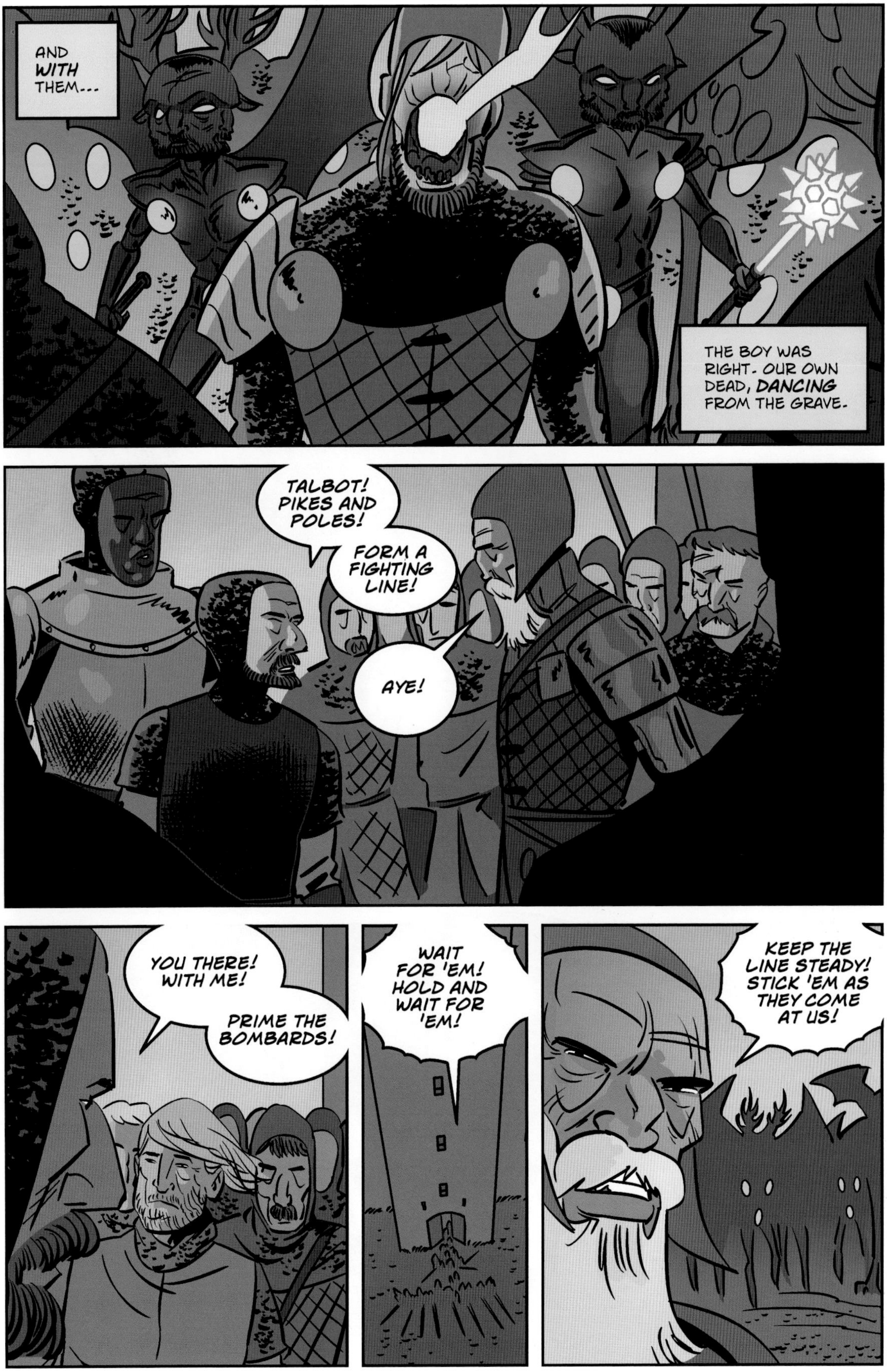
AND WITH THEM...
THE BOY WAS RIGHT. OUR OWN DEAD, DANCING FROM THE GRAVE.
TALBOT! PIKES AND POLES!
FORM A FIGHTING LINE!
AYE!
YOU THERE! WITH ME!
PRIME THE BOMBARDS!
WAIT FOR 'EM! HOLD AND WAIT FOR 'EM!
KEEP THE LINE STEADY! STICK 'EM AS THEY COME AT US!

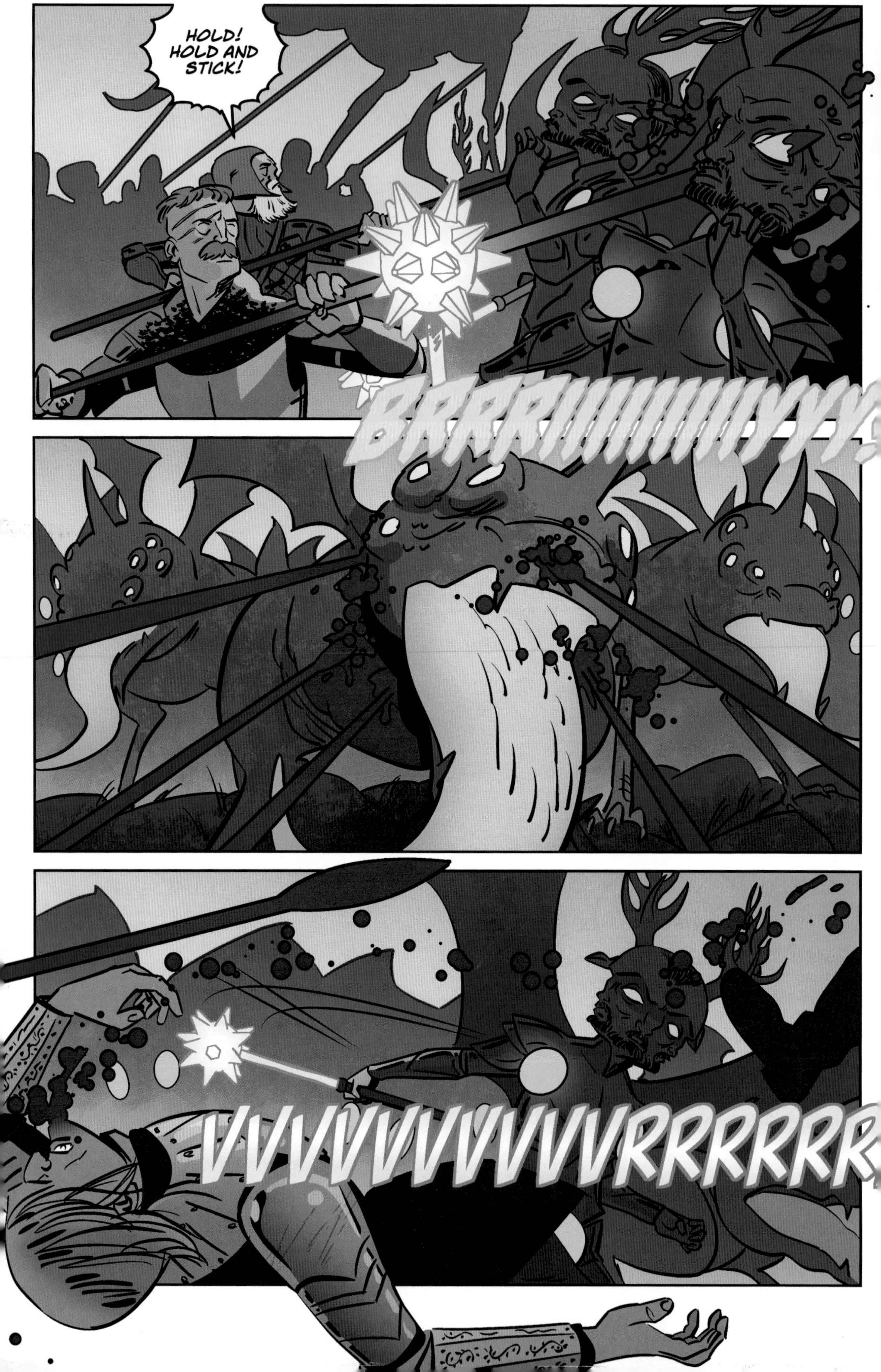
HOLD! HOLD AND STICK!
BRRRIIIIIIIIIYYY!
VVVVVVVVVVVVRRRRRR

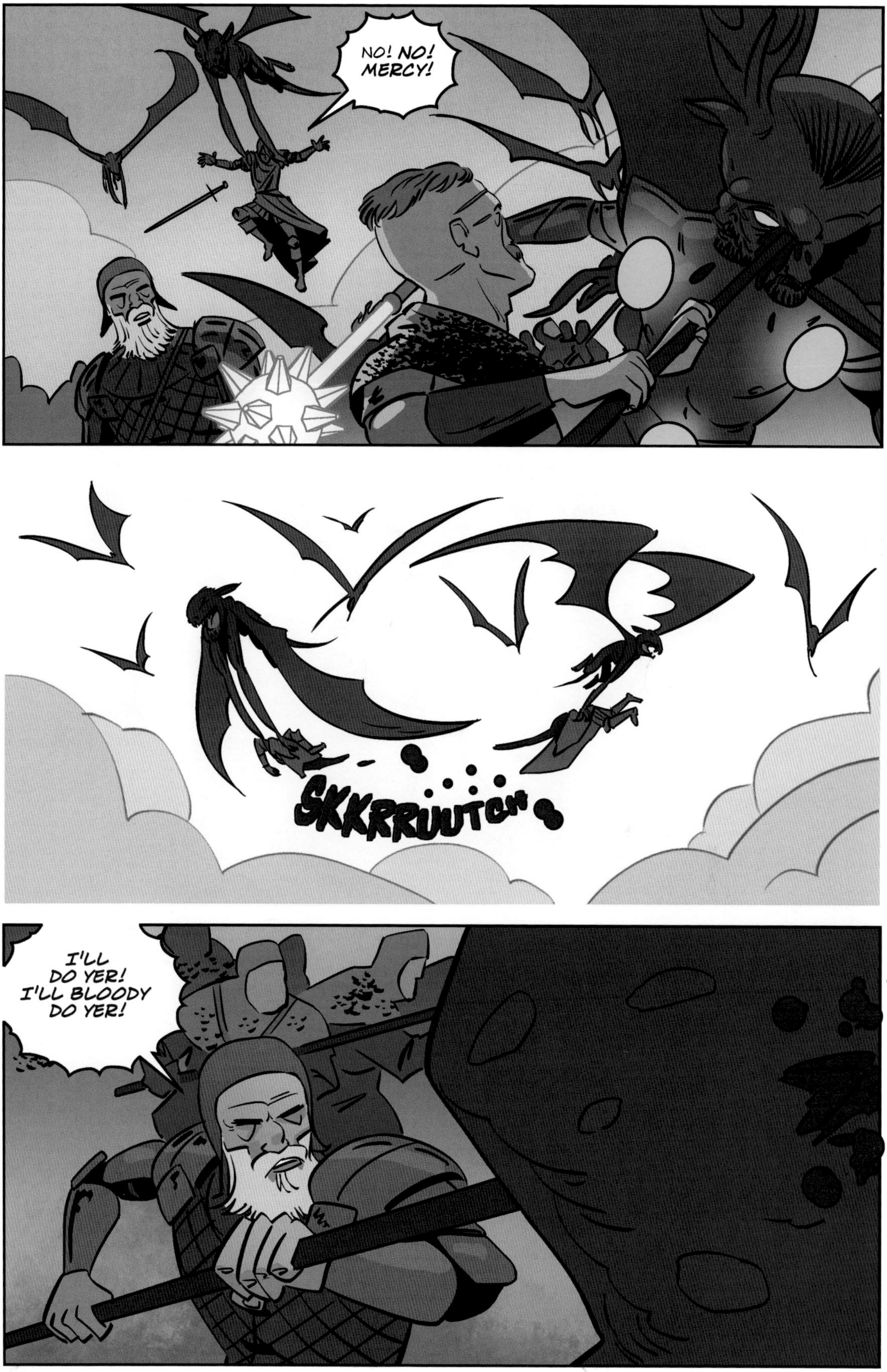
NO! NO! MERCY!
SKKRRUUTCH
I'LL DO YER! I'LL BLOODY DO YER!

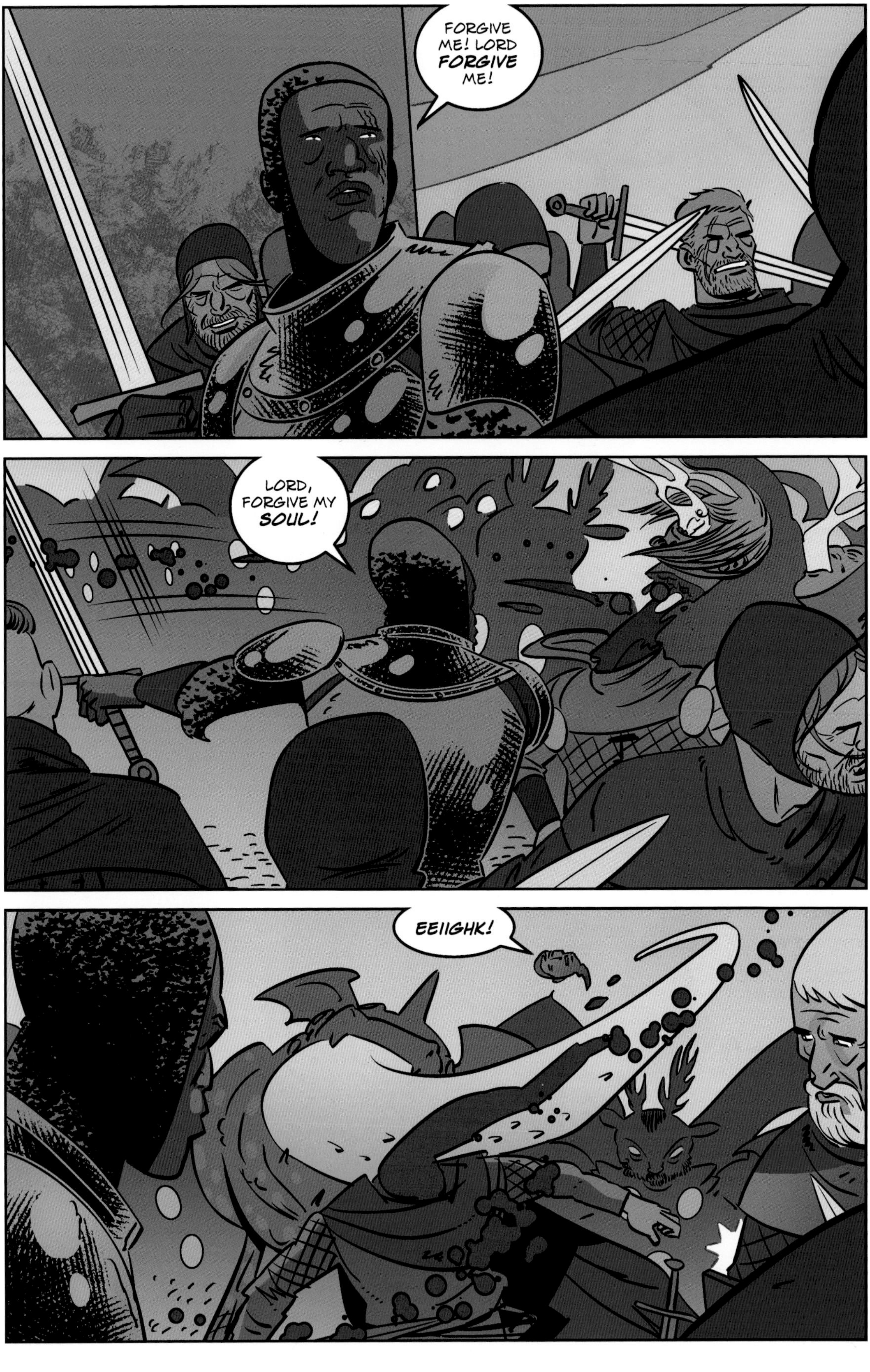
FORGIVE ME! LORD FORGIVE ME!
LORD, FORGIVE MY SOUL!
EEIIGHK!

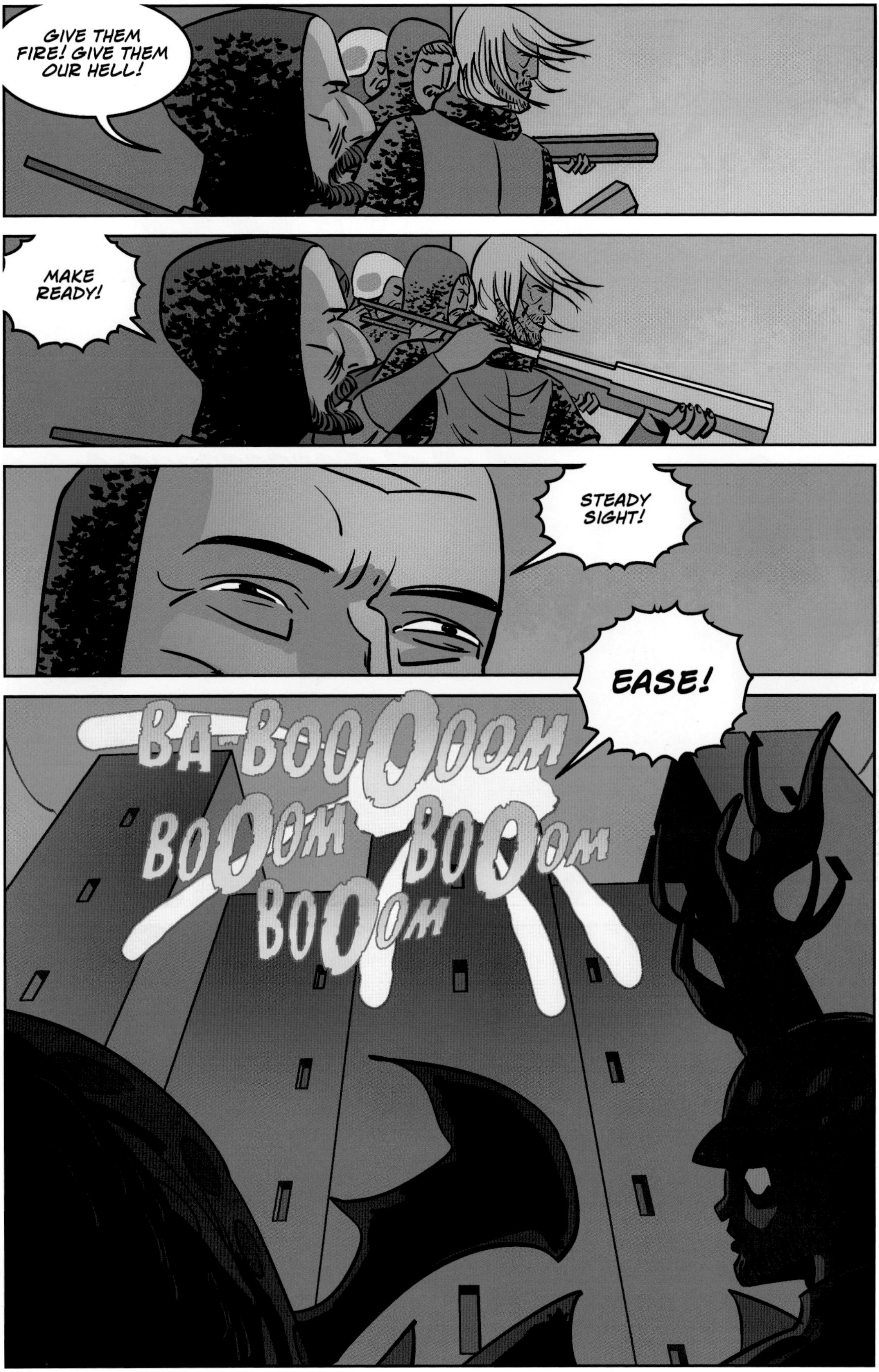
GIVE THEM FIRE! GIVE THEM OUR HELL!
MAKE READY!
STEADY SIGHT!
EASE!
BA-BOOOOOM
BOOOM BOOOM
BOOOM

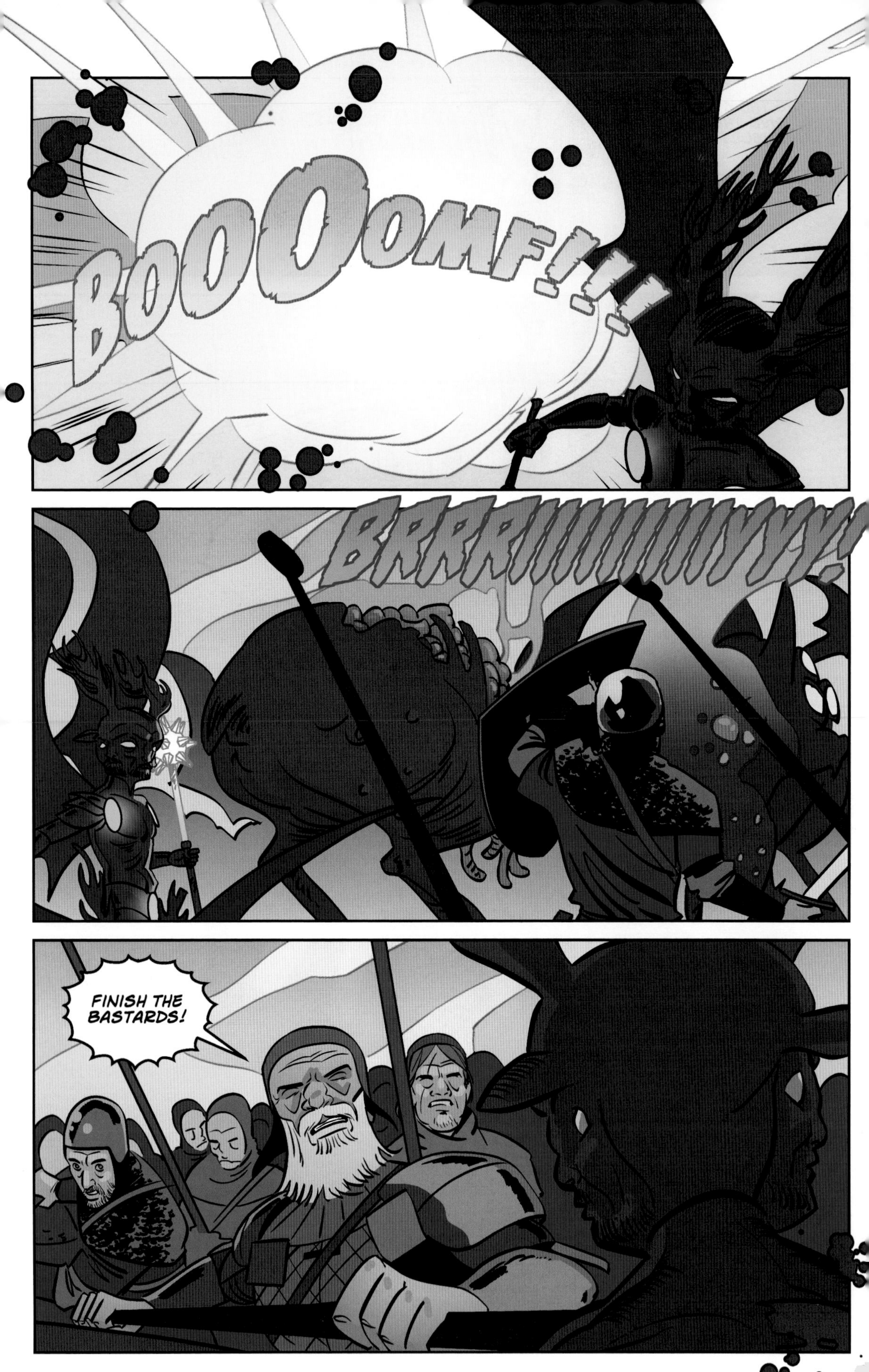
BOOOOMF!!!
BRRRIIIIIIIIIINNN!!
FINISH THE BASTARDS!

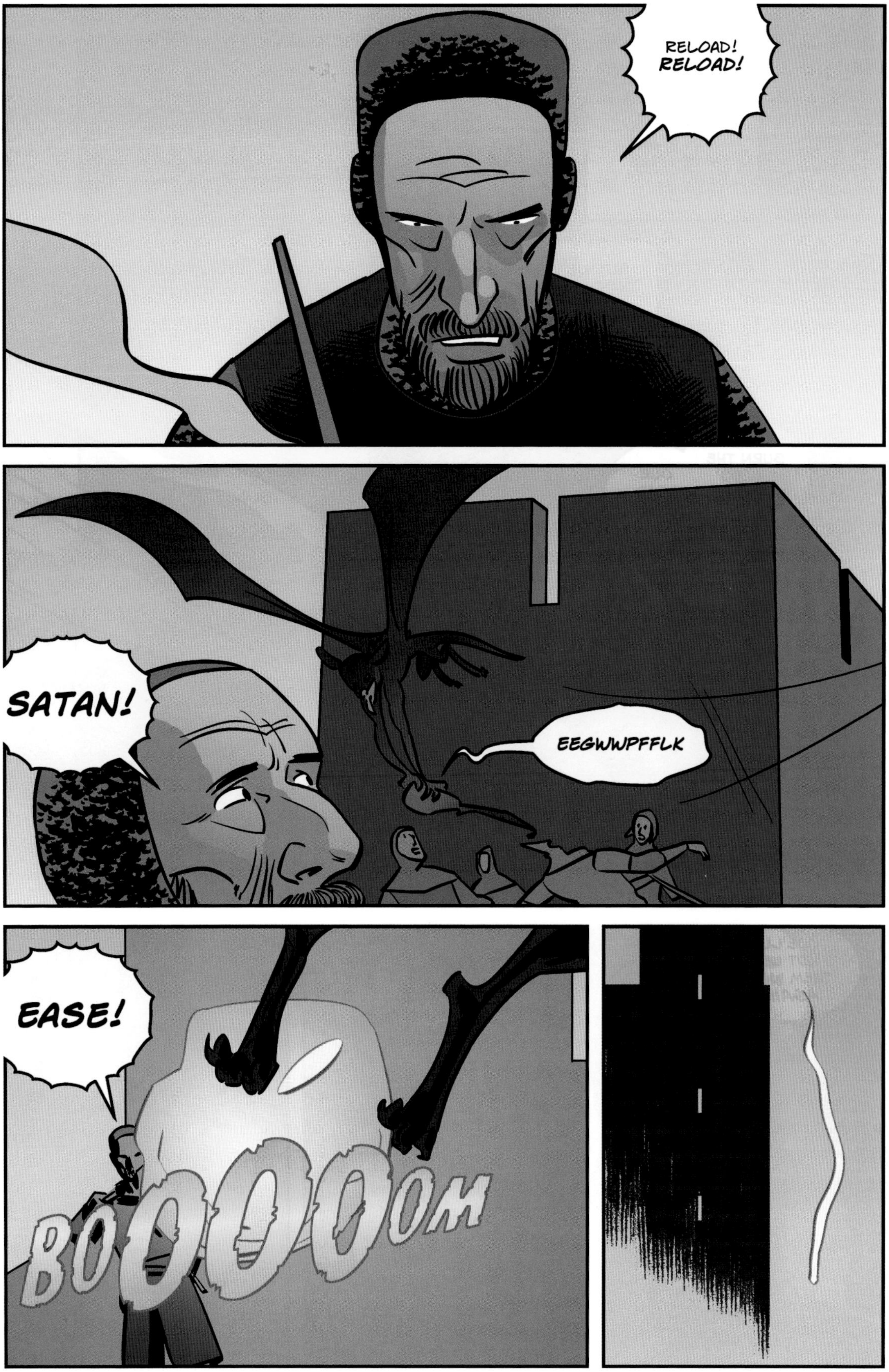
RELOAD!
RELOAD!
SATAN!
EEGWWPFFLK
EASE!
BOOOOOM

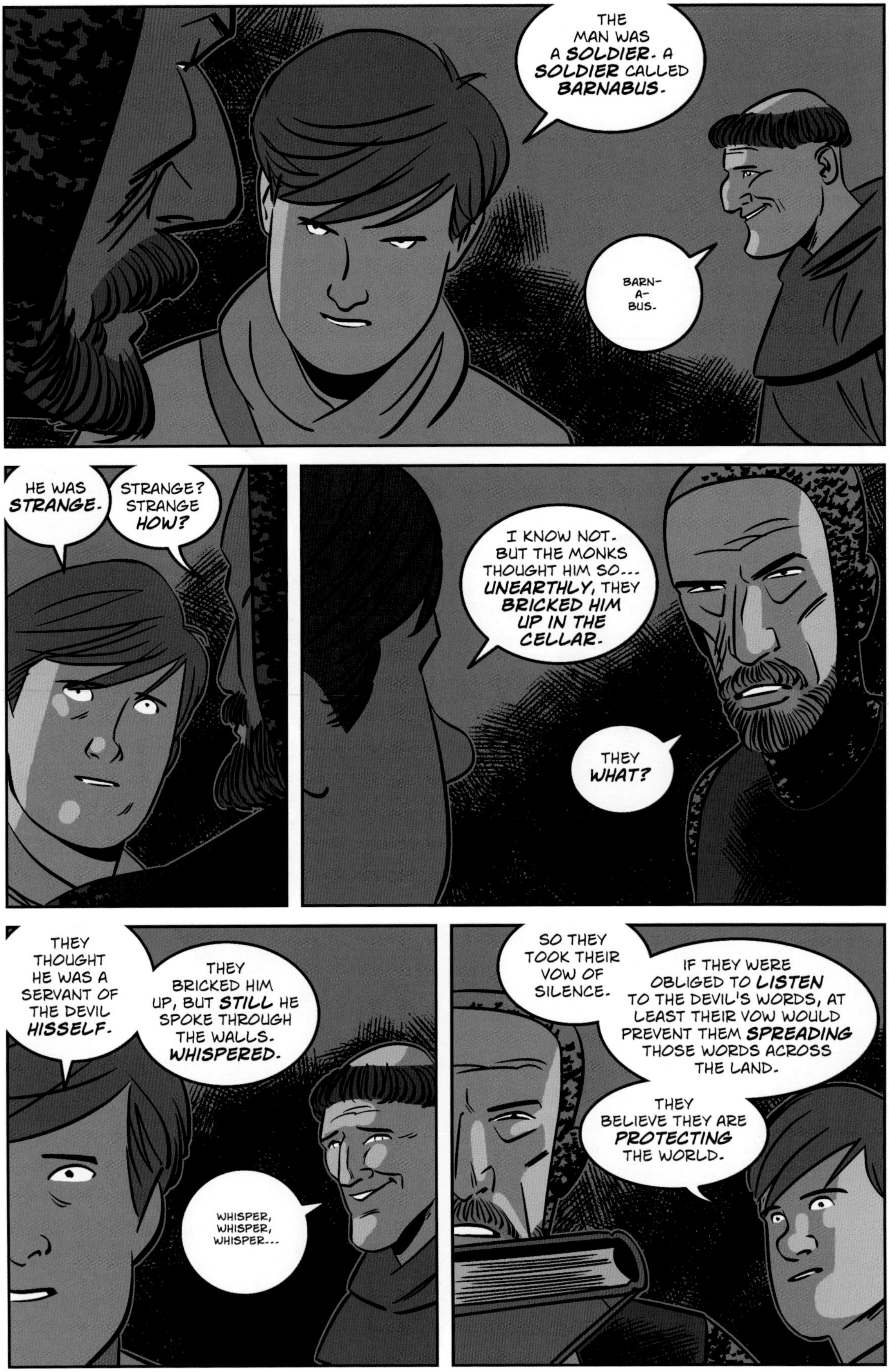
THE MAN WAS A SOLDIER. A SOLDIER CALLED BARNABUS.
BARN-A-BUS.
HE WAS STRANGE.
STRANGE? STRANGE HOW?
I KNOW NOT. BUT THE MONKS THOUGHT HIM SO... UNEARTHLY, THEY BRICKED HIM UP IN THE CELLAR.
THEY WHAT?
THEY THOUGHT HE WAS A SERVANT OF THE DEVIL HISSELF.
THEY BRICKED HIM UP, BUT STILL HE SPOKE THROUGH THE WALLS. WHISPERED.
WHISPER, WHISPER, WHISPER...
SO THEY TOOK THEIR VOW OF SILENCE.
IF THEY WERE OBLIGED TO LISTEN TO THE DEVIL'S WORDS, AT LEAST THEIR VOW WOULD PREVENT THEM SPREADING THOSE WORDS ACROSS THE LAND.
THEY BELIEVE THEY ARE PROTECTING THE WORLD.

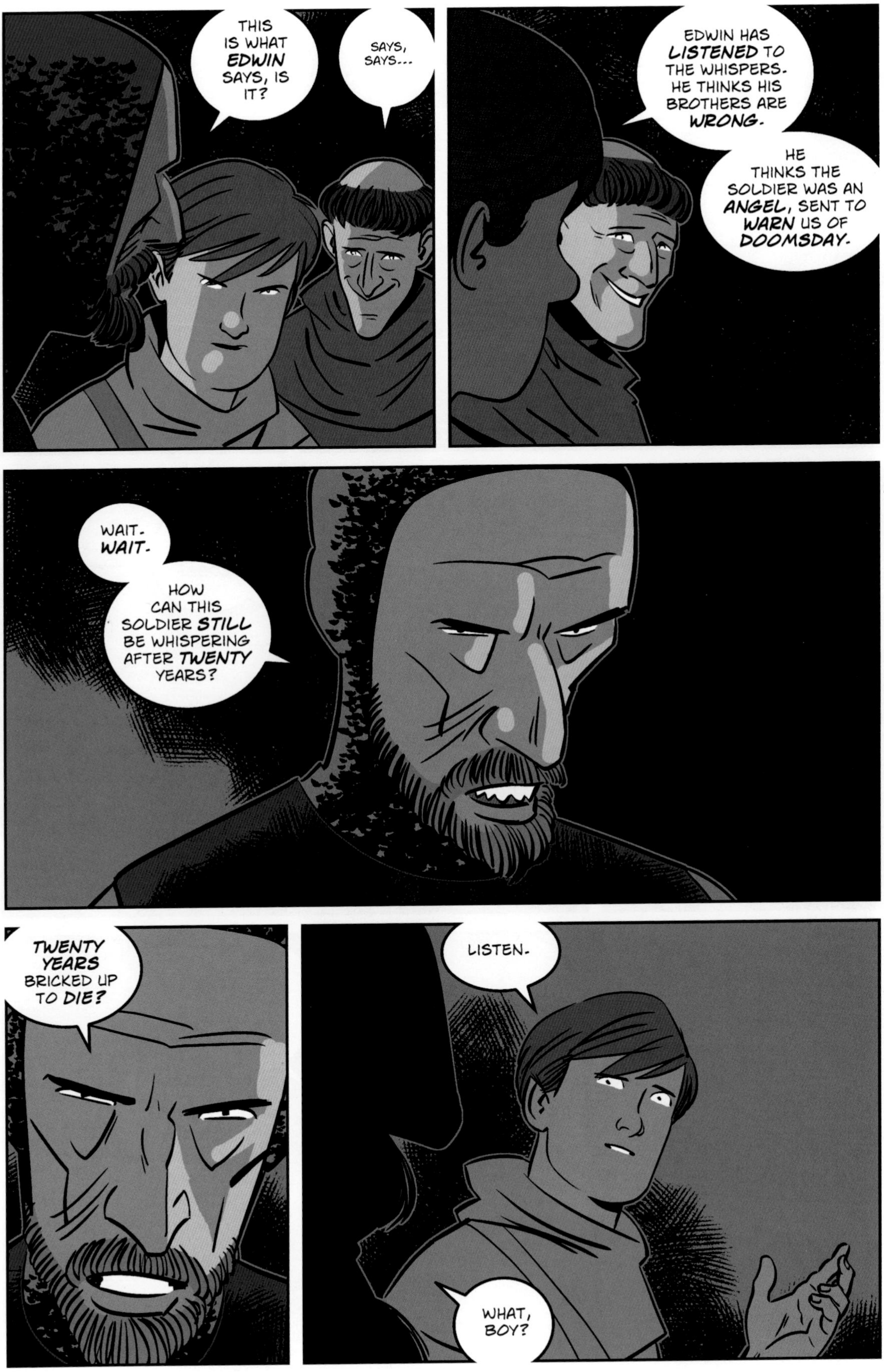
THIS IS WHAT EDWIN SAYS, IS IT?
SAYS, SAYS...
EDWIN HAS LISTENED TO THE WHISPERS. HE THINKS HIS BROTHERS ARE WRONG.
HE THINKS THE SOLDIER WAS AN ANGEL, SENT TO WARN US OF DOOMSDAY.
WAIT. WAIT.
HOW CAN THIS SOLDIER STILL BE WHISPERING AFTER TWENTY YEARS?
TWENTY YEARS BRICKED UP TO DIE?
LISTEN.
WHAT, BOY?

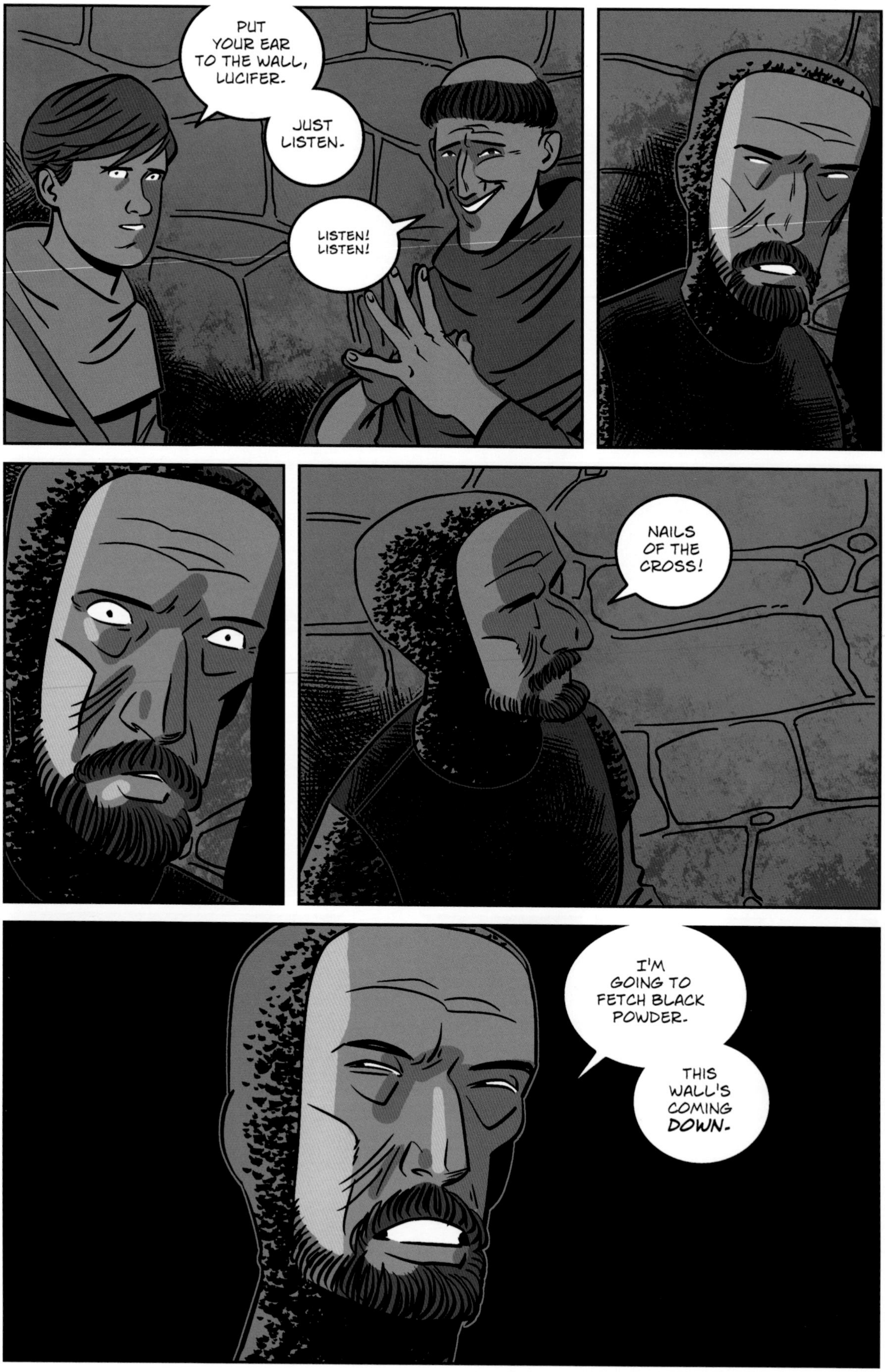
PUT YOUR EAR TO THE WALL, LUCIFER.
JUST LISTEN.
LISTEN! LISTEN!
NAILS OF THE CROSS!
I'M GOING TO FETCH BLACK POWDER.
THIS WALL'S COMING **DOWN**.

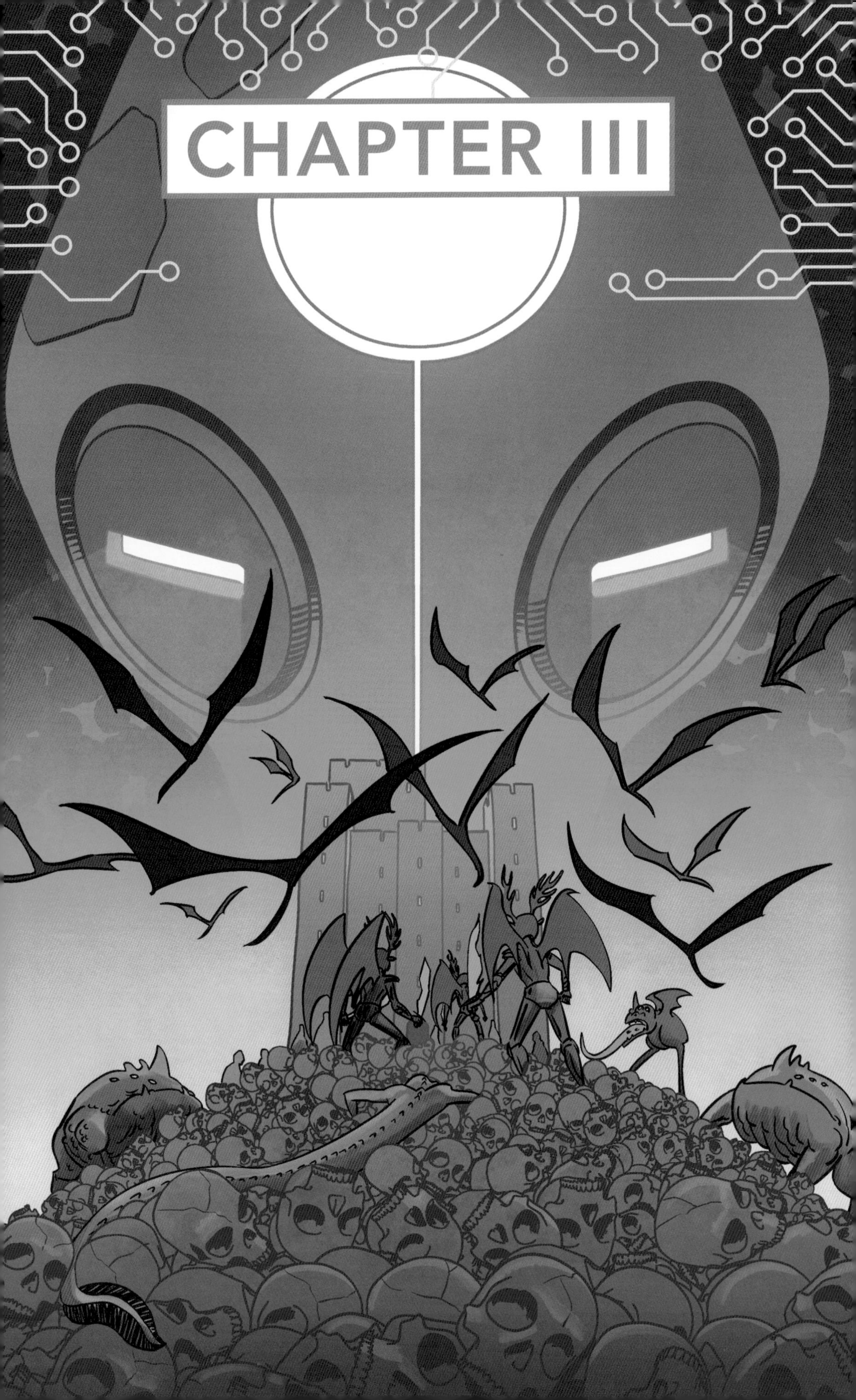
CHAPTER III

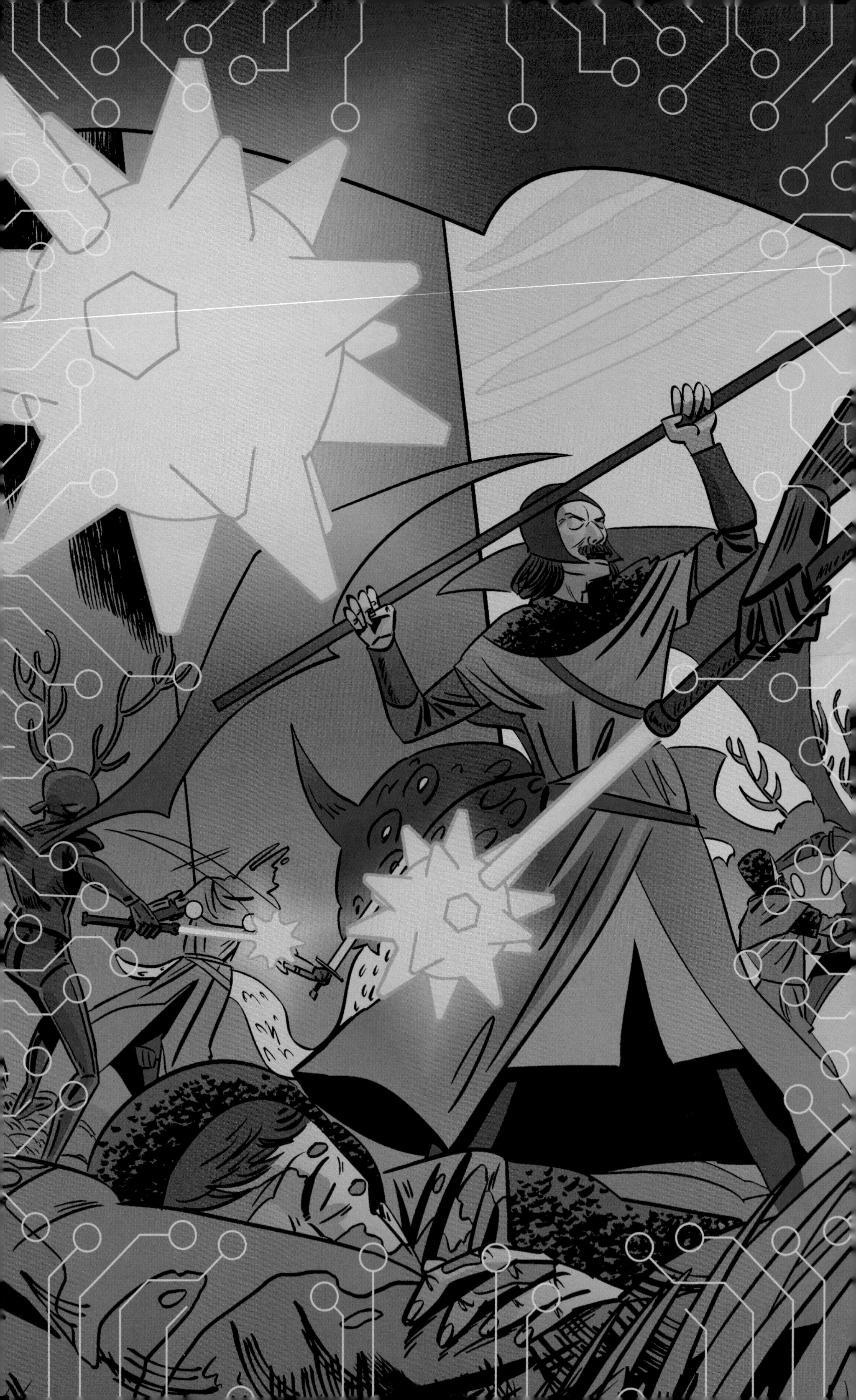

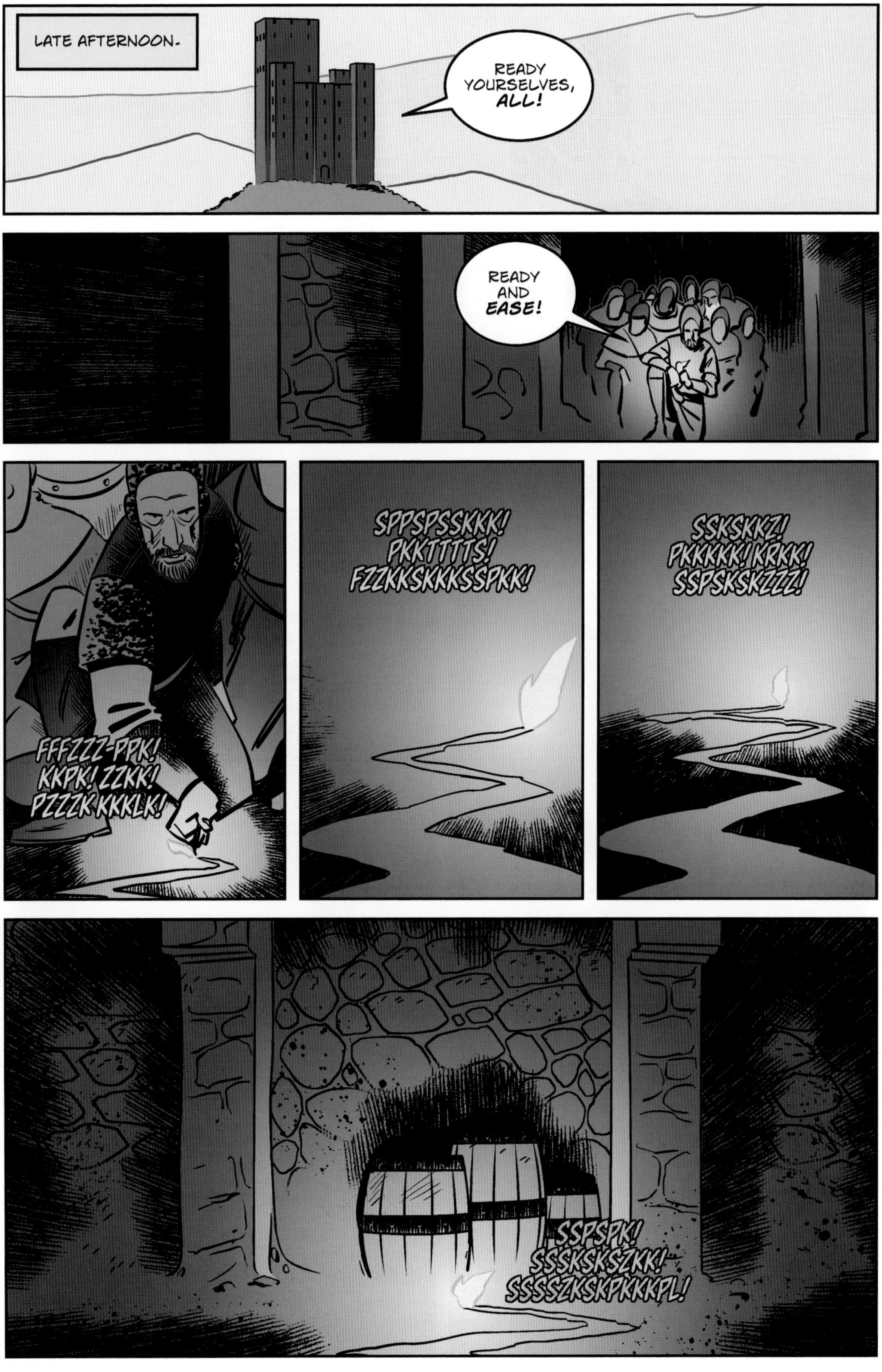
LATE AFTERNOON.
READY YOURSELVES, ALL!
READY AND EASE!
FFFZZZ-PPK! KKPK! ZZKK! PZZZK KKKLK!
SPPSPSSKKK! PKKTTTTS! FZZKKSKKKSSPKK!
SSKSKKZ! PKKKKK! KRKK! SSPSKSKZZZ!
SSPSPK! SSSKSKSZKK! SSSSZKSKPKKKPL!

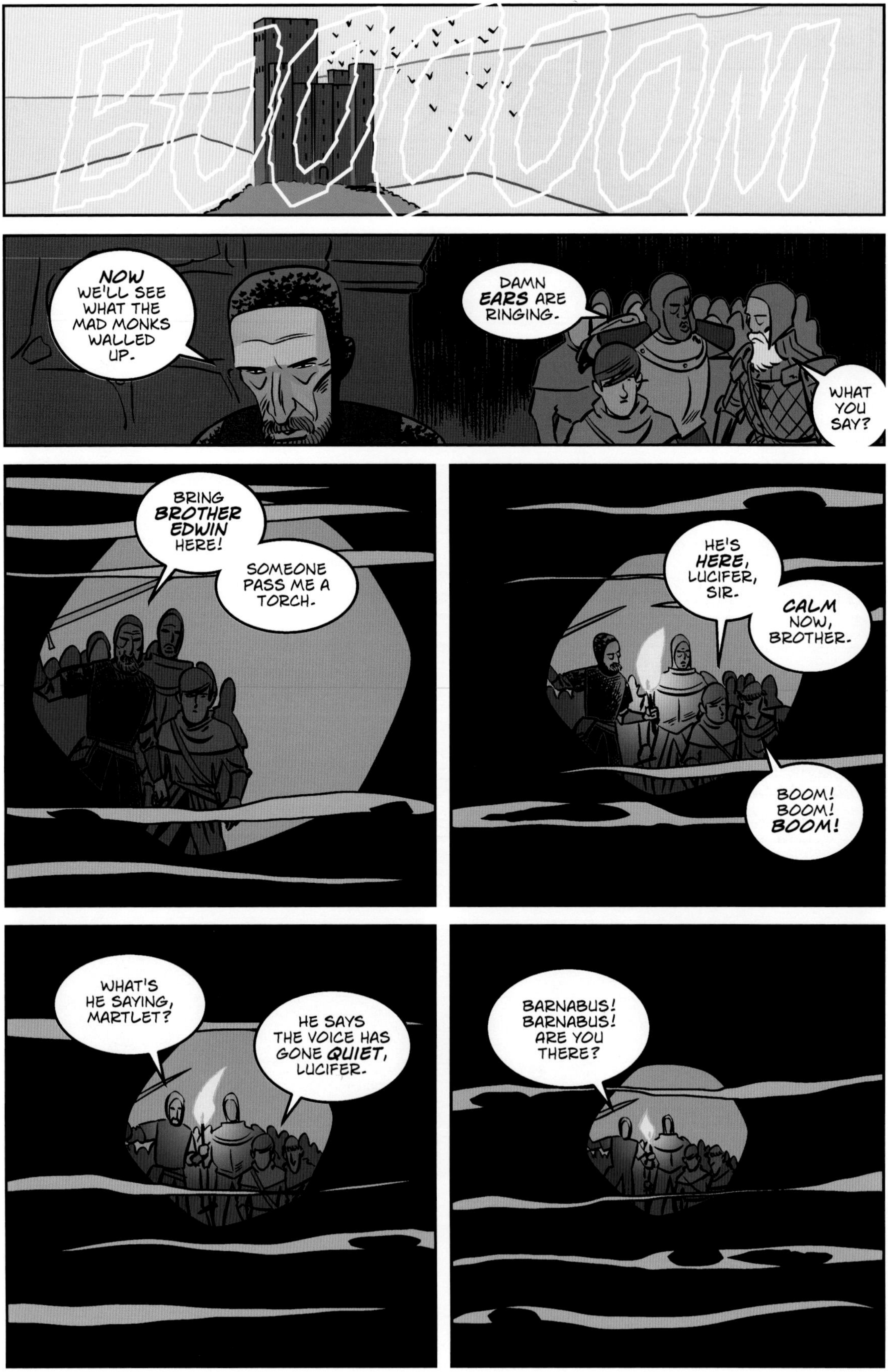
BOOOOOM
NOW WE'LL SEE WHAT THE MAD MONKS WALLED UP.
DAMN EARS ARE RINGING.
WHAT YOU SAY?
BRING BROTHER EDWIN HERE!
SOMEONE PASS ME A TORCH.
HE'S HERE, LUCIFER, SIR.
CALM NOW, BROTHER.
BOOM! BOOM! BOOM!
WHAT'S HE SAYING, MARTLET?
HE SAYS THE VOICE HAS GONE QUIET, LUCIFER.
BARNABUS! BARNABUS! ARE YOU THERE?

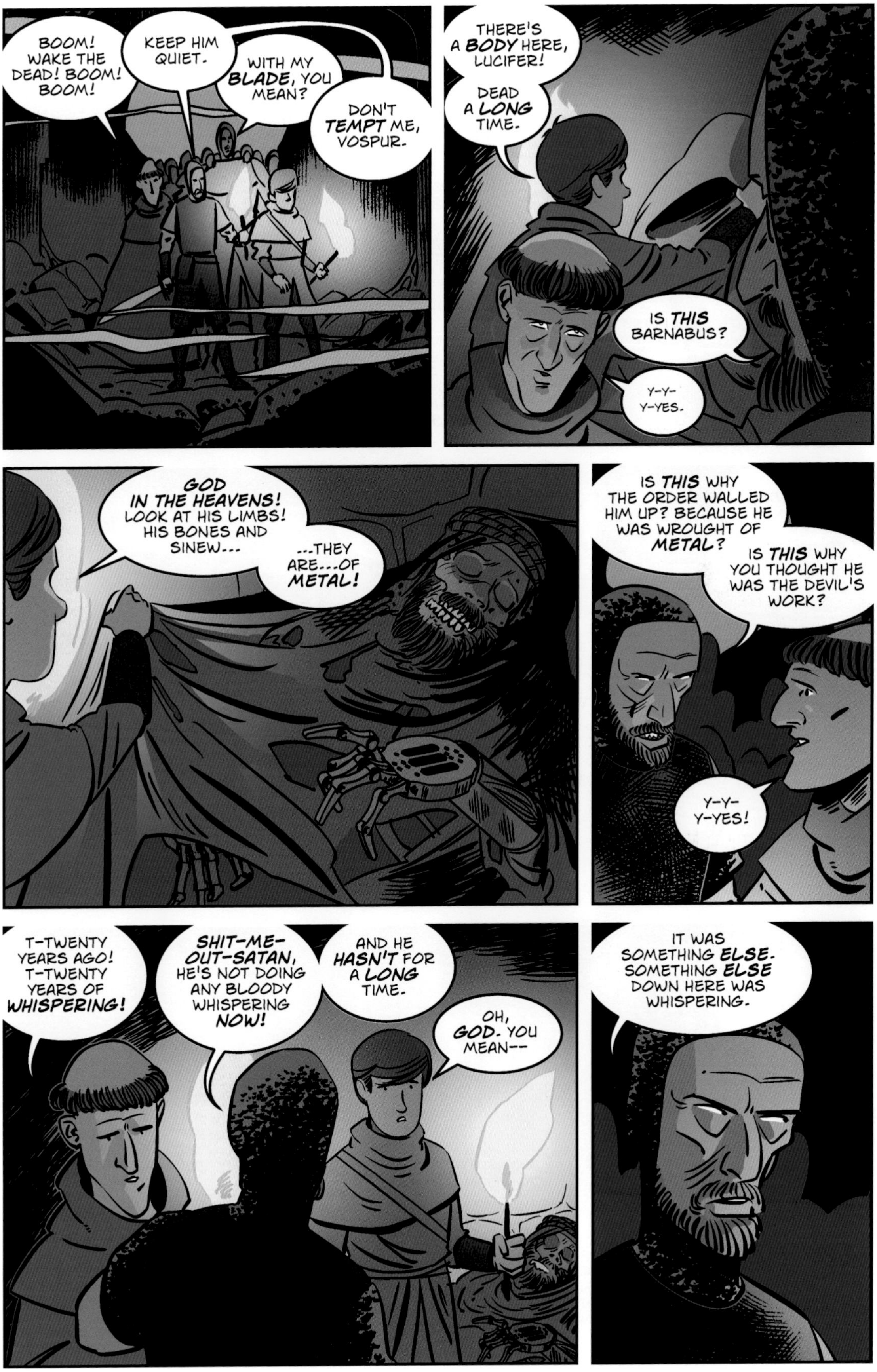
BOOM! WAKE THE DEAD! BOOM! BOOM!
KEEP HIM QUIET.
WITH MY BLADE, YOU MEAN?
DON'T TEMPT ME, VOSPUR.
THERE'S A BODY HERE, LUCIFER!
DEAD A LONG TIME.
IS THIS BARNABUS?
Y-Y-Y-YES.
GOD IN THE HEAVENS! LOOK AT HIS LIMBS! HIS BONES AND SINEW...
...THEY ARE...OF METAL!
IS THIS WHY THE ORDER WALLED HIM UP? BECAUSE HE WAS WROUGHT OF METAL?
IS THIS WHY YOU THOUGHT HE WAS THE DEVIL'S WORK?
Y-Y-Y-YES!
T-TWENTY YEARS AGO! T-TWENTY YEARS OF WHISPERING!
SHIT-ME-OUT-SATAN, HE'S NOT DOING ANY BLOODY WHISPERING NOW!
AND HE HASN'T FOR A LONG TIME.
OH, GOD. YOU MEAN--
IT WAS SOMETHING ELSE. SOMETHING ELSE DOWN HERE WAS WHISPERING.

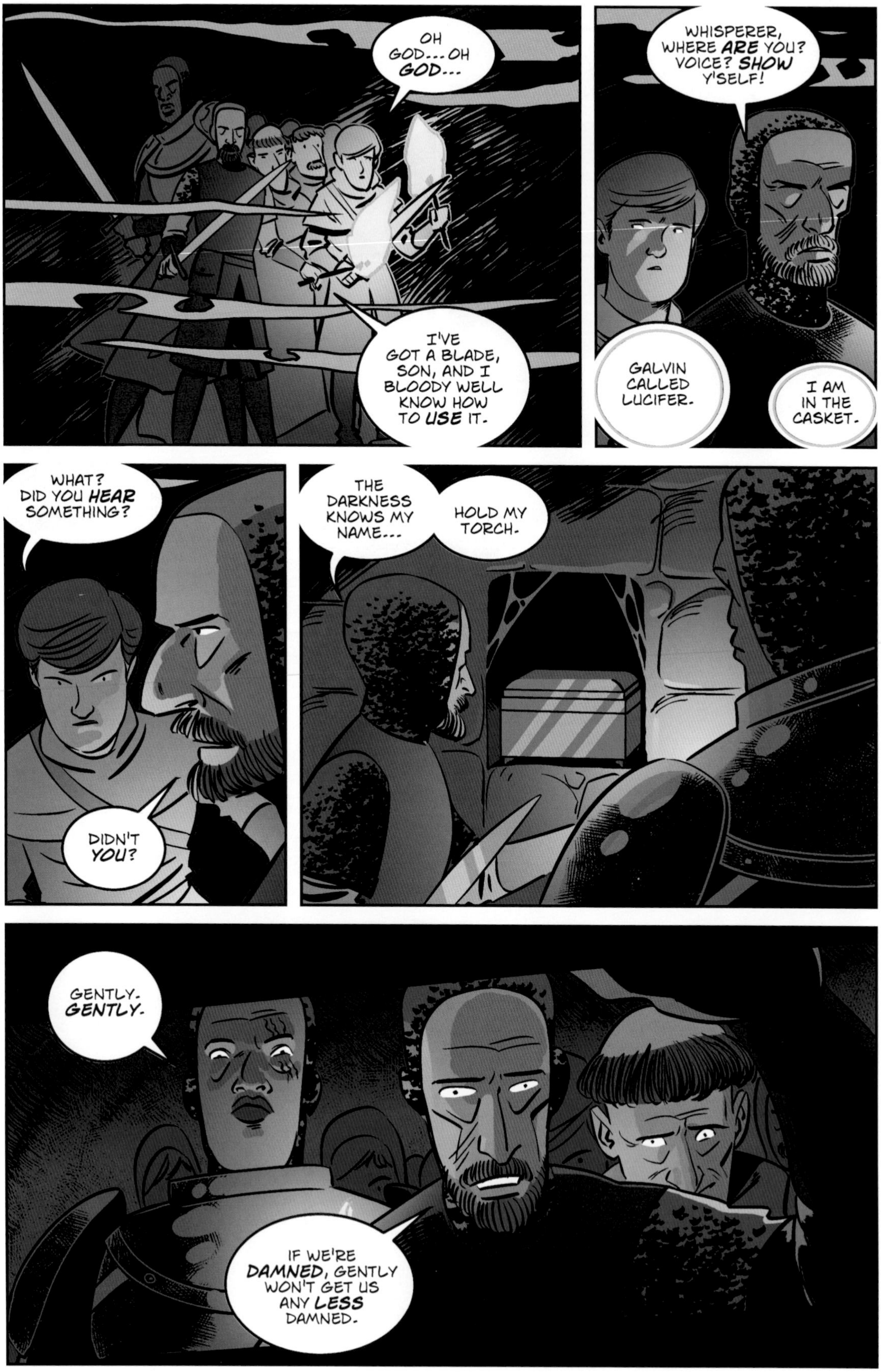
OH GOD... OH GOD...
I'VE GOT A BLADE, SON, AND I BLOODY WELL KNOW HOW TO USE IT.
WHISPERER, WHERE ARE YOU? VOICE? SHOW Y'SELF!
GALVIN CALLED LUCIFER.
I AM IN THE CASKET.
WHAT? DID YOU HEAR SOMETHING?
DIDN'T YOU?
THE DARKNESS KNOWS MY NAME...
HOLD MY TORCH.
GENTLY. GENTLY.
IF WE'RE DAMNED, GENTLY WON'T GET US ANY LESS DAMNED.

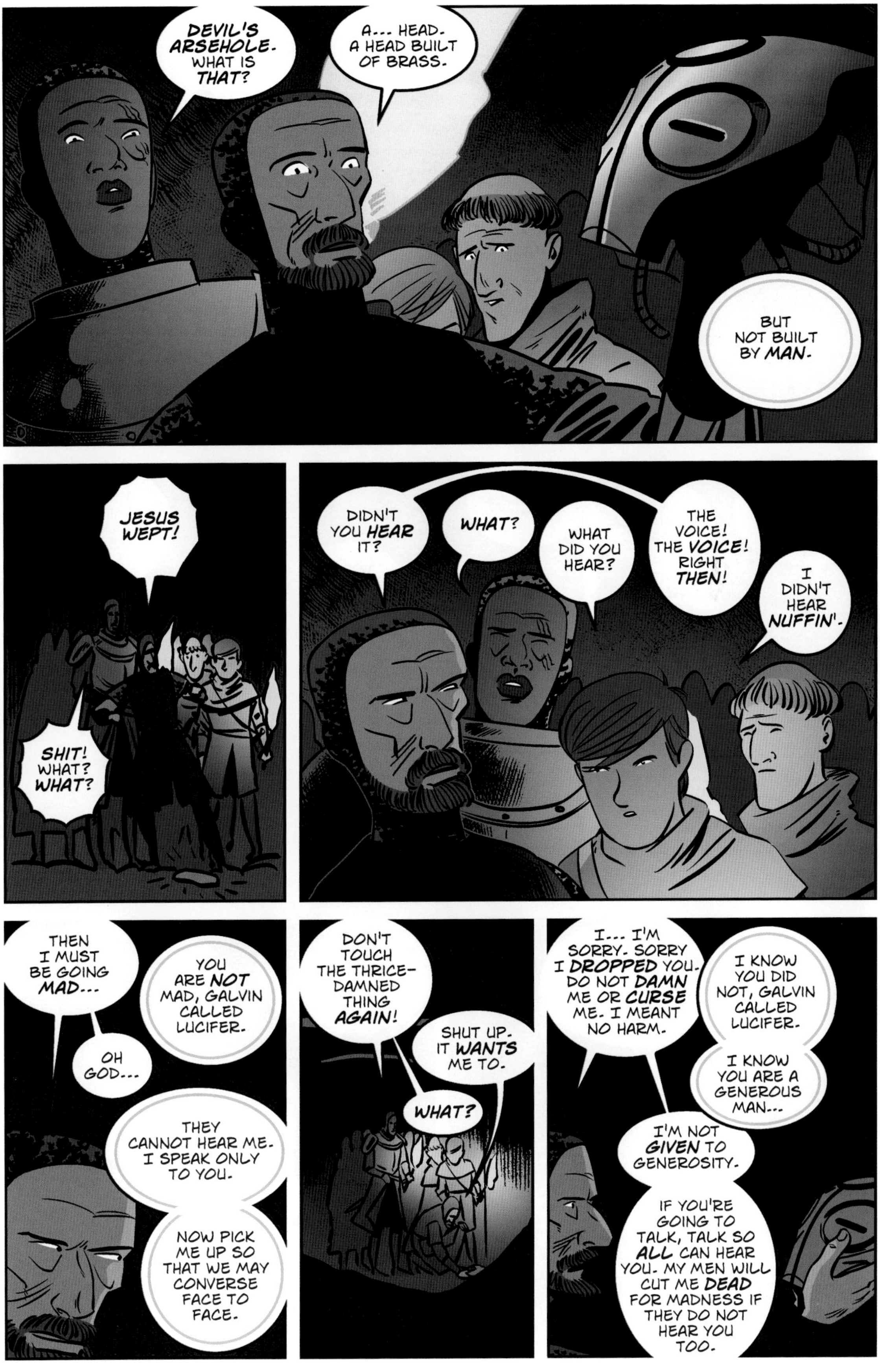
DEVIL'S ARSEHOLE. WHAT IS THAT?
A... HEAD. A HEAD BUILT OF BRASS.
BUT NOT BUILT BY MAN.
JESUS WEPT!
SHIT! WHAT? WHAT?
DIDN'T YOU HEAR IT?
WHAT?
WHAT DID YOU HEAR?
THE VOICE! THE VOICE! RIGHT THEN!
I DIDN'T HEAR NUFFIN'.
THEN I MUST BE GOING MAD...
YOU ARE NOT MAD, GALVIN CALLED LUCIFER.
OH GOD...
THEY CANNOT HEAR ME. I SPEAK ONLY TO YOU.
NOW PICK ME UP SO THAT WE MAY CONVERSE FACE TO FACE.
DON'T TOUCH THE THRICE-DAMNED THING AGAIN!
SHUT UP. IT WANTS ME TO.
WHAT?
I... I'M SORRY. SORRY I DROPPED YOU. DO NOT DAMN ME OR CURSE ME. I MEANT NO HARM.
I KNOW YOU DID NOT, GALVIN CALLED LUCIFER.
I KNOW YOU ARE A GENEROUS MAN...
I'M NOT GIVEN TO GENEROSITY.
IF YOU'RE GOING TO TALK, TALK SO ALL CAN HEAR YOU. MY MEN WILL CUT ME DEAD FOR MADNESS IF THEY DO NOT HEAR YOU TOO.

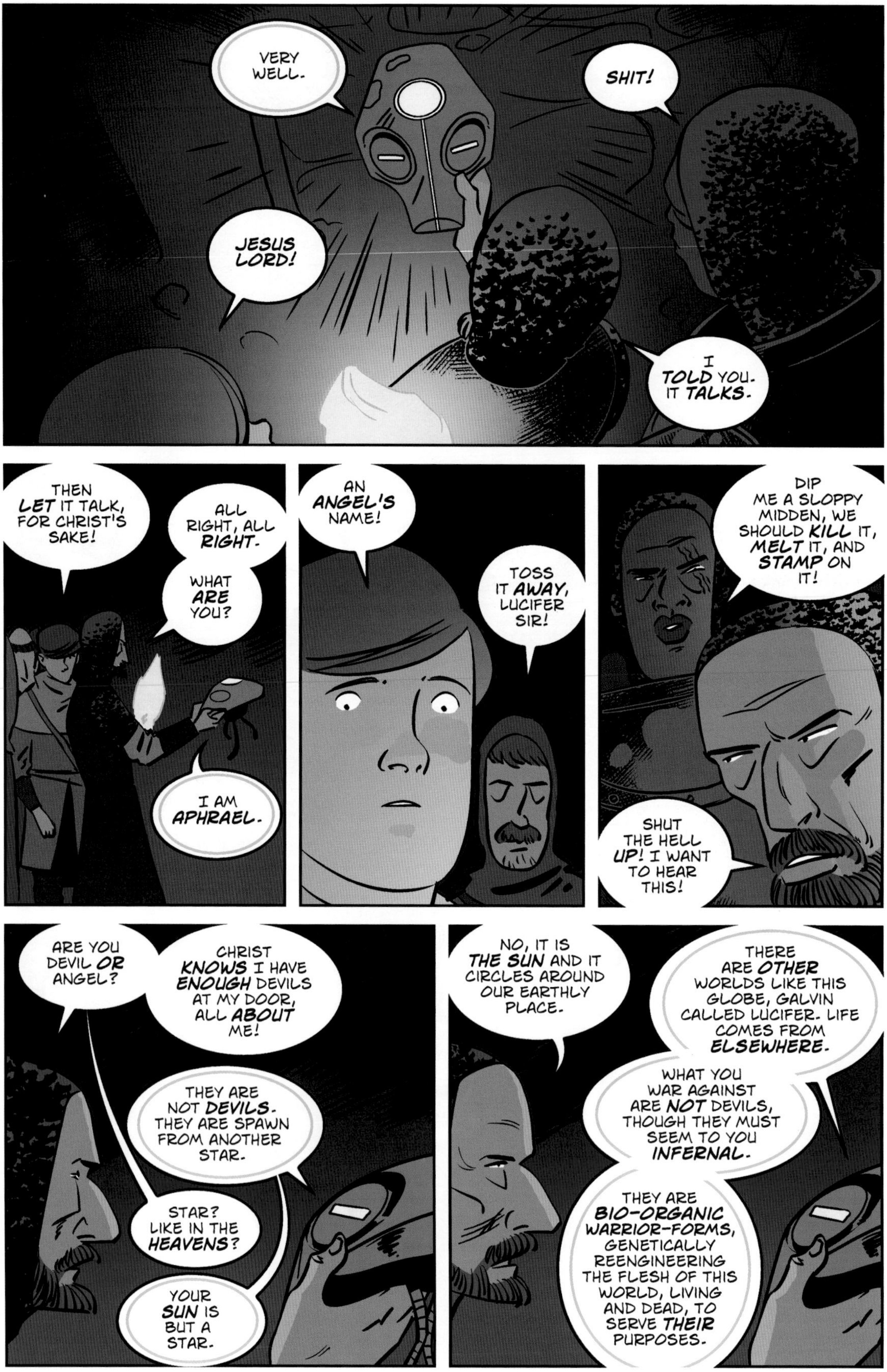
VERY WELL.
SHIT!
JESUS LORD!
I TOLD YOU. IT TALKS.
THEN LET IT TALK, FOR CHRIST'S SAKE!
ALL RIGHT, ALL RIGHT.
WHAT ARE YOU?
I AM APHRAEL.
AN ANGEL'S NAME!
TOSS IT AWAY, LUCIFER SIR!
DIP ME A SLOPPY MIDDEN, WE SHOULD KILL IT, MELT IT, AND STAMP ON IT!
SHUT THE HELL UP! I WANT TO HEAR THIS!
ARE YOU DEVIL OR ANGEL?
CHRIST KNOWS I HAVE ENOUGH DEVILS AT MY DOOR, ALL ABOUT ME!
THEY ARE NOT DEVILS. THEY ARE SPAWN FROM ANOTHER STAR.
STAR? LIKE IN THE HEAVENS?
YOUR SUN IS BUT A STAR.
NO, IT IS THE SUN AND IT CIRCLES AROUND OUR EARTHLY PLACE.
THERE ARE OTHER WORLDS LIKE THIS GLOBE, GALVIN CALLED LUCIFER. LIFE COMES FROM ELSEWHERE.
WHAT YOU WAR AGAINST ARE NOT DEVILS, THOUGH THEY MUST SEEM TO YOU INFERNAL.
THEY ARE BIO-ORGANIC WARRIOR-FORMS, GENETICALLY REENGINEERING THE FLESH OF THIS WORLD, LIVING AND DEAD, TO SERVE THEIR PURPOSES.

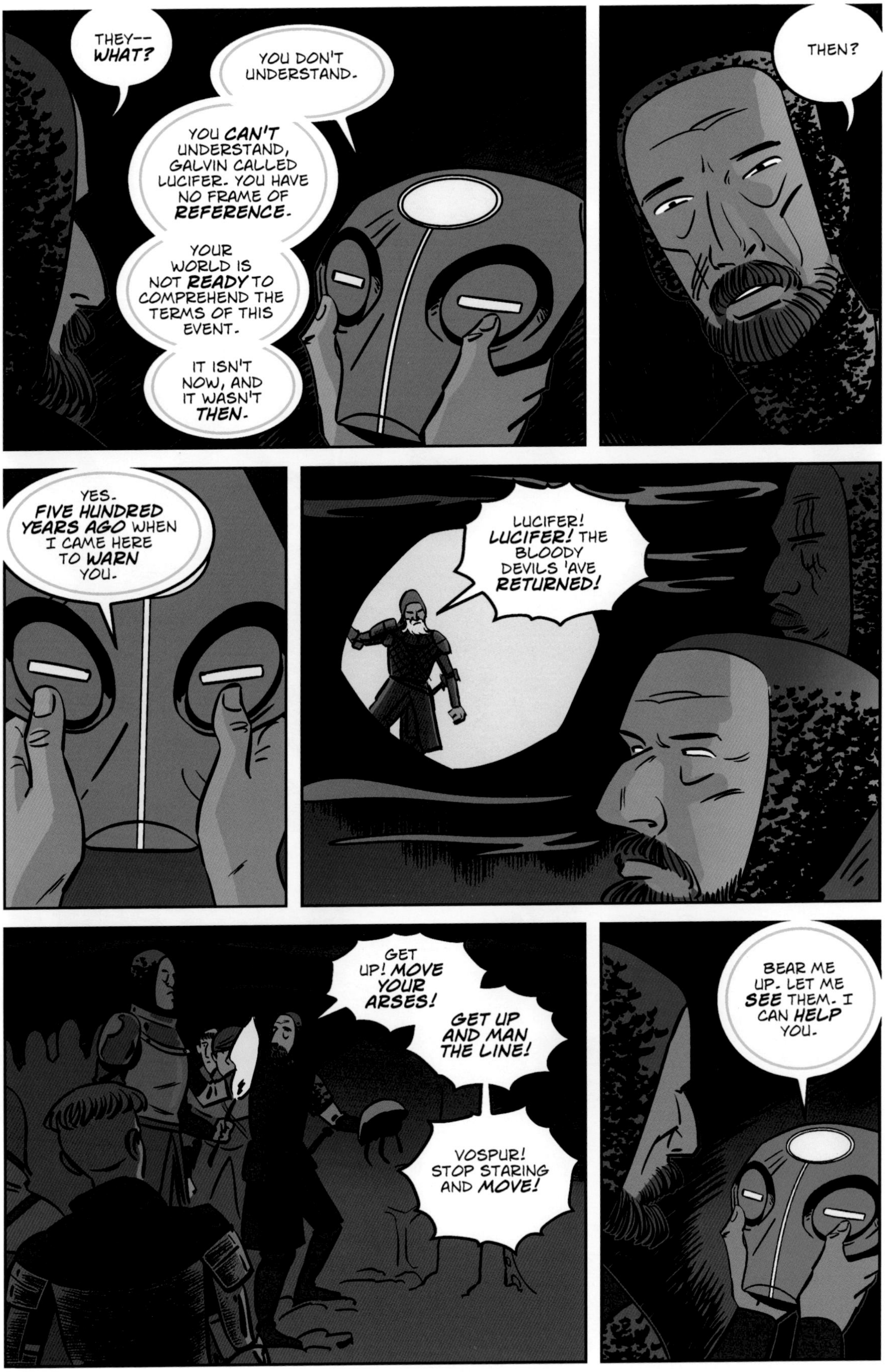
THEY-- WHAT?
YOU DON'T UNDERSTAND.
YOU CAN'T UNDERSTAND, GALVIN CALLED LUCIFER. YOU HAVE NO FRAME OF REFERENCE.
YOUR WORLD IS NOT READY TO COMPREHEND THE TERMS OF THIS EVENT.
IT ISN'T NOW, AND IT WASN'T THEN.
THEN?
YES. FIVE HUNDRED YEARS AGO WHEN I CAME HERE TO WARN YOU.
LUCIFER! LUCIFER! THE BLOODY DEVILS 'AVE RETURNED!
GET UP! MOVE YOUR ARSES!
GET UP AND MAN THE LINE!
VOSPUR! STOP STARING AND MOVE!
BEAR ME UP. LET ME SEE THEM. I CAN HELP YOU.

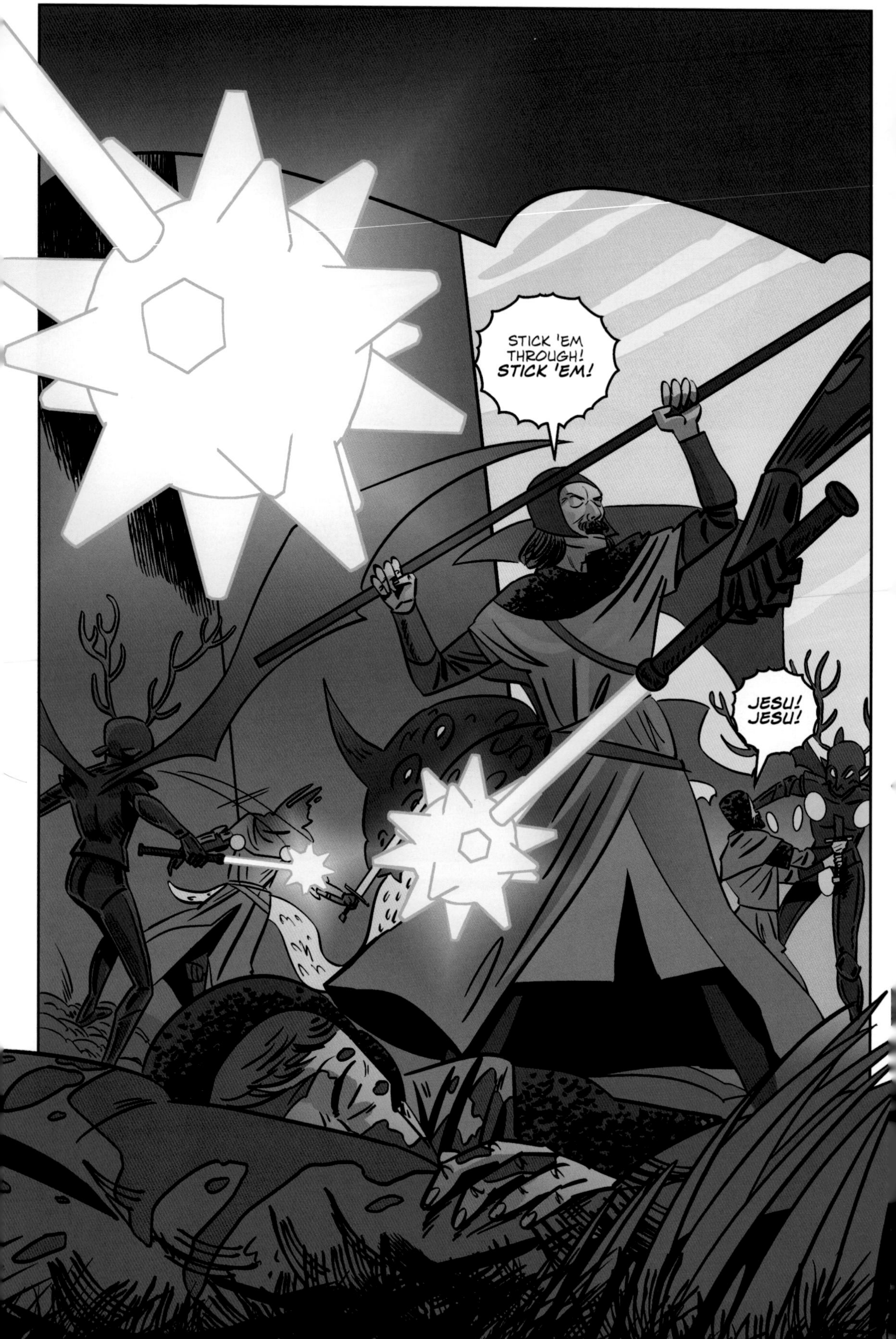
STICK 'EM THROUGH! STICK 'EM!
JESU! JESU!

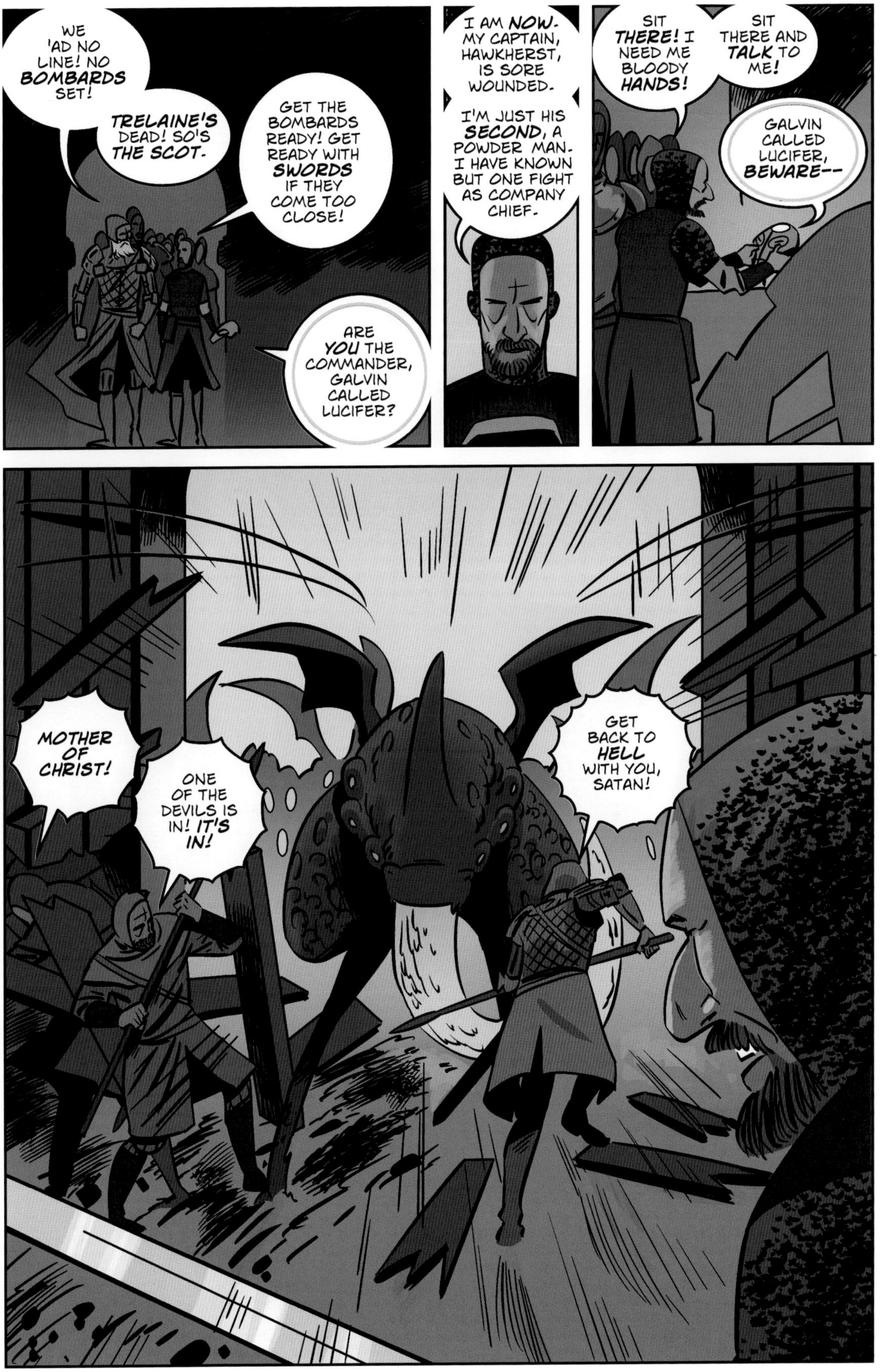

WE 'AD NO LINE! NO BOMBARDS SET!
TRELAINE'S DEAD! SO'S THE SCOT.
GET THE BOMBARDS READY! GET READY WITH SWORDS IF THEY COME TOO CLOSE!
ARE YOU THE COMMANDER, GALVIN CALLED LUCIFER?
I AM NOW. MY CAPTAIN, HAWKHERST, IS SORE WOUNDED.
I'M JUST HIS SECOND, A POWDER MAN. I HAVE KNOWN BUT ONE FIGHT AS COMPANY CHIEF.
SIT THERE! I NEED ME BLOODY HANDS!
SIT THERE AND TALK TO ME!
GALVIN CALLED LUCIFER, BEWARE--
MOTHER OF CHRIST!
ONE OF THE DEVILS IS IN! IT'S IN!
GET BACK TO HELL WITH YOU, SATAN!

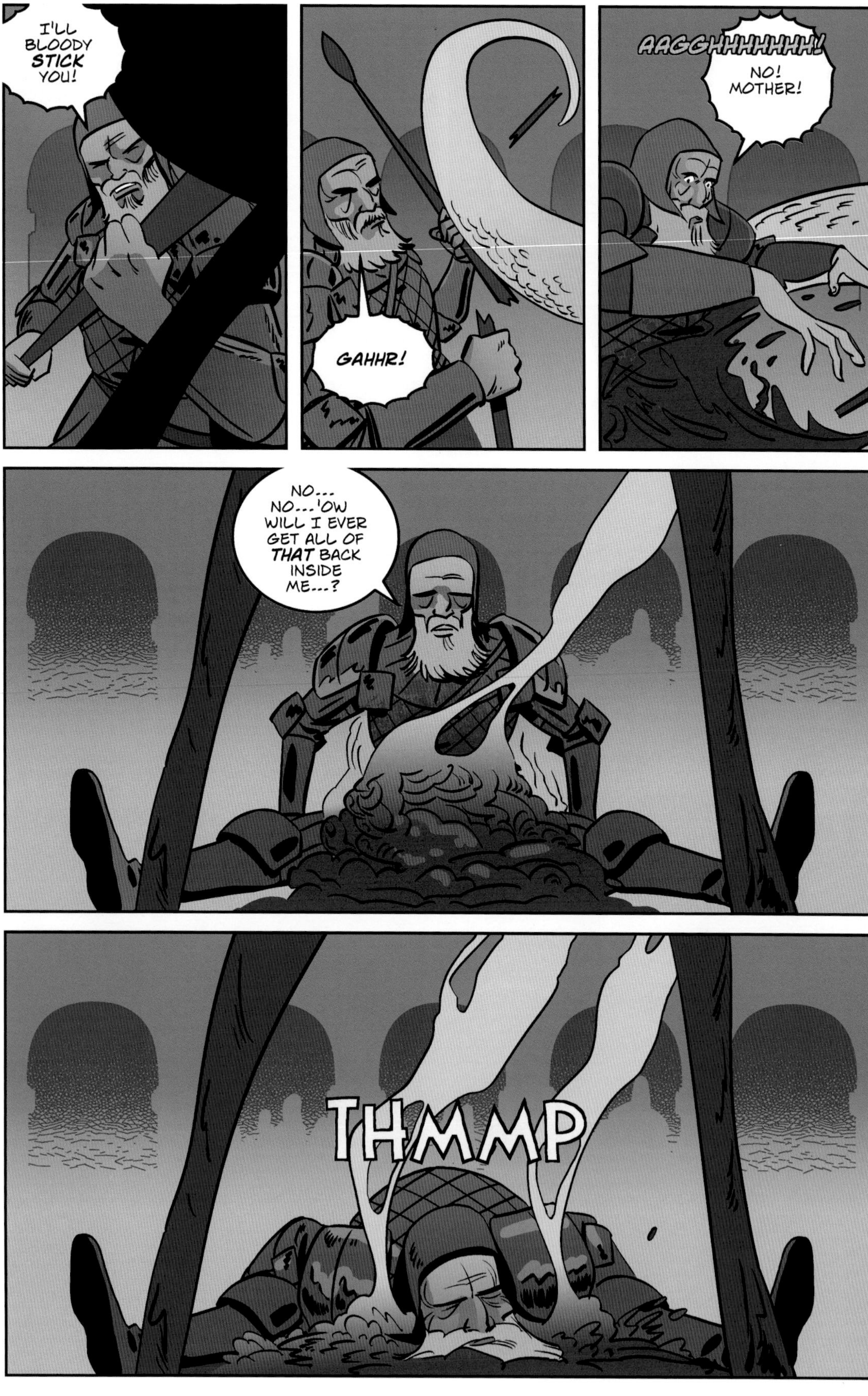

I'LL BLOODY STICK YOU!
GAHHR!
AAGGHHHHHHH!
NO! MOTHER!
NO... NO... 'OW WILL I EVER GET ALL OF THAT BACK INSIDE ME...?
THMMP

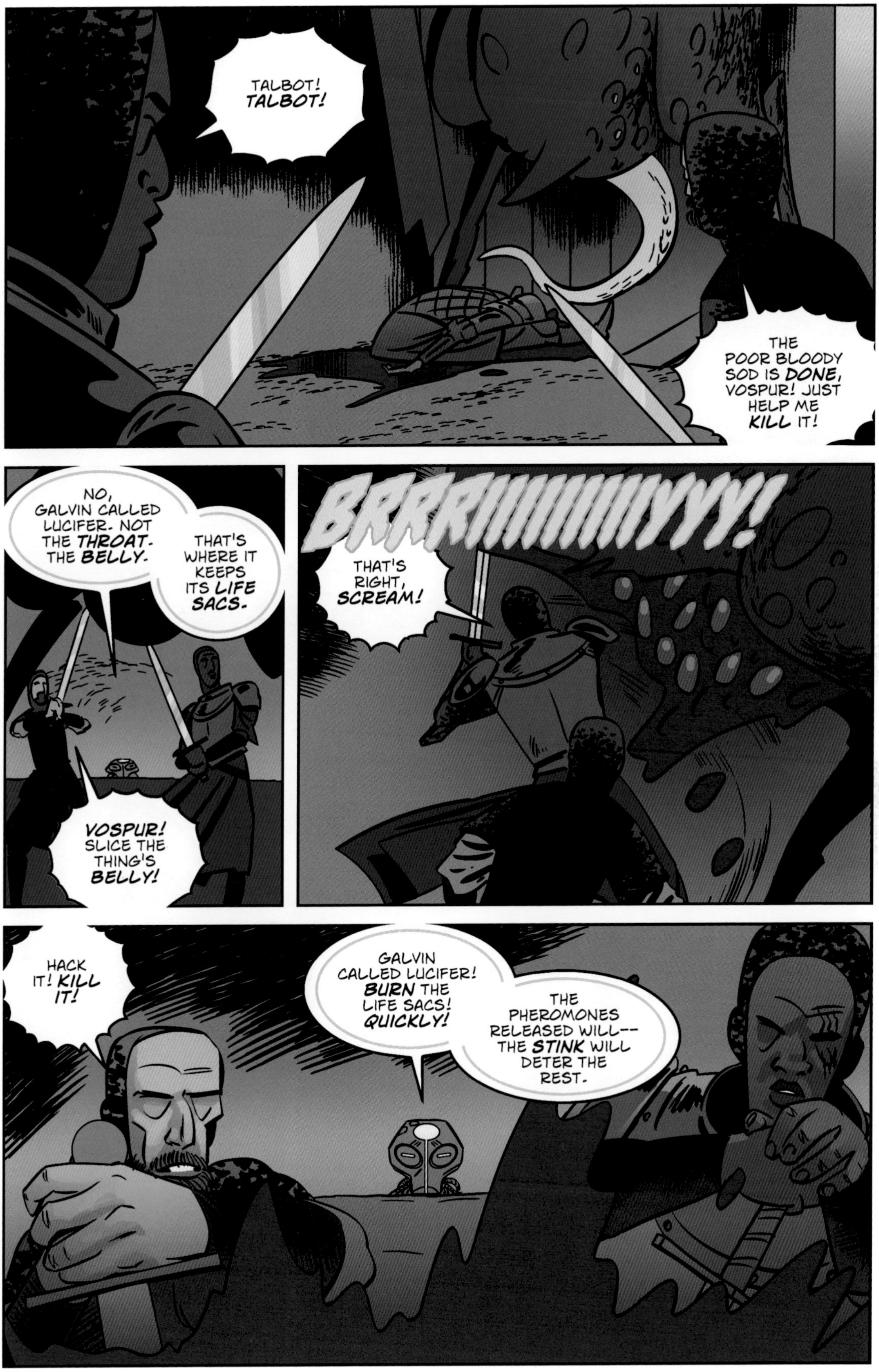
TALBOT! TALBOT!
THE POOR BLOODY SOD IS DONE, VOSPUR! JUST HELP ME KILL IT!
NO, GALVIN CALLED LUCIFER. NOT THE THROAT- THE BELLY.
THAT'S WHERE IT KEEPS ITS LIFE SACS.
VOSPUR! SLICE THE THING'S BELLY!
BRRRIIIIIIIIIIYYY!
THAT'S RIGHT, SCREAM!
HACK IT! KILL IT!
GALVIN CALLED LUCIFER! BURN THE LIFE SACS! QUICKLY!
THE PHEROMONES RELEASED WILL-- THE STINK WILL DETER THE REST.

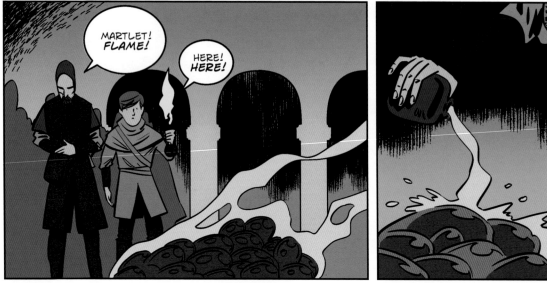

MARTLET! FLAME!

HERE! HERE!

WHHHOOMMMFFF!

BURN. IN HELL. OR WHATEVER STAR YOU CAME TO US FROM.

LUCIFER! SIR!

DONNE?

THE DEVILS ARE FALLING BACK! THEY'RE FLEEING!

GET SHOVELS. ROPES. GET THIS THING OUTSIDE, THE ASHES TOO.

THEN BRING THE MEN IN AND SEAL THE BLOODY GATES.

SIR!

HOW MANY, DONNE?

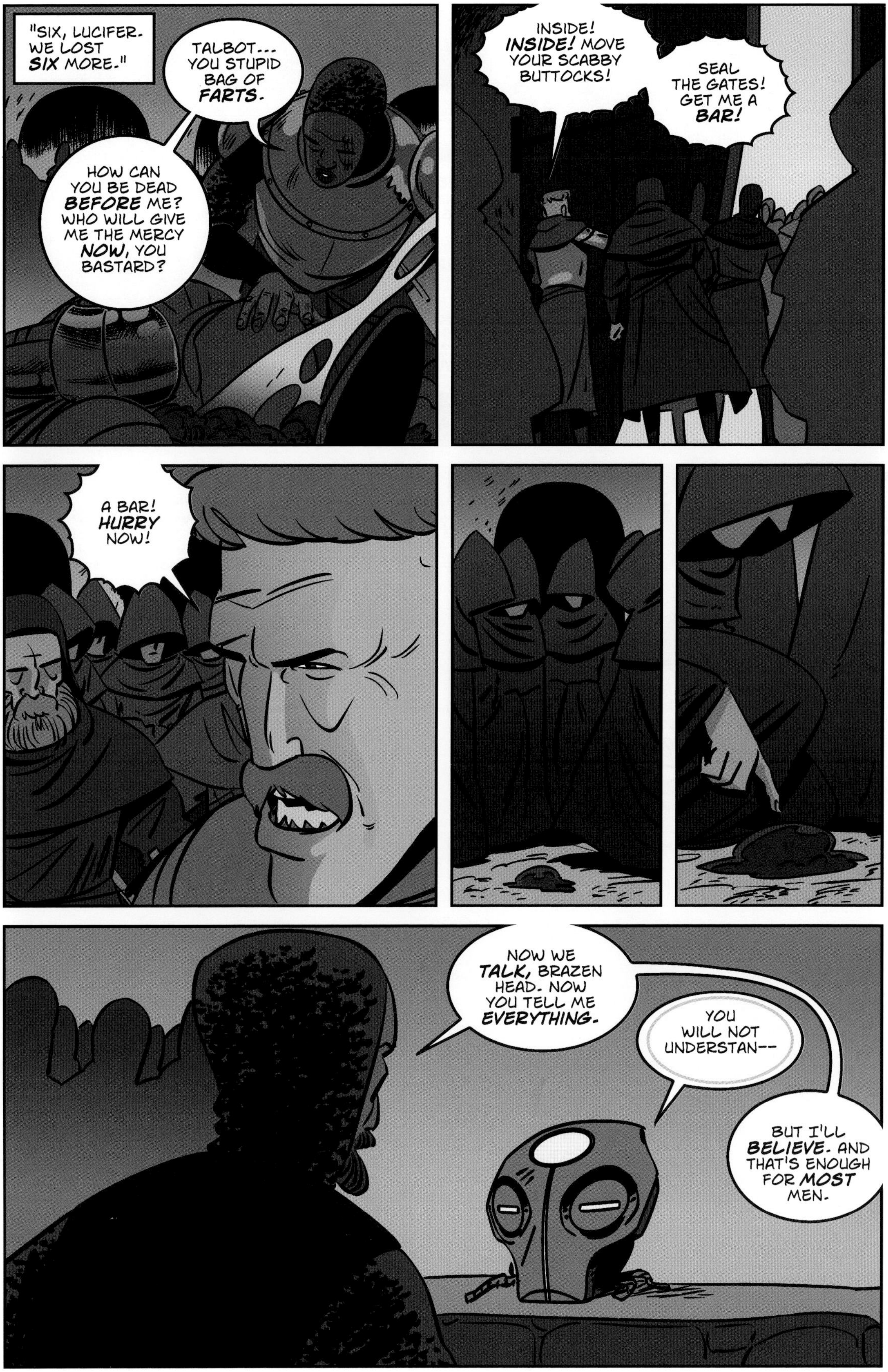
"SIX, LUCIFER. WE LOST SIX MORE."
TALBOT... YOU STUPID BAG OF FARTS.
HOW CAN YOU BE DEAD BEFORE ME? WHO WILL GIVE ME THE MERCY NOW, YOU BASTARD?
INSIDE! INSIDE! MOVE YOUR SCABBY BUTTOCKS!
SEAL THE GATES! GET ME A BAR!
A BAR! HURRY NOW!
NOW WE TALK, BRAZEN HEAD. NOW YOU TELL ME EVERYTHING.
YOU WILL NOT UNDERSTAN--
BUT I'LL BELIEVE. AND THAT'S ENOUGH FOR MOST MEN.

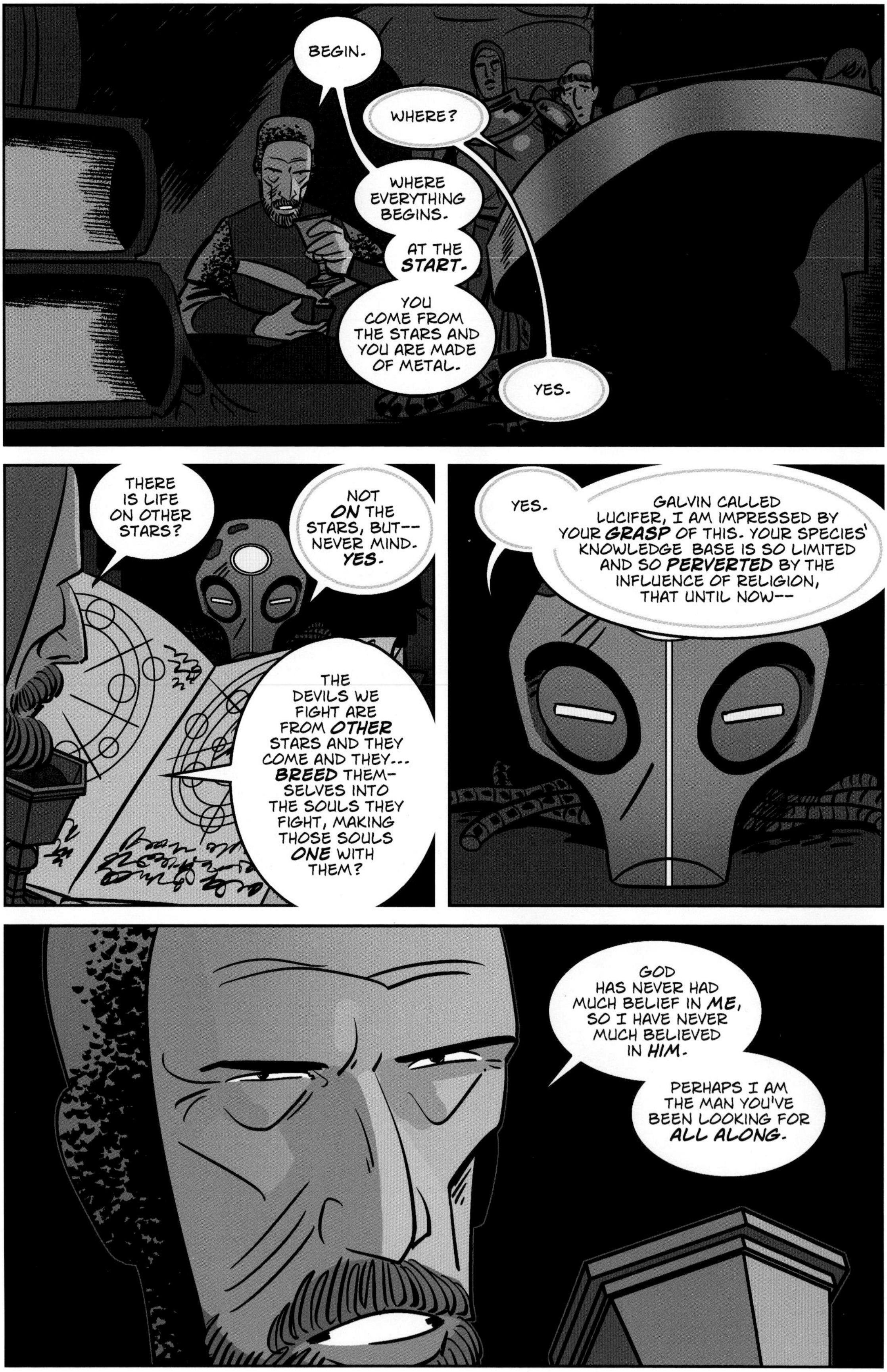

BEGIN.
WHERE?
WHERE EVERYTHING BEGINS.
AT THE START.
YOU COME FROM THE STARS AND YOU ARE MADE OF METAL.
YES.
THERE IS LIFE ON OTHER STARS?
NOT ON THE STARS, BUT-- NEVER MIND. YES.
THE DEVILS WE FIGHT ARE FROM OTHER STARS AND THEY COME AND THEY... BREED THEMSELVES INTO THE SOULS THEY FIGHT, MAKING THOSE SOULS ONE WITH THEM?
YES.
GALVIN CALLED LUCIFER, I AM IMPRESSED BY YOUR GRASP OF THIS. YOUR SPECIES' KNOWLEDGE BASE IS SO LIMITED AND SO PERVERTED BY THE INFLUENCE OF RELIGION, THAT UNTIL NOW--
GOD HAS NEVER HAD MUCH BELIEF IN ME, SO I HAVE NEVER MUCH BELIEVED IN HIM.
PERHAPS I AM THE MAN YOU'VE BEEN LOOKING FOR ALL ALONG.

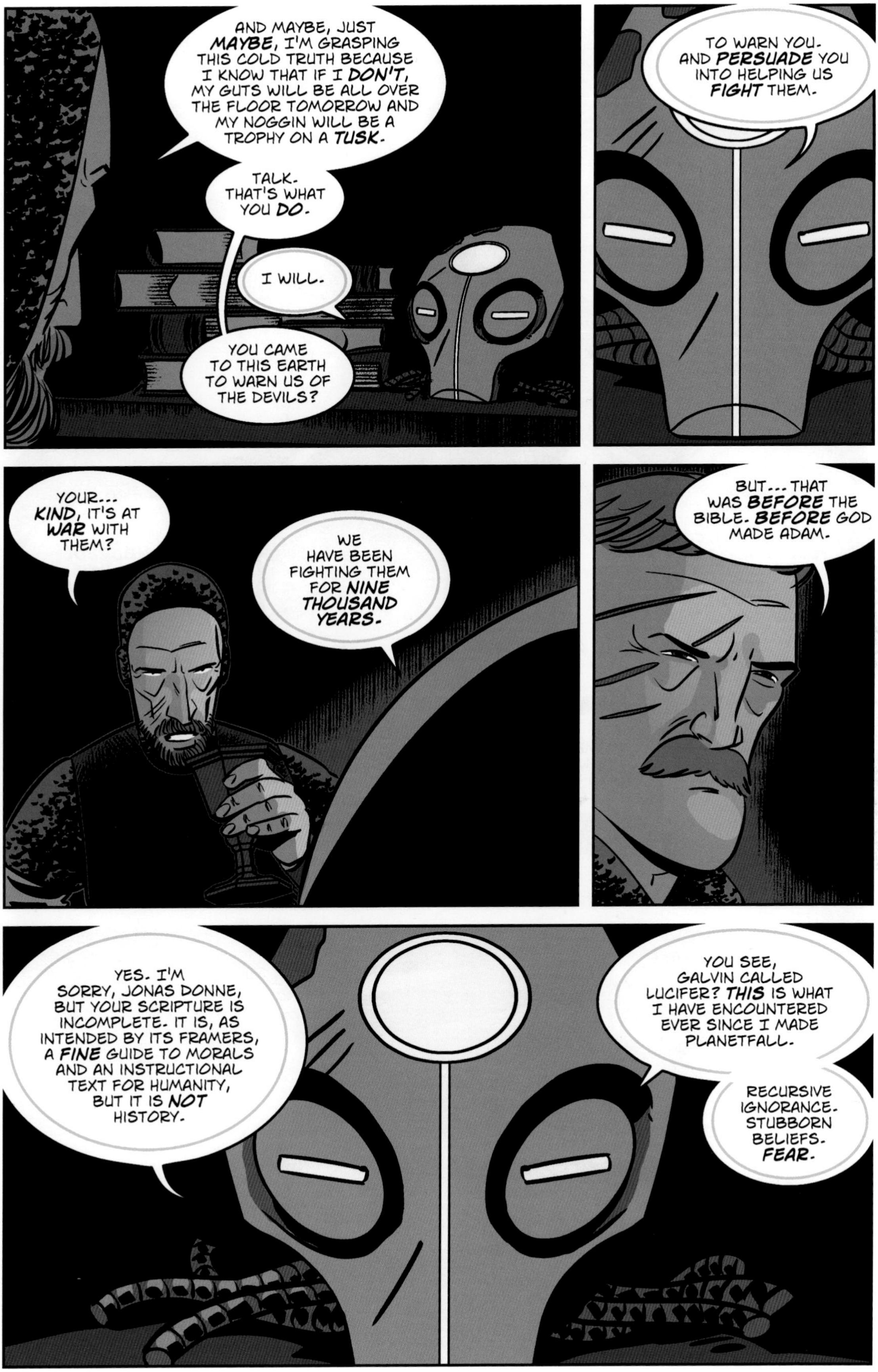
AND MAYBE, JUST MAYBE, I'M GRASPING THIS COLD TRUTH BECAUSE I KNOW THAT IF I DON'T, MY GUTS WILL BE ALL OVER THE FLOOR TOMORROW AND MY NOGGIN WILL BE A TROPHY ON A TUSK.
TALK. THAT'S WHAT YOU DO.
I WILL.
YOU CAME TO THIS EARTH TO WARN US OF THE DEVILS?
TO WARN YOU. AND PERSUADE YOU INTO HELPING US FIGHT THEM.
YOUR... KIND, IT'S AT WAR WITH THEM?
WE HAVE BEEN FIGHTING THEM FOR NINE THOUSAND YEARS.
BUT... THAT WAS BEFORE THE BIBLE. BEFORE GOD MADE ADAM.
YES. I'M SORRY, JONAS DONNE, BUT YOUR SCRIPTURE IS INCOMPLETE. IT IS, AS INTENDED BY ITS FRAMERS, A FINE GUIDE TO MORALS AND AN INSTRUCTIONAL TEXT FOR HUMANITY, BUT IT IS NOT HISTORY.
YOU SEE, GALVIN CALLED LUCIFER? THIS IS WHAT I HAVE ENCOUNTERED EVER SINCE I MADE PLANETFALL.
RECURSIVE IGNORANCE. STUBBORN BELIEFS. FEAR.

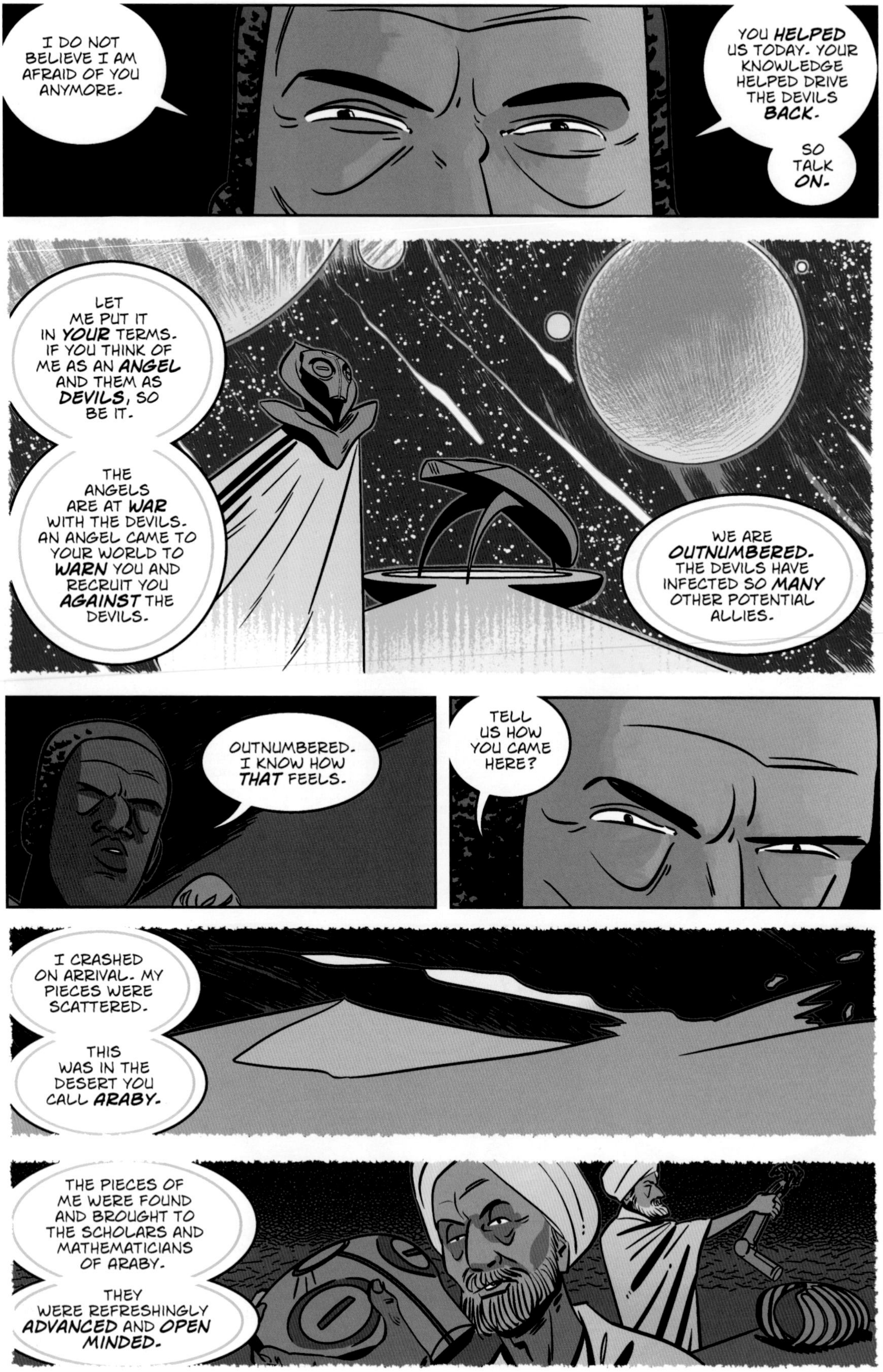
I DO NOT BELIEVE I AM AFRAID OF YOU ANYMORE.
YOU HELPED US TODAY. YOUR KNOWLEDGE HELPED DRIVE THE DEVILS BACK.
SO TALK ON.
LET ME PUT IT IN YOUR TERMS. IF YOU THINK OF ME AS AN ANGEL AND THEM AS DEVILS, SO BE IT.
THE ANGELS ARE AT WAR WITH THE DEVILS. AN ANGEL CAME TO YOUR WORLD TO WARN YOU AND RECRUIT YOU AGAINST THE DEVILS.
WE ARE OUTNUMBERED. THE DEVILS HAVE INFECTED SO MANY OTHER POTENTIAL ALLIES.
OUTNUMBERED. I KNOW HOW THAT FEELS.
TELL US HOW YOU CAME HERE?
I CRASHED ON ARRIVAL. MY PIECES WERE SCATTERED.
THIS WAS IN THE DESERT YOU CALL ARABY.
THE PIECES OF ME WERE FOUND AND BROUGHT TO THE SCHOLARS AND MATHEMATICIANS OF ARABY.
THEY WERE REFRESHINGLY ADVANCED AND OPEN MINDED.

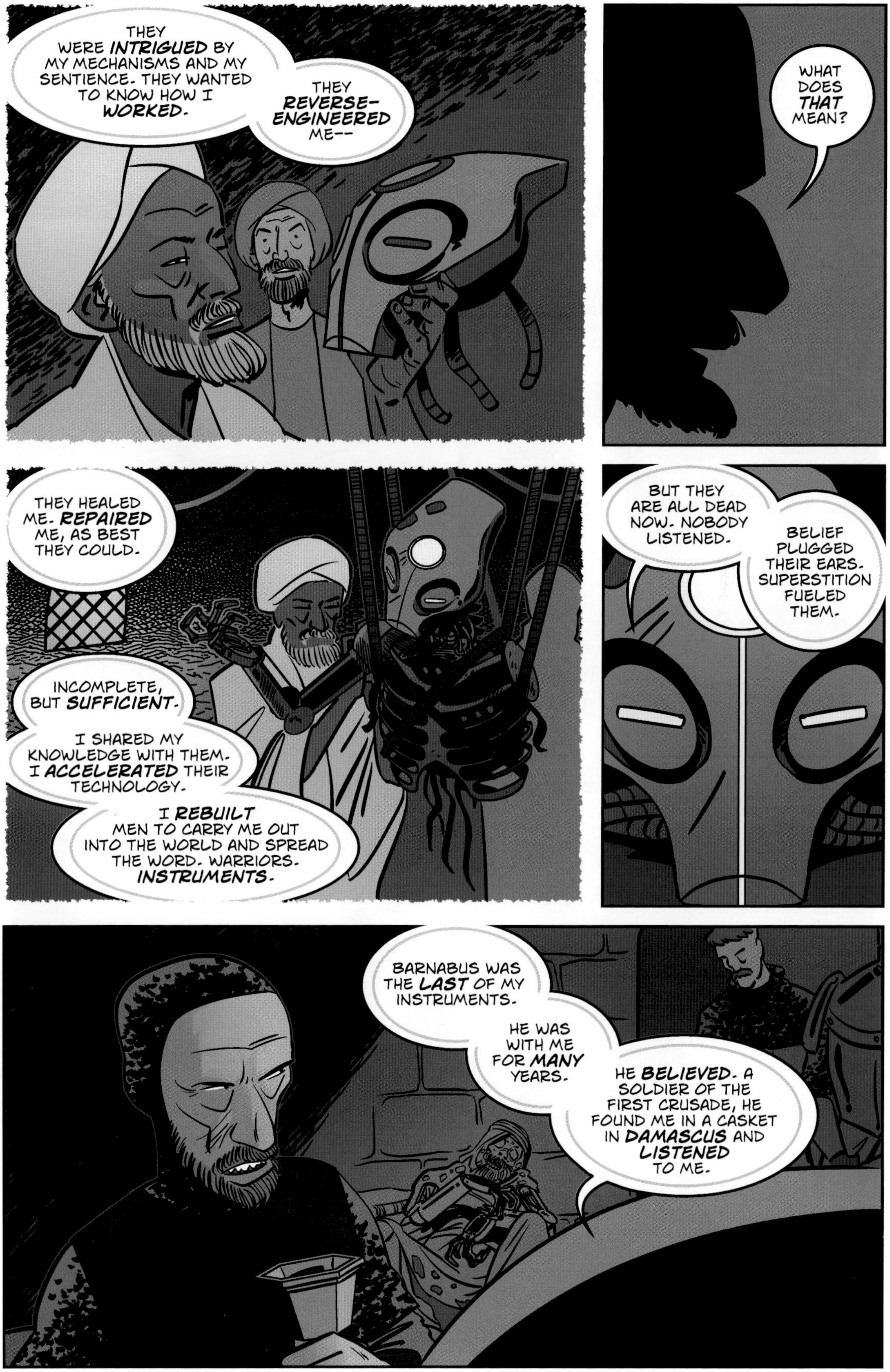
THEY WERE **INTRIGUED** BY MY MECHANISMS AND MY SENTIENCE. THEY WANTED TO KNOW HOW I **WORKED**.
THEY **REVERSE-ENGINEERED** ME--
WHAT DOES **THAT** MEAN?
THEY HEALED ME. **REPAIRED** ME, AS BEST THEY COULD.
INCOMPLETE, BUT **SUFFICIENT**.
I SHARED MY KNOWLEDGE WITH THEM. I **ACCELERATED** THEIR TECHNOLOGY.
I **REBUILT** MEN TO CARRY ME OUT INTO THE WORLD AND SPREAD THE WORD. WARRIORS. **INSTRUMENTS**.
BUT THEY ARE ALL DEAD NOW. NOBODY LISTENED.
BELIEF PLUGGED THEIR EARS. SUPERSTITION FUELED THEM.
BARNABUS WAS THE **LAST** OF MY INSTRUMENTS.
HE WAS WITH ME FOR **MANY** YEARS.
HE **BELIEVED**. A SOLDIER OF THE FIRST CRUSADE, HE FOUND ME IN A CASKET IN **DAMASCUS** AND **LISTENED** TO ME.

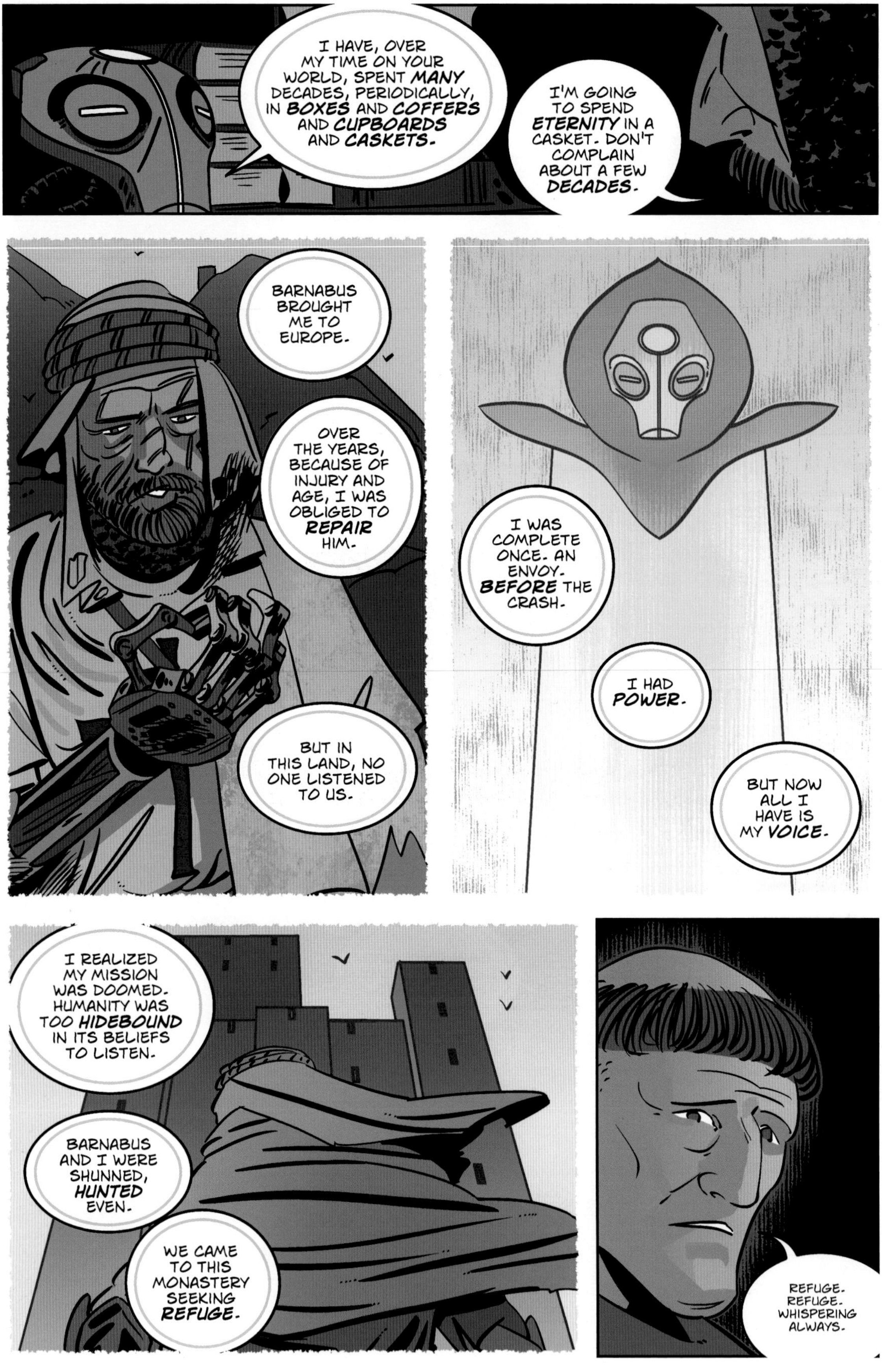
I HAVE, OVER MY TIME ON YOUR WORLD, SPENT MANY DECADES, PERIODICALLY, IN BOXES AND COFFERS AND CUPBOARDS AND CASKETS.
I'M GOING TO SPEND ETERNITY IN A CASKET. DON'T COMPLAIN ABOUT A FEW DECADES.
BARNABUS BROUGHT ME TO EUROPE.
OVER THE YEARS, BECAUSE OF INJURY AND AGE, I WAS OBLIGED TO REPAIR HIM.
BUT IN THIS LAND, NO ONE LISTENED TO US.
I WAS COMPLETE ONCE. AN ENVOY. BEFORE THE CRASH.
I HAD POWER.
BUT NOW ALL I HAVE IS MY VOICE.
I REALIZED MY MISSION WAS DOOMED. HUMANITY WAS TOO HIDEBOUND IN ITS BELIEFS TO LISTEN.
BARNABUS AND I WERE SHUNNED, HUNTED EVEN.
WE CAME TO THIS MONASTERY SEEKING REFUGE.
REFUGE. REFUGE. WHISPERING ALWAYS.

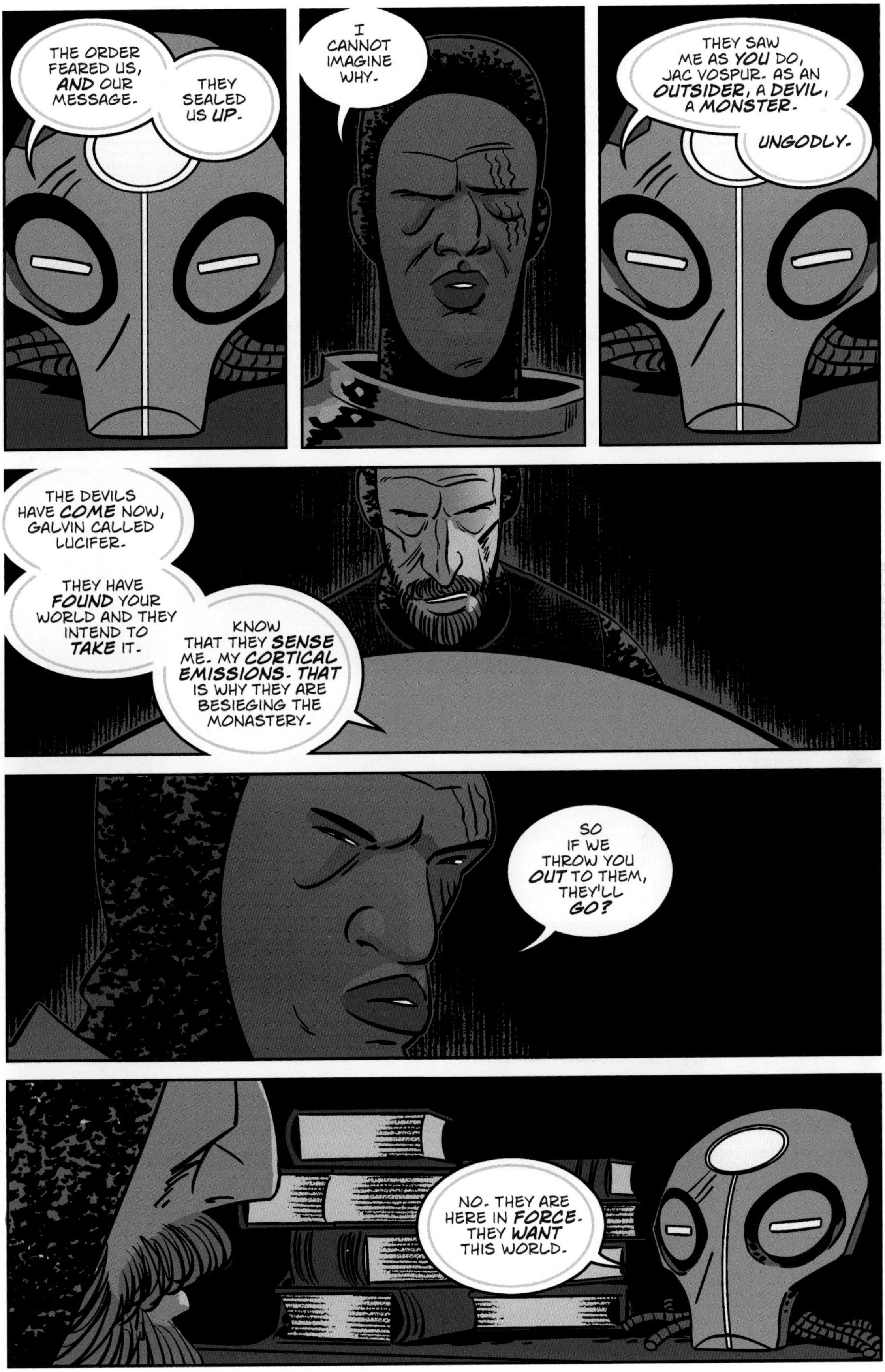
THE ORDER FEARED US, AND OUR MESSAGE.
THEY SEALED US UP.
I CANNOT IMAGINE WHY.
THEY SAW ME AS YOU DO, JAC VOSPUR. AS AN OUTSIDER, A DEVIL, A MONSTER.
UNGODLY.
THE DEVILS HAVE COME NOW, GALVIN CALLED LUCIFER.
THEY HAVE FOUND YOUR WORLD AND THEY INTEND TO TAKE IT.
KNOW THAT THEY SENSE ME. MY CORTICAL EMISSIONS. THAT IS WHY THEY ARE BESIEGING THE MONASTERY.
SO IF WE THROW YOU OUT TO THEM, THEY'LL GO?
NO. THEY ARE HERE IN FORCE. THEY WANT THIS WORLD.

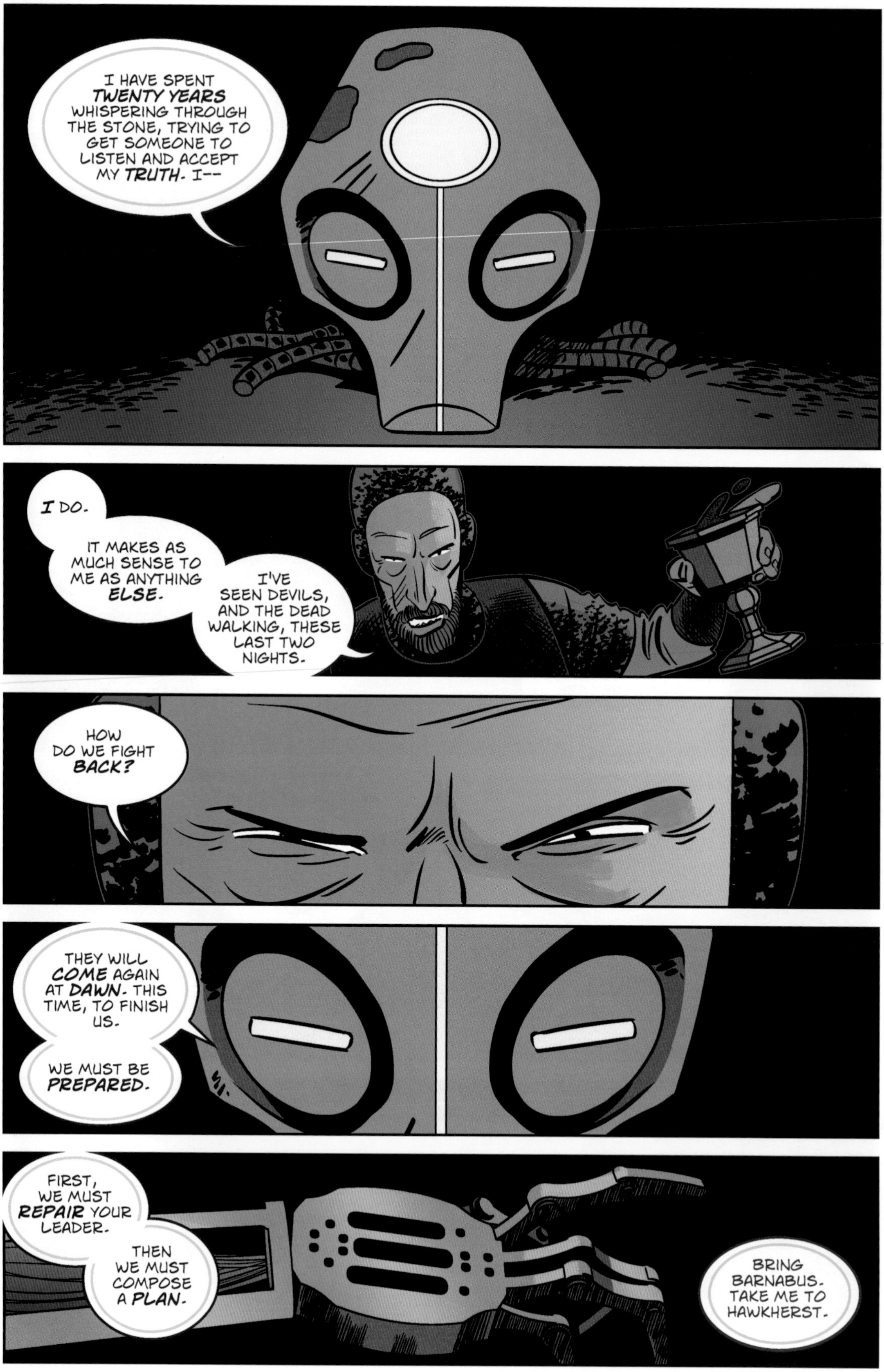
I HAVE SPENT TWENTY YEARS WHISPERING THROUGH THE STONE, TRYING TO GET SOMEONE TO LISTEN AND ACCEPT MY TRUTH. I--
I DO.
IT MAKES AS MUCH SENSE TO ME AS ANYTHING ELSE.
I'VE SEEN DEVILS, AND THE DEAD WALKING, THESE LAST TWO NIGHTS.
HOW DO WE FIGHT BACK?
THEY WILL COME AGAIN AT DAWN. THIS TIME, TO FINISH US.
WE MUST BE PREPARED.
FIRST, WE MUST REPAIR YOUR LEADER.
THEN WE MUST COMPOSE A PLAN.
BRING BARNABUS. TAKE ME TO HAWKHERST.

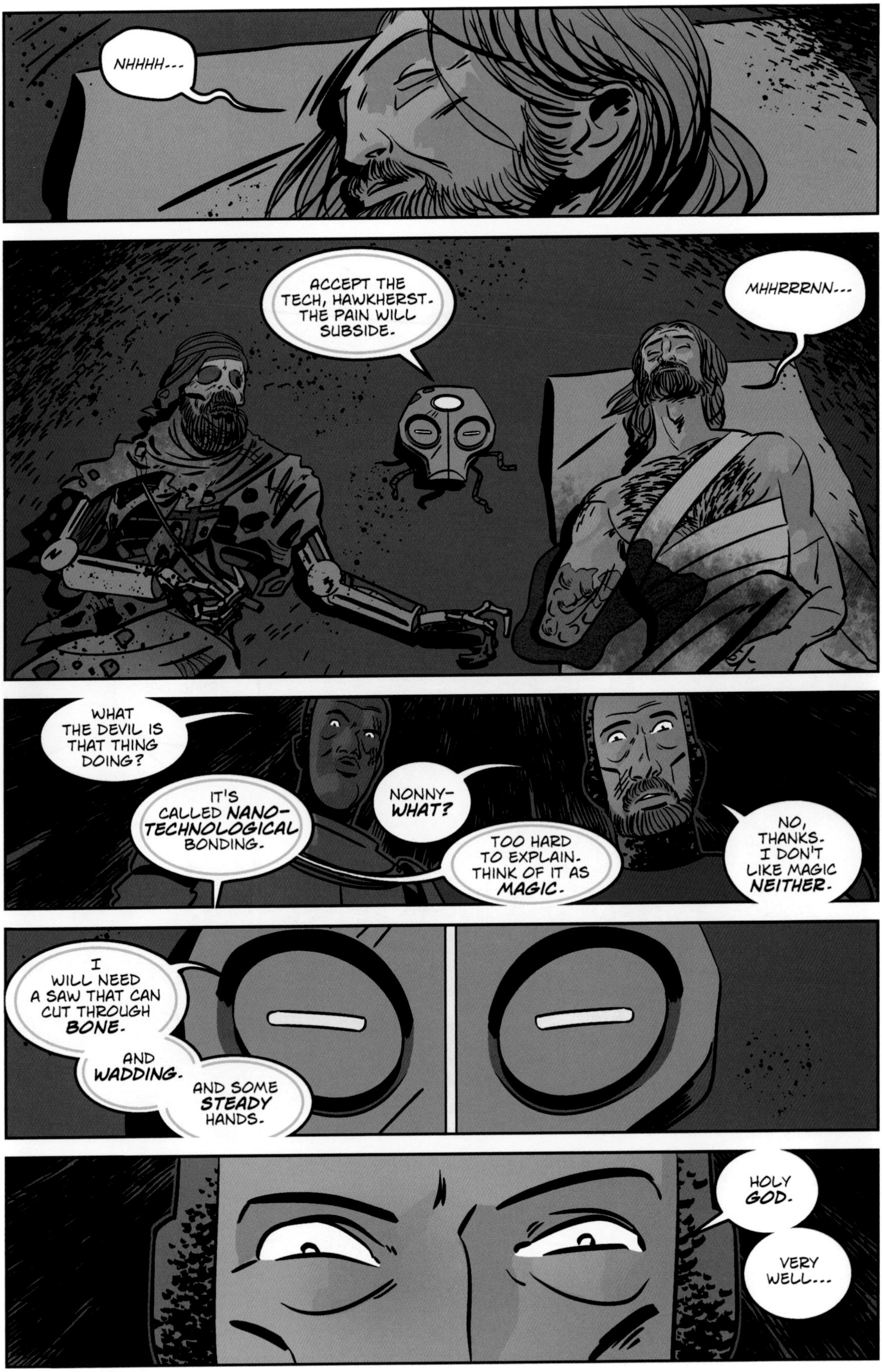
NHHHH---
ACCEPT THE TECH, HAWKHERST. THE PAIN WILL SUBSIDE.
MHHRRRNN---
WHAT THE DEVIL IS THAT THING DOING?
IT'S CALLED NANO-TECHNOLOGICAL BONDING.
NONNY-WHAT?
TOO HARD TO EXPLAIN. THINK OF IT AS MAGIC.
NO, THANKS. I DON'T LIKE MAGIC NEITHER.
I WILL NEED A SAW THAT CAN CUT THROUGH BONE.
AND WADDING.
AND SOME STEADY HANDS.
HOLY GOD.
VERY WELL---

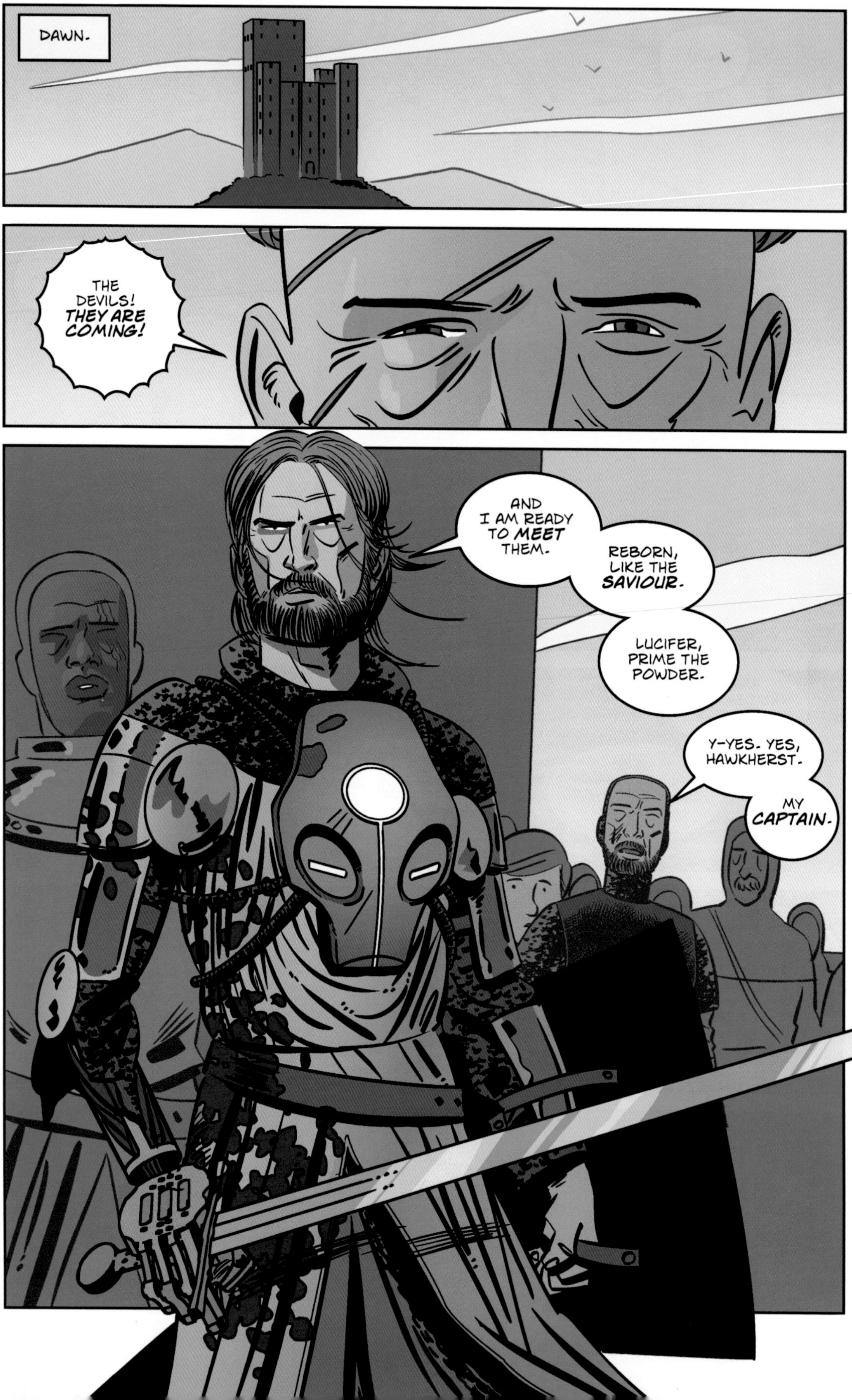
DAWN.
THE DEVILS! THEY ARE COMING!
AND I AM READY TO MEET THEM.
REBORN, LIKE THE SAVIOUR.
LUCIFER, PRIME THE POWDER.
Y-YES. YES, HAWKHERST.
MY CAPTAIN.

CHAPTER IV

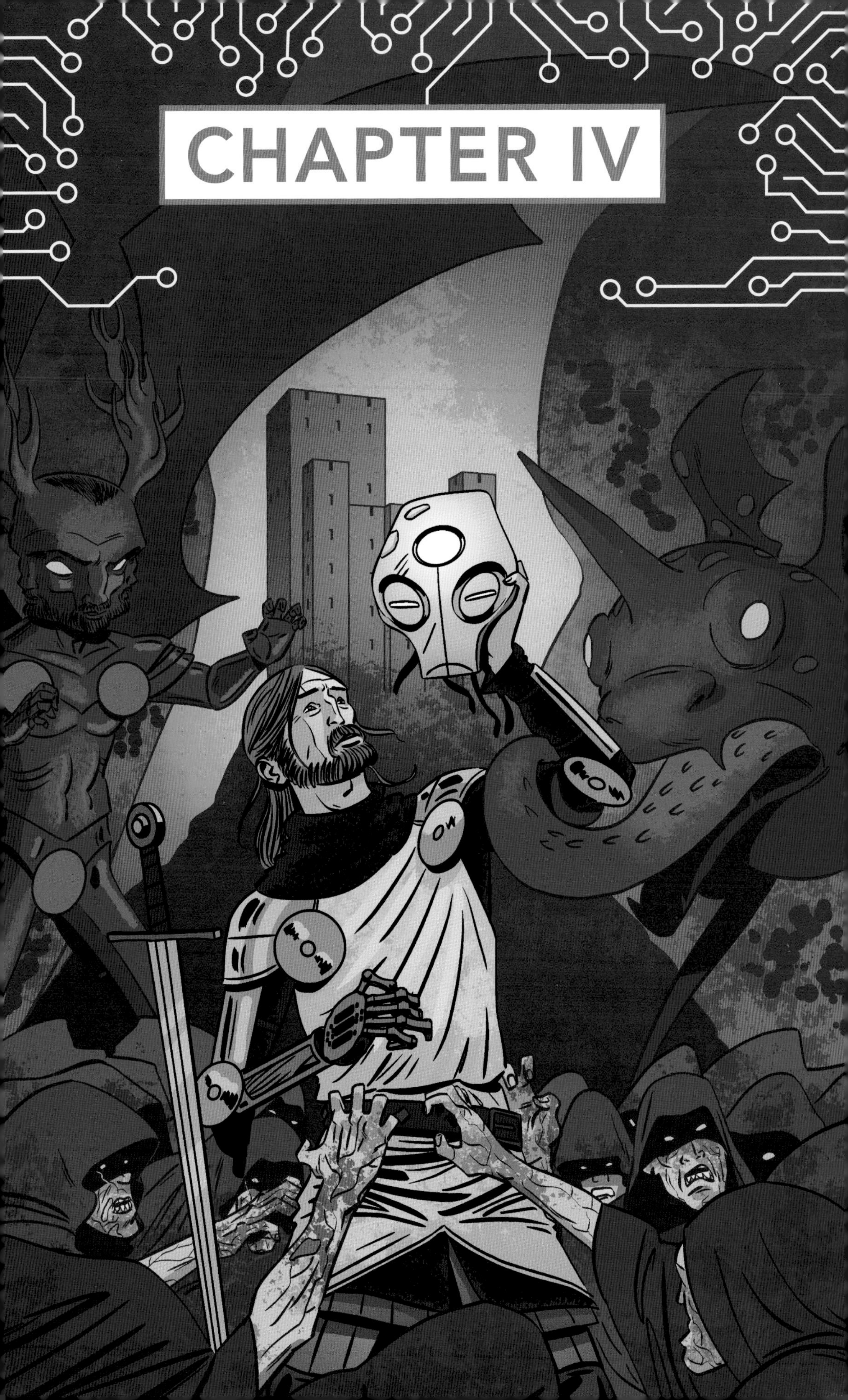

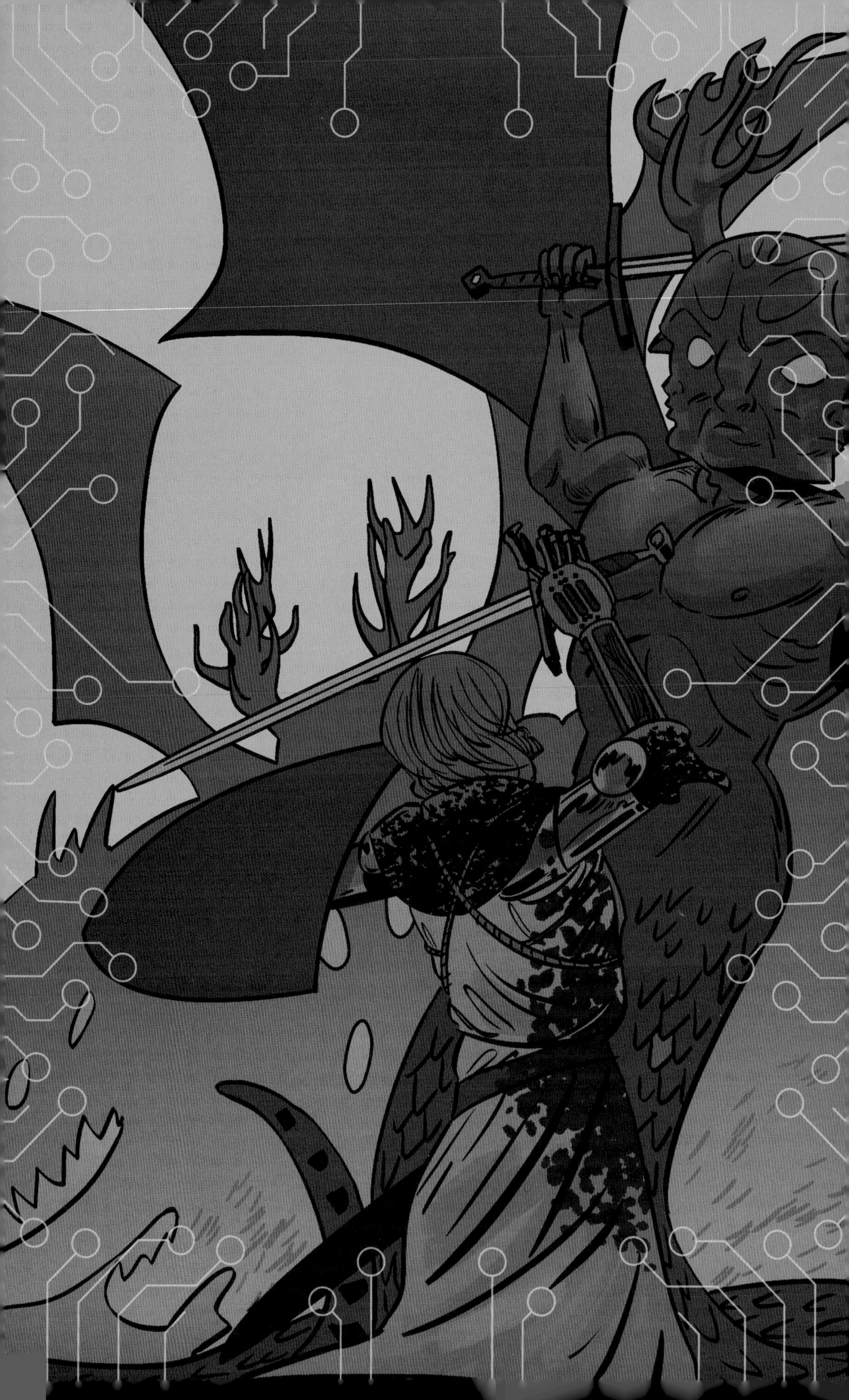

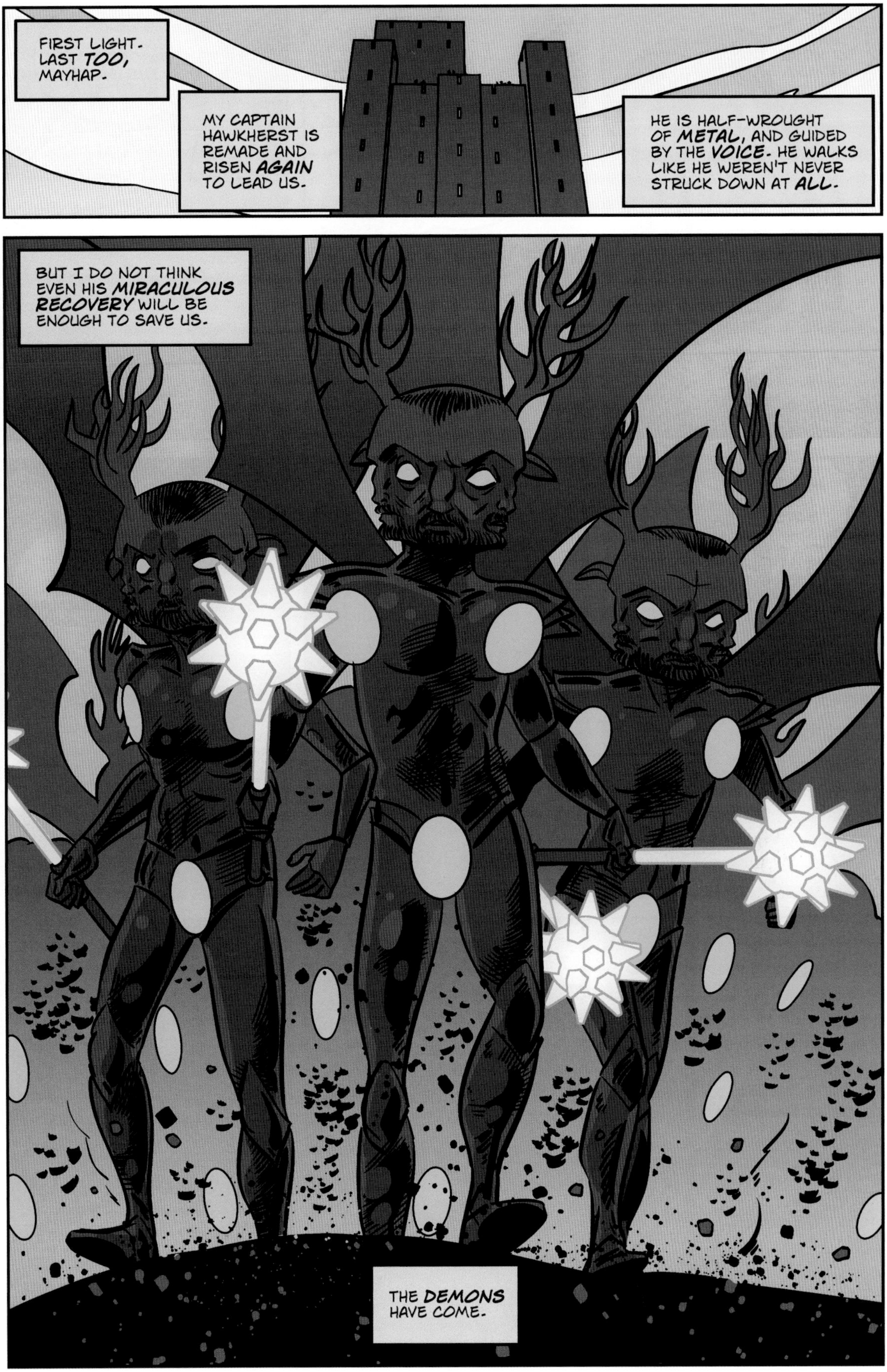
FIRST LIGHT. LAST TOO, MAYHAP.
MY CAPTAIN HAWKHERST IS REMADE AND RISEN AGAIN TO LEAD US.
HE IS HALF-WROUGHT OF METAL, AND GUIDED BY THE VOICE. HE WALKS LIKE HE WEREN'T NEVER STRUCK DOWN AT ALL.
BUT I DO NOT THINK EVEN HIS MIRACULOUS RECOVERY WILL BE ENOUGH TO SAVE US.
THE DEMONS HAVE COME.

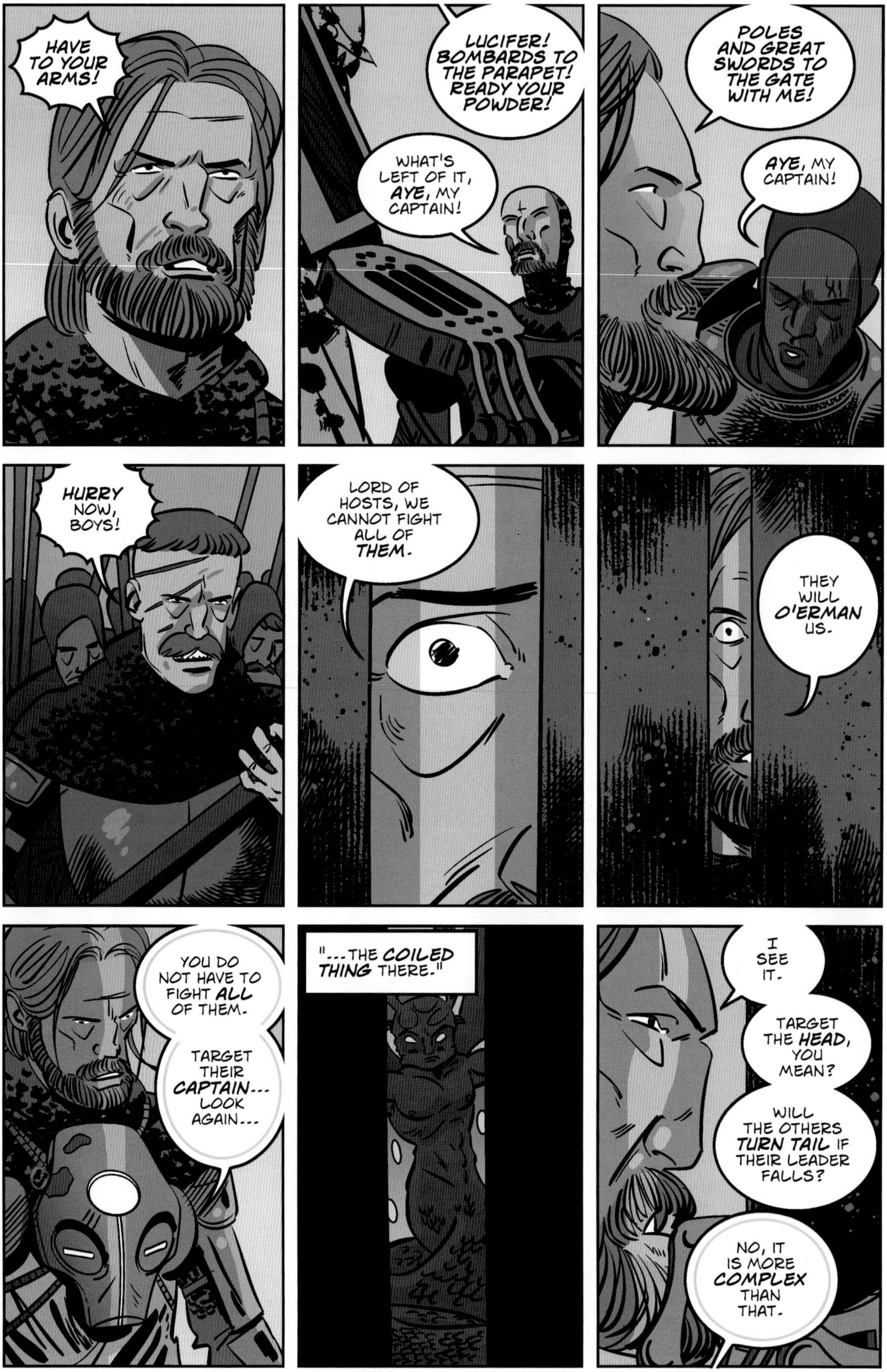
HAVE TO YOUR ARMS!
LUCIFER! BOMBARDS TO THE PARAPET! READY YOUR POWDER!
WHAT'S LEFT OF IT, AYE, MY CAPTAIN!
POLES AND GREAT SWORDS TO THE GATE WITH ME!
AYE, MY CAPTAIN!
HURRY NOW, BOYS!
LORD OF HOSTS, WE CANNOT FIGHT ALL OF THEM.
THEY WILL O'ERMAN US.
YOU DO NOT HAVE TO FIGHT ALL OF THEM.
TARGET THEIR CAPTAIN... LOOK AGAIN...
"...THE COILED THING THERE."
I SEE IT.
TARGET THE HEAD, YOU MEAN?
WILL THE OTHERS TURN TAIL IF THEIR LEADER FALLS?
NO, IT IS MORE COMPLEX THAN THAT.

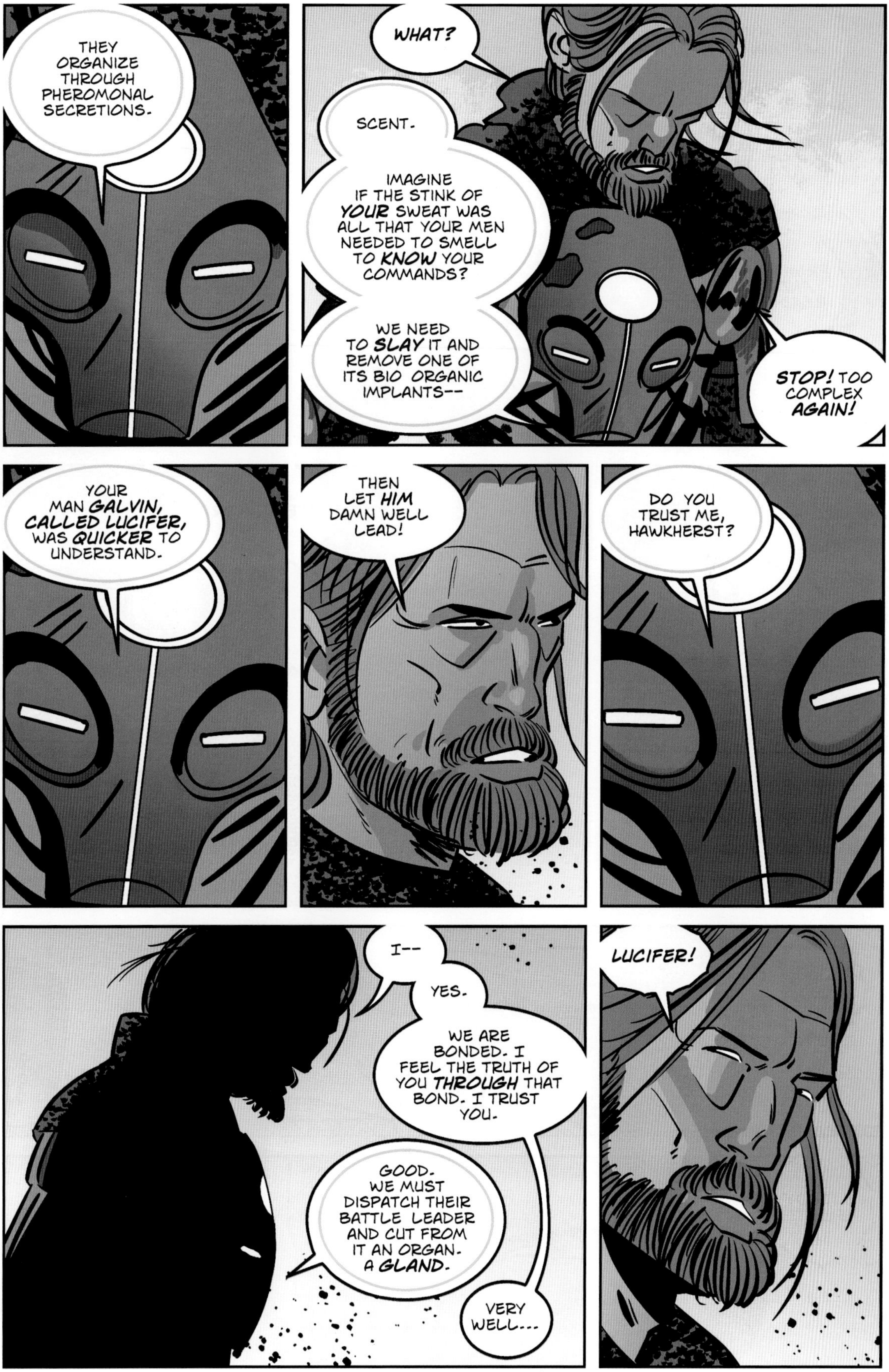
THEY ORGANIZE THROUGH PHEROMONAL SECRETIONS.
WHAT?
SCENT.
IMAGINE IF THE STINK OF YOUR SWEAT WAS ALL THAT YOUR MEN NEEDED TO SMELL TO KNOW YOUR COMMANDS?
WE NEED TO SLAY IT AND REMOVE ONE OF ITS BIO ORGANIC IMPLANTS--
STOP! TOO COMPLEX AGAIN!
YOUR MAN GALVIN, CALLED LUCIFER, WAS QUICKER TO UNDERSTAND.
THEN LET HIM DAMN WELL LEAD!
DO YOU TRUST ME, HAWKHERST?
I--
YES.
WE ARE BONDED. I FEEL THE TRUTH OF YOU THROUGH THAT BOND. I TRUST YOU.
GOOD. WE MUST DISPATCH THEIR BATTLE LEADER AND CUT FROM IT AN ORGAN. A GLAND.
VERY WELL...
LUCIFER!

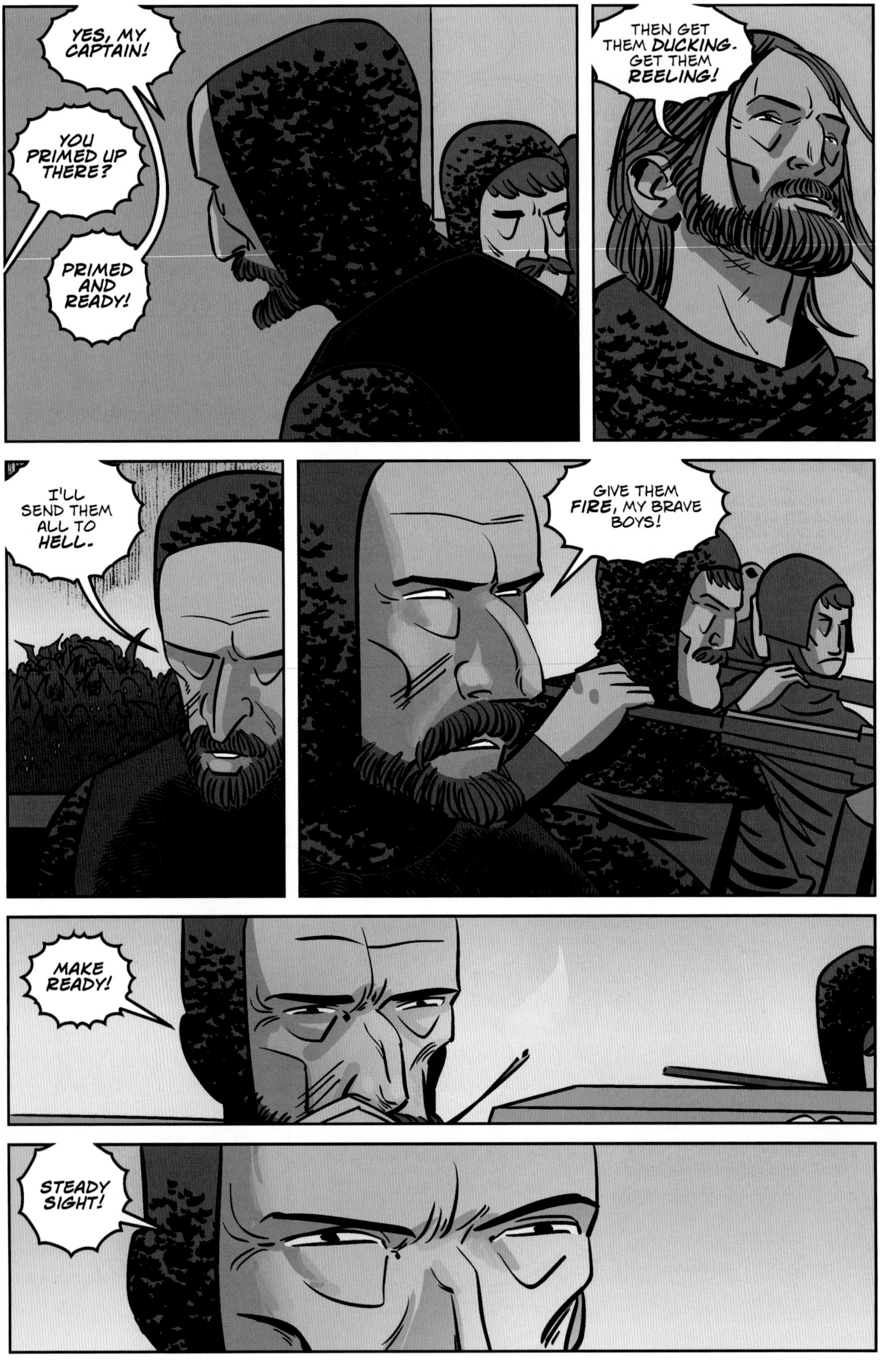
YES, MY CAPTAIN!
YOU PRIMED UP THERE?
PRIMED AND READY!
THEN GET THEM DUCKING. GET THEM REELING!
I'LL SEND THEM ALL TO HELL.
GIVE THEM FIRE, MY BRAVE BOYS!
MAKE READY!
STEADY SIGHT!

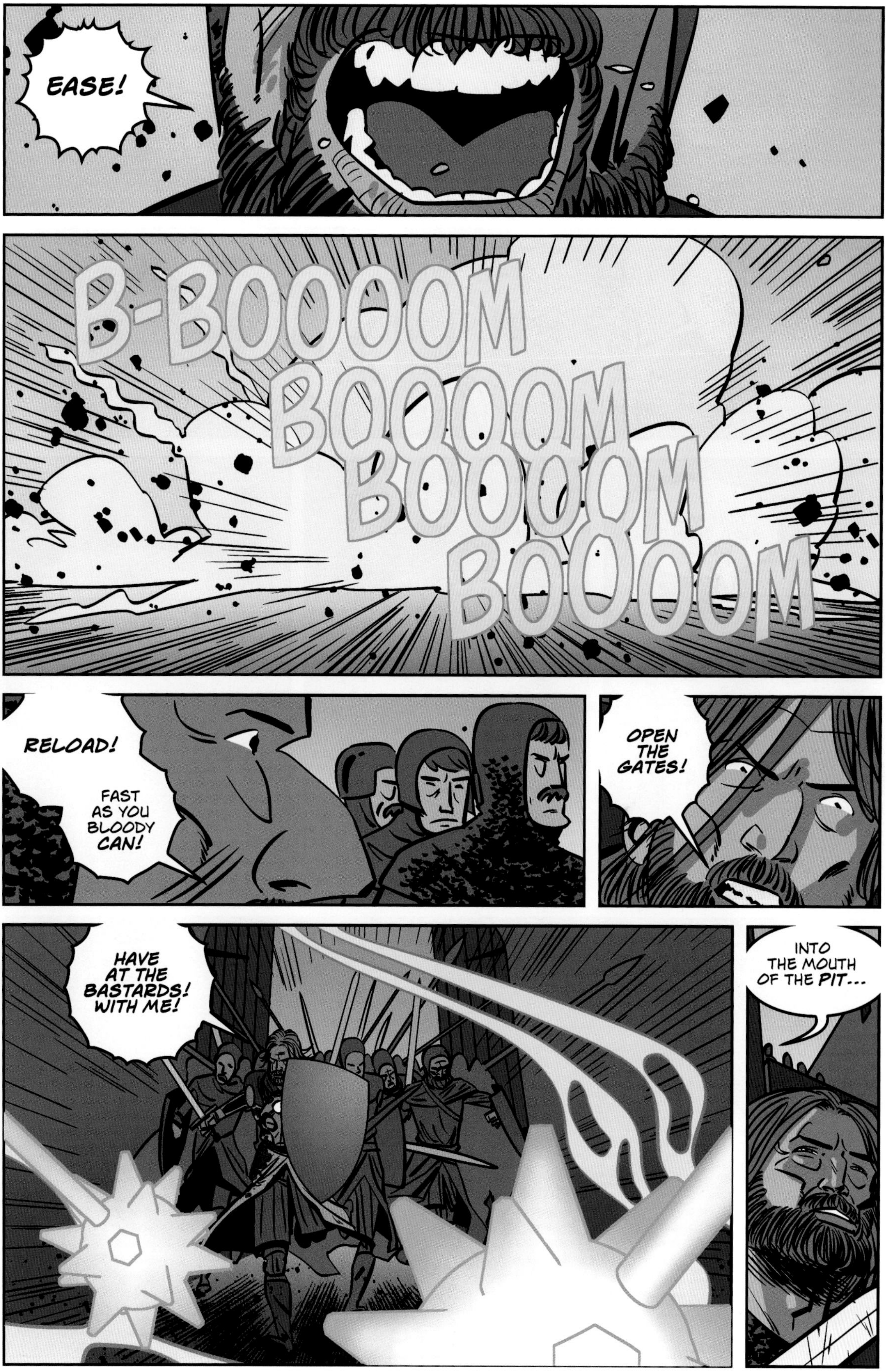
EASE!
B-BOOOOM BOOOOM BOOOOM BOOOOM
RELOAD!
FAST AS YOU BLOODY CAN!
OPEN THE GATES!
HAVE AT THE BASTARDS! WITH ME!
INTO THE MOUTH OF THE PIT...

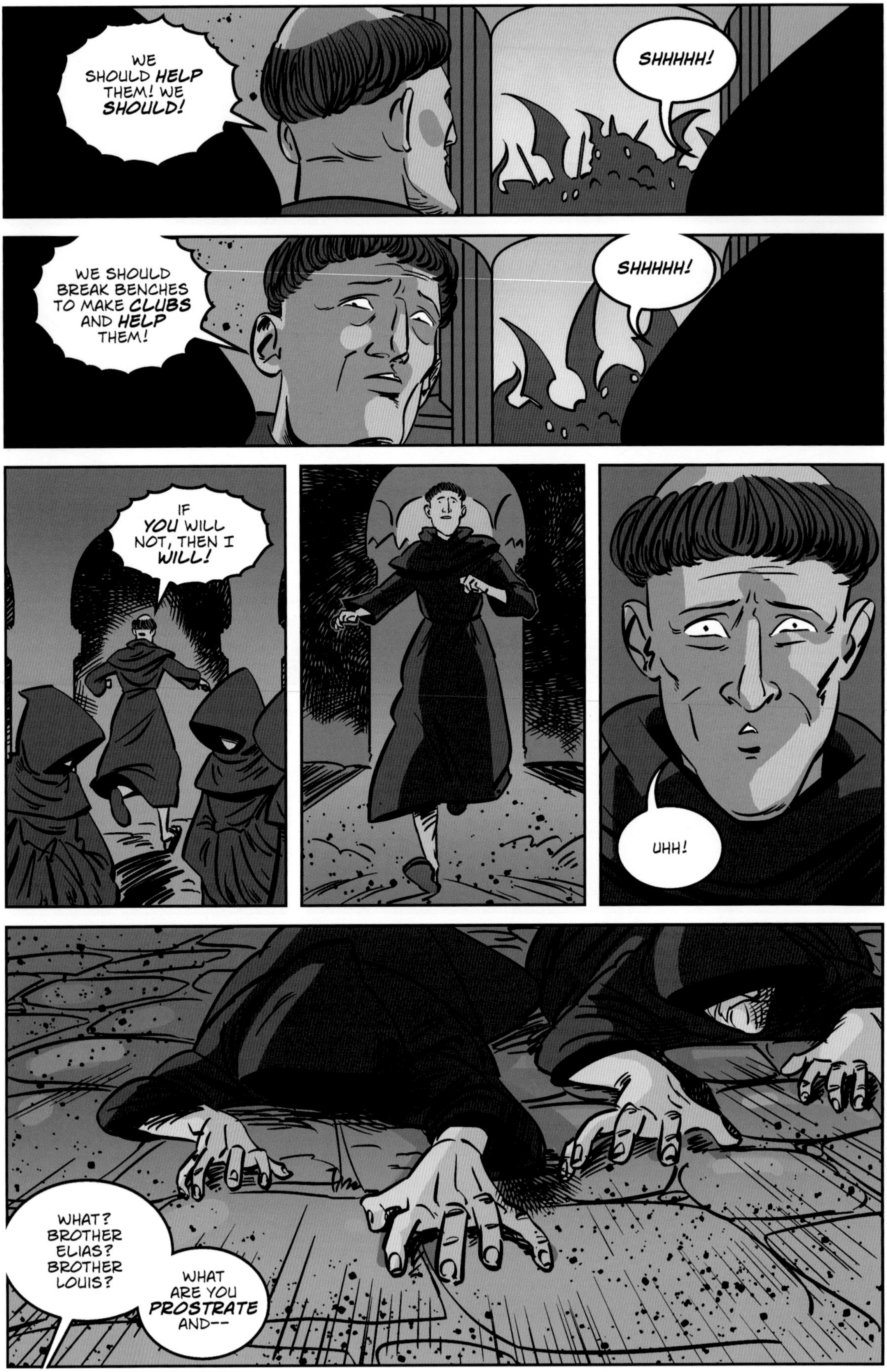
WE SHOULD HELP THEM! WE SHOULD!
SHHHHH!
WE SHOULD BREAK BENCHES TO MAKE CLUBS AND HELP THEM!
SHHHHH!
IF YOU WILL NOT, THEN I WILL!
UHH!
WHAT? BROTHER ELIAS? BROTHER LOUIS?
WHAT ARE YOU PROSTRATE AND--

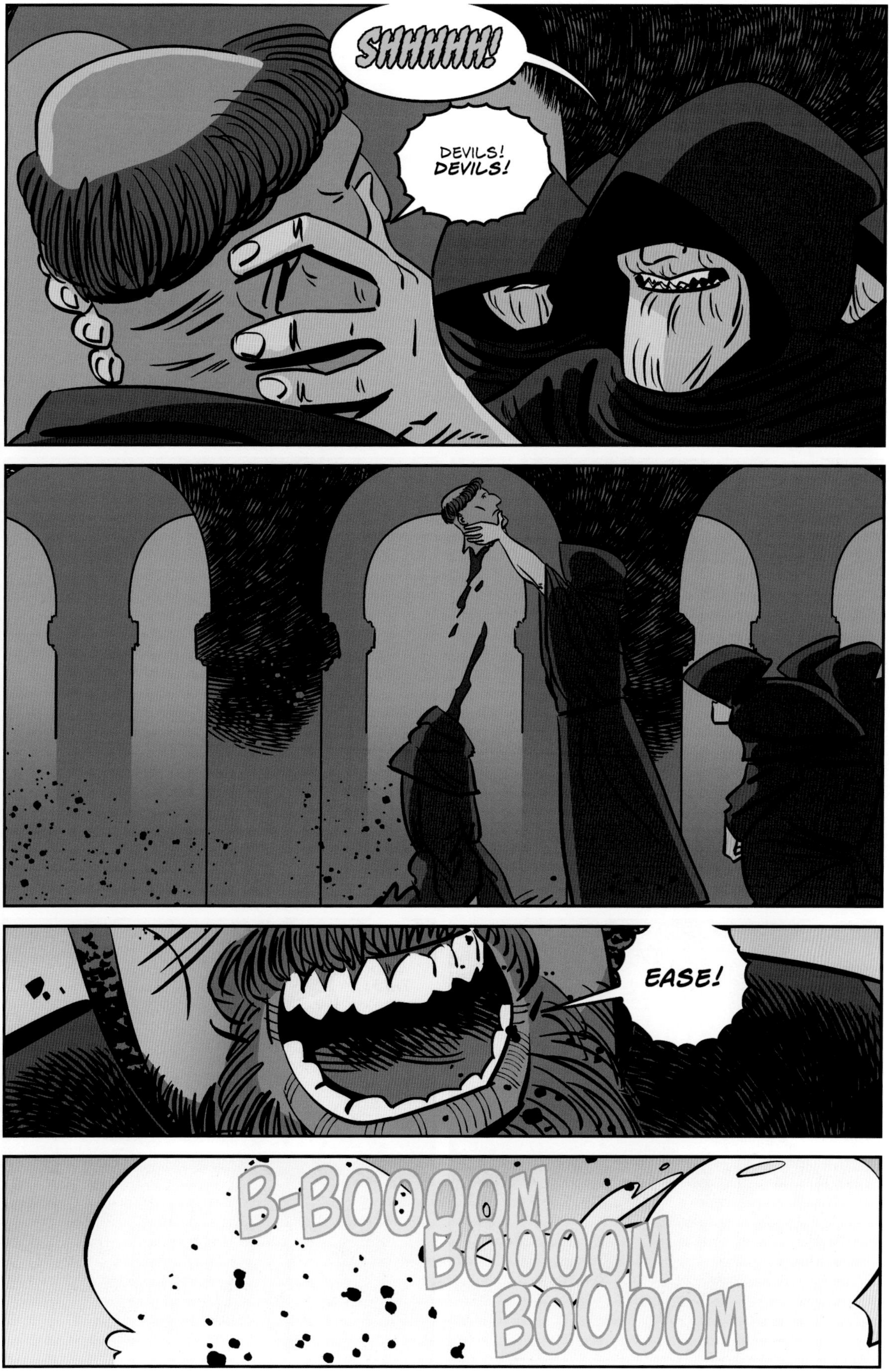
SHHHHH!
DEVILS! DEVILS!
EASE!
B-BOOOOM
BOOOOM
BOOOOM

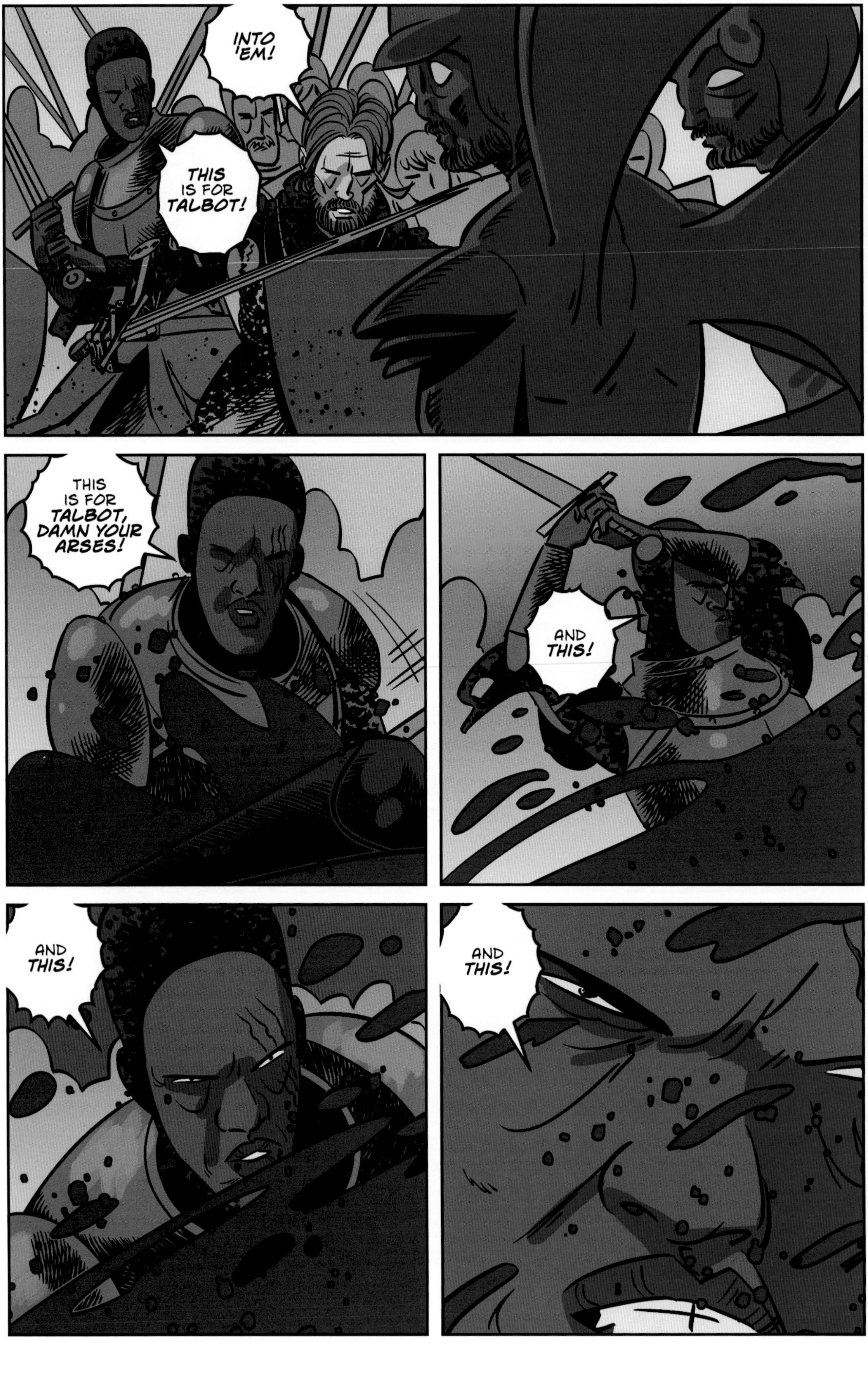
INTO 'EM!
THIS IS FOR TALBOT!
THIS IS FOR TALBOT, DAMN YOUR ARSES!
AND THIS!
AND THIS!
AND THIS!

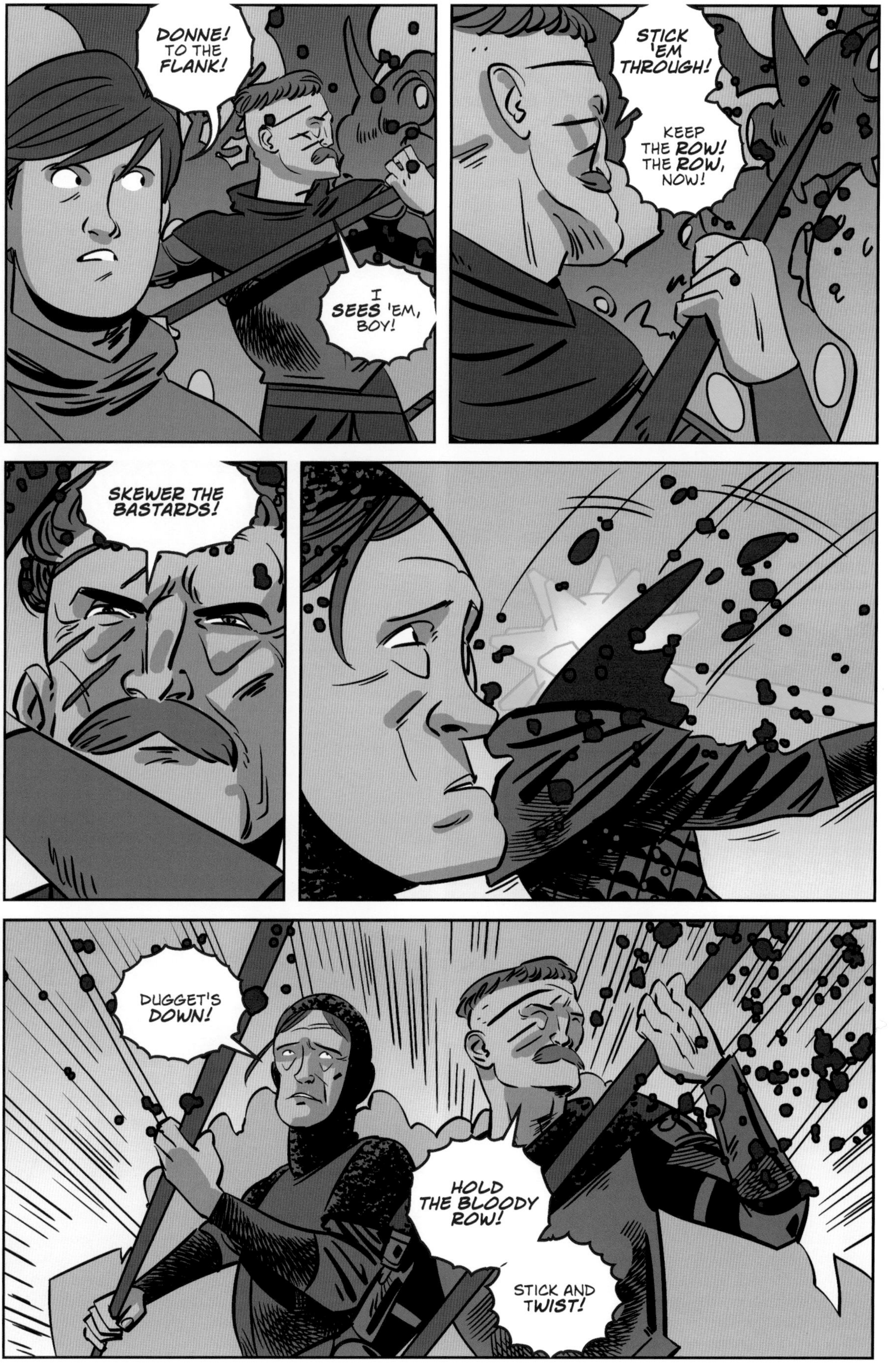
DONNE! TO THE FLANK!
I SEES 'EM, BOY!
STICK 'EM THROUGH!
KEEP THE ROW! THE ROW, NOW!
SKEWER THE BASTARDS!
DUGGET'S DOWN!
HOLD THE BLOODY ROW!
STICK AND TWIST!

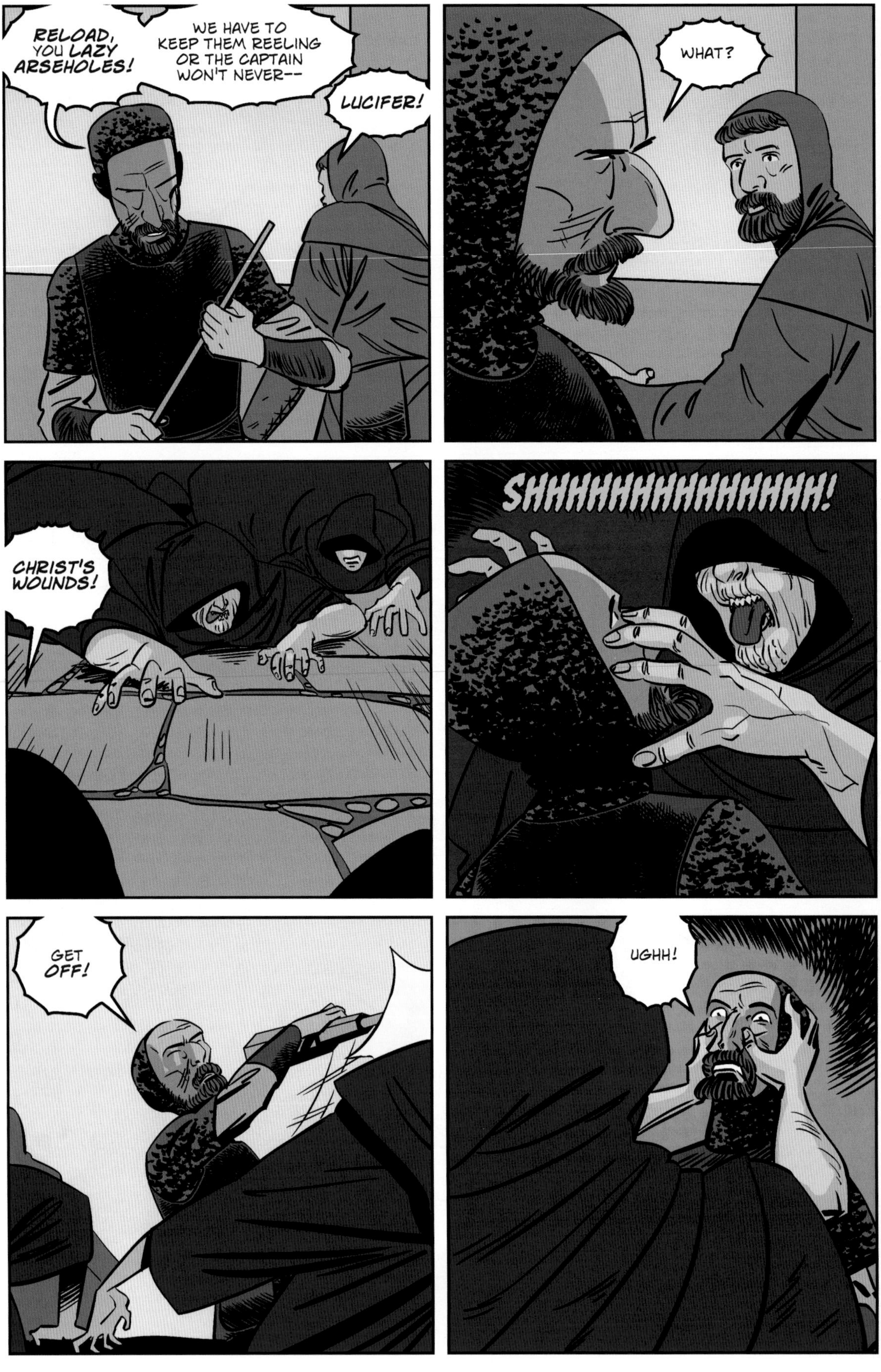
RELOAD, YOU LAZY ARSEHOLES!
WE HAVE TO KEEP THEM REELING OR THE CAPTAIN WON'T NEVER--
LUCIFER!
WHAT?
CHRIST'S WOUNDS!
SHHHHHHHHHHHHHH!
GET OFF!
UGHH!

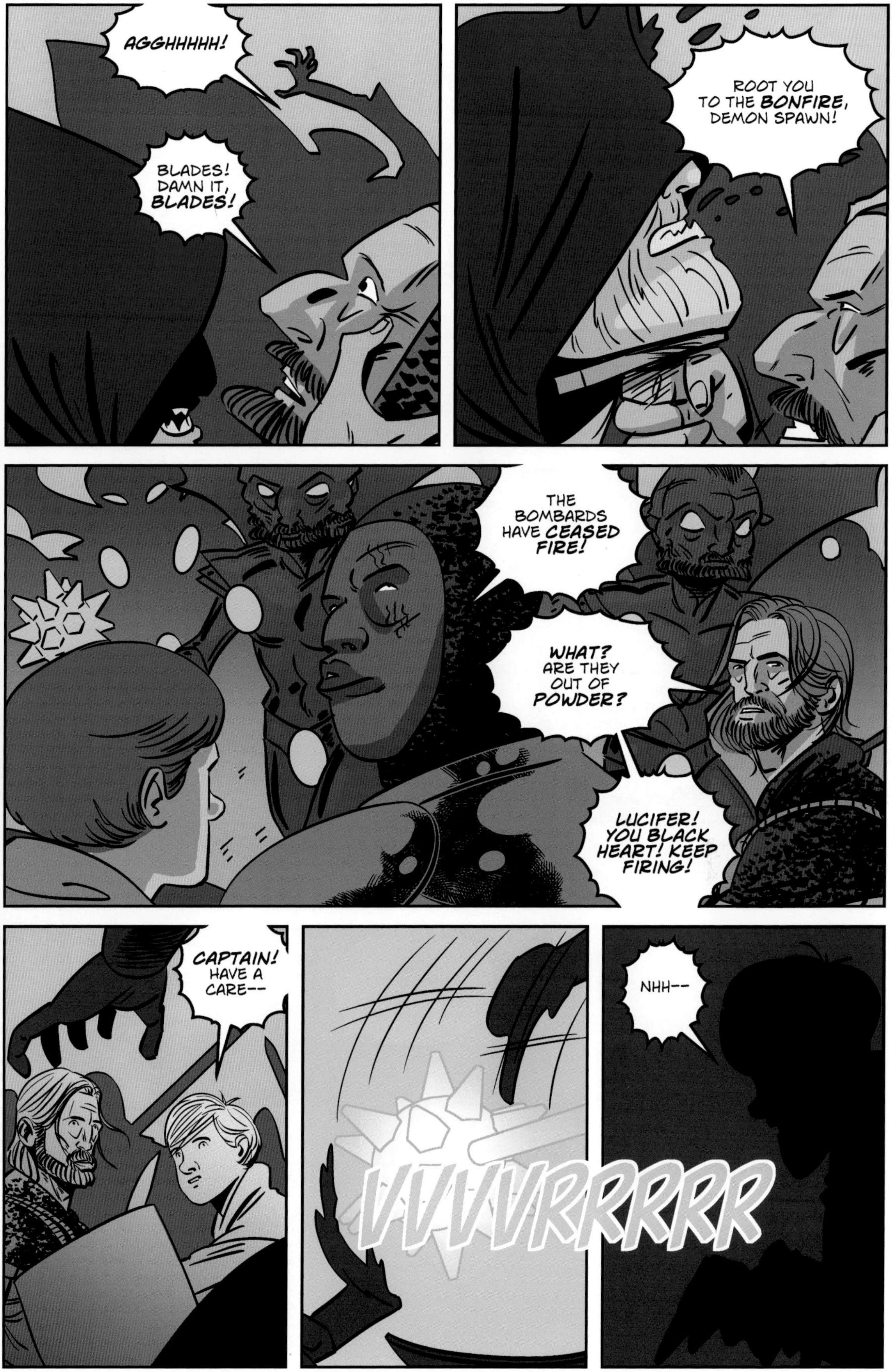
AGGHHHHH!
BLADES! DAMN IT, BLADES!
ROOT YOU TO THE BONFIRE, DEMON SPAWN!
THE BOMBARDS HAVE CEASED FIRE!
WHAT? ARE THEY OUT OF POWDER?
LUCIFER! YOU BLACK HEART! KEEP FIRING!
CAPTAIN! HAVE A CARE--
VVVVRRRRR
NHH--

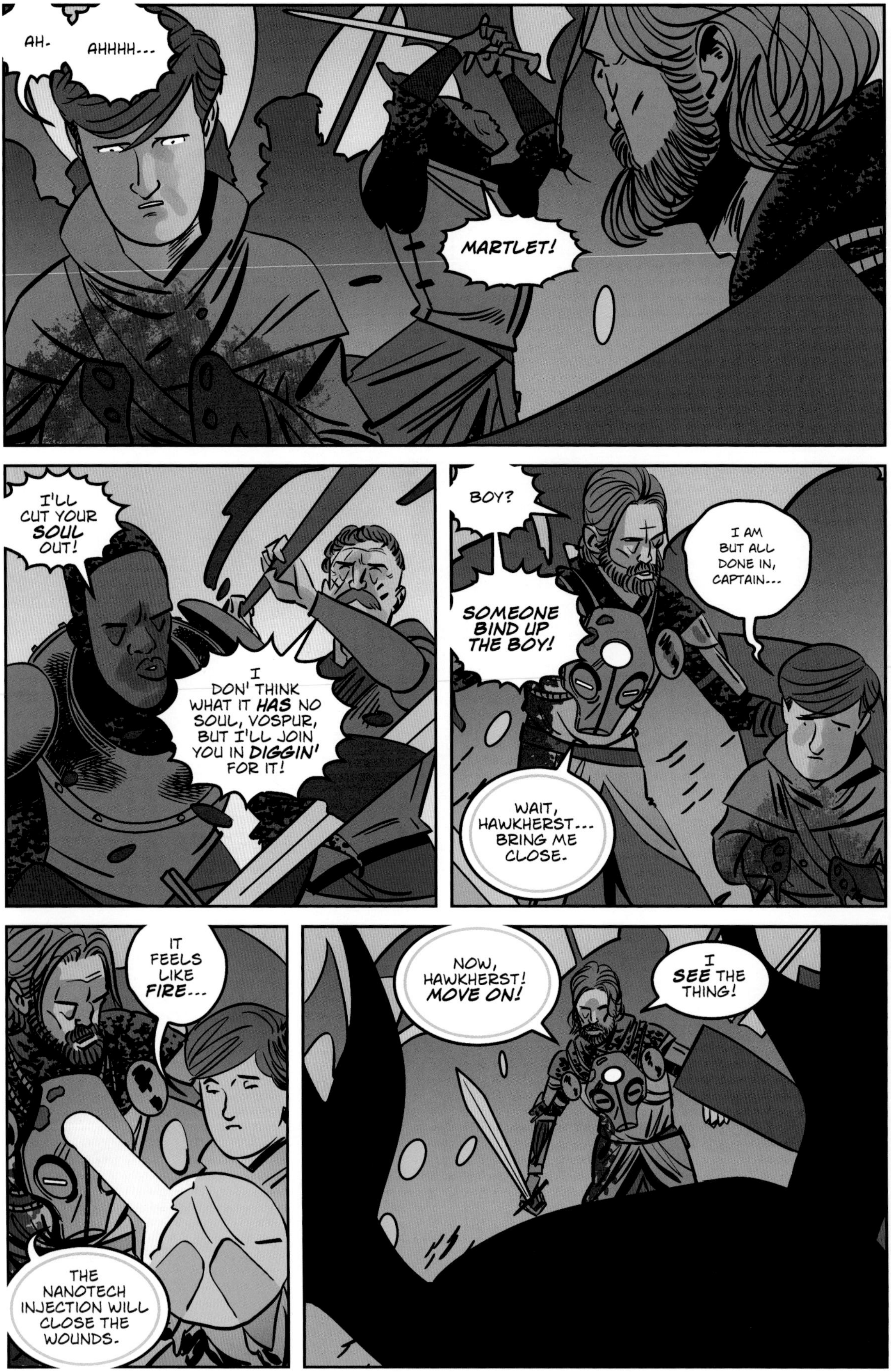

AH-
AHHHH...
MARTLET!
I'LL CUT YOUR SOUL OUT!
I DON' THINK WHAT IT HAS NO SOUL, VOSPUR, BUT I'LL JOIN YOU IN DIGGIN' FOR IT!
BOY?
SOMEONE BIND UP THE BOY!
I AM BUT ALL DONE IN, CAPTAIN...
WAIT, HAWKHERST... BRING ME CLOSE.
IT FEELS LIKE FIRE...
THE NANOTECH INJECTION WILL CLOSE THE WOUNDS.
NOW, HAWKHERST! MOVE ON!
I SEE THE THING!

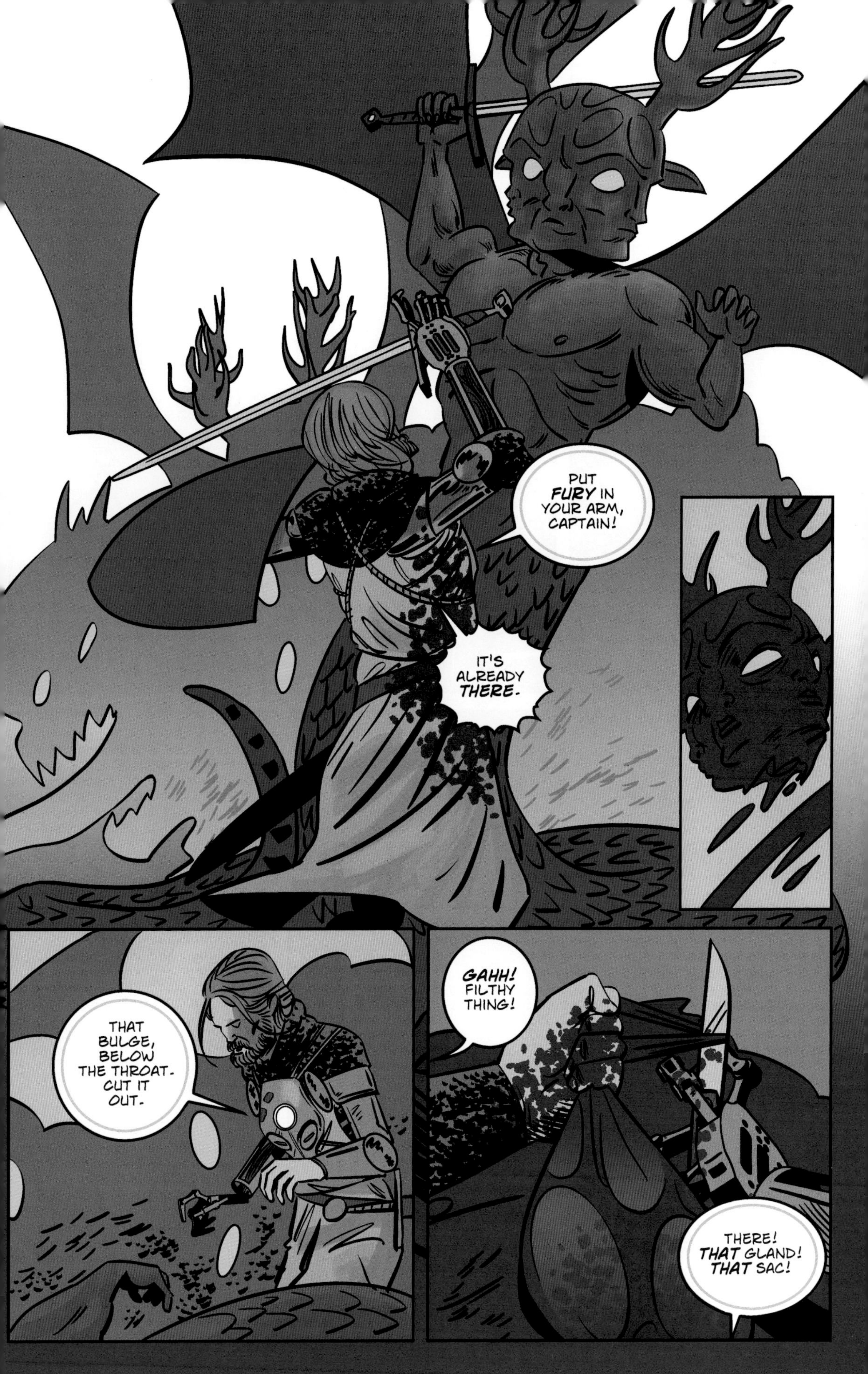
PUT FURY IN YOUR ARM, CAPTAIN!
IT'S ALREADY THERE.
THAT BULGE, BELOW THE THROAT. CUT IT OUT.
GAHH! FILTHY THING!
THERE! THAT GLAND! THAT SAC!

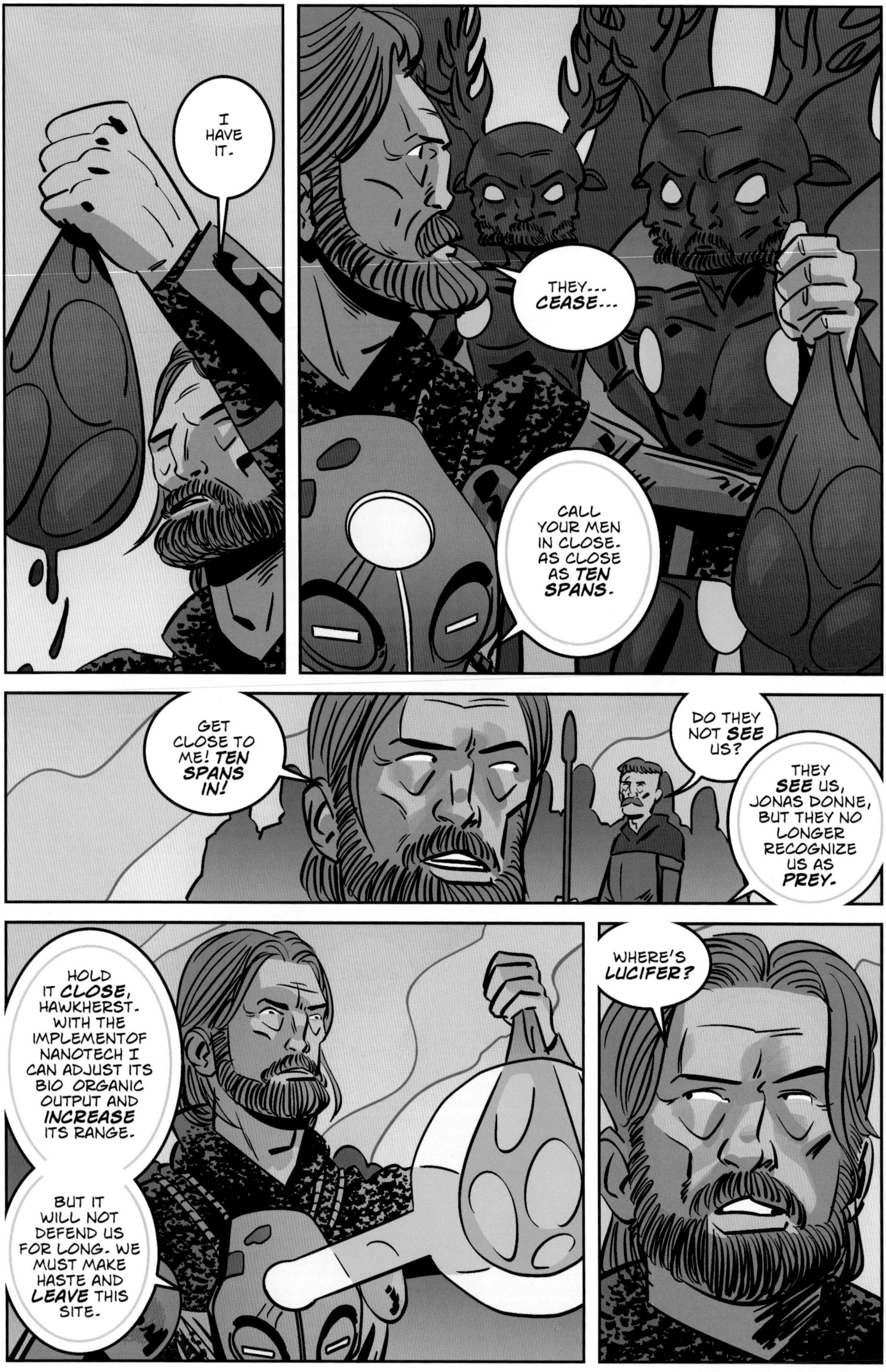
I HAVE IT.
THEY... CEASE...
CALL YOUR MEN IN CLOSE. AS CLOSE AS TEN SPANS.
GET CLOSE TO ME! TEN SPANS IN!
DO THEY NOT SEE US?
THEY SEE US, JONAS DONNE, BUT THEY NO LONGER RECOGNIZE US AS PREY.
HOLD IT CLOSE, HAWKHERST. WITH THE IMPLEMENTOF NANOTECH I CAN ADJUST ITS BIO ORGANIC OUTPUT AND INCREASE ITS RANGE.
BUT IT WILL NOT DEFEND US FOR LONG. WE MUST MAKE HASTE AND LEAVE THIS SITE.
WHERE'S LUCIFER?

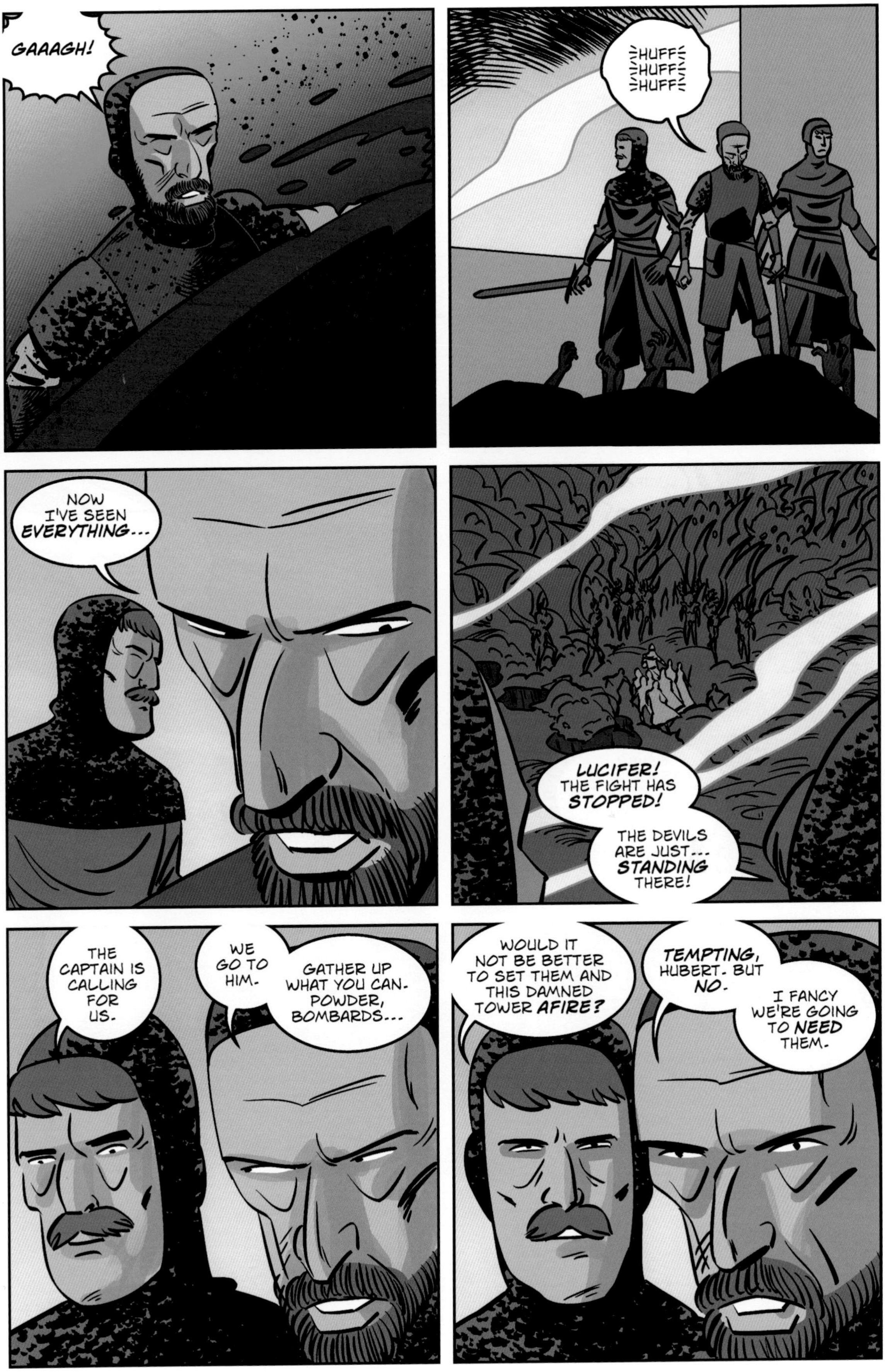
GAAAGH!
HUFF HUFF HUFF
NOW I'VE SEEN EVERYTHING...
LUCIFER! THE FIGHT HAS STOPPED!
THE DEVILS ARE JUST... STANDING THERE!
THE CAPTAIN IS CALLING FOR US.
WE GO TO HIM.
GATHER UP WHAT YOU CAN. POWDER, BOMBARDS...
WOULD IT NOT BE BETTER TO SET THEM AND THIS DAMNED TOWER AFIRE?
TEMPTING, HUBERT. BUT NO.
I FANCY WE'RE GOING TO NEED THEM.

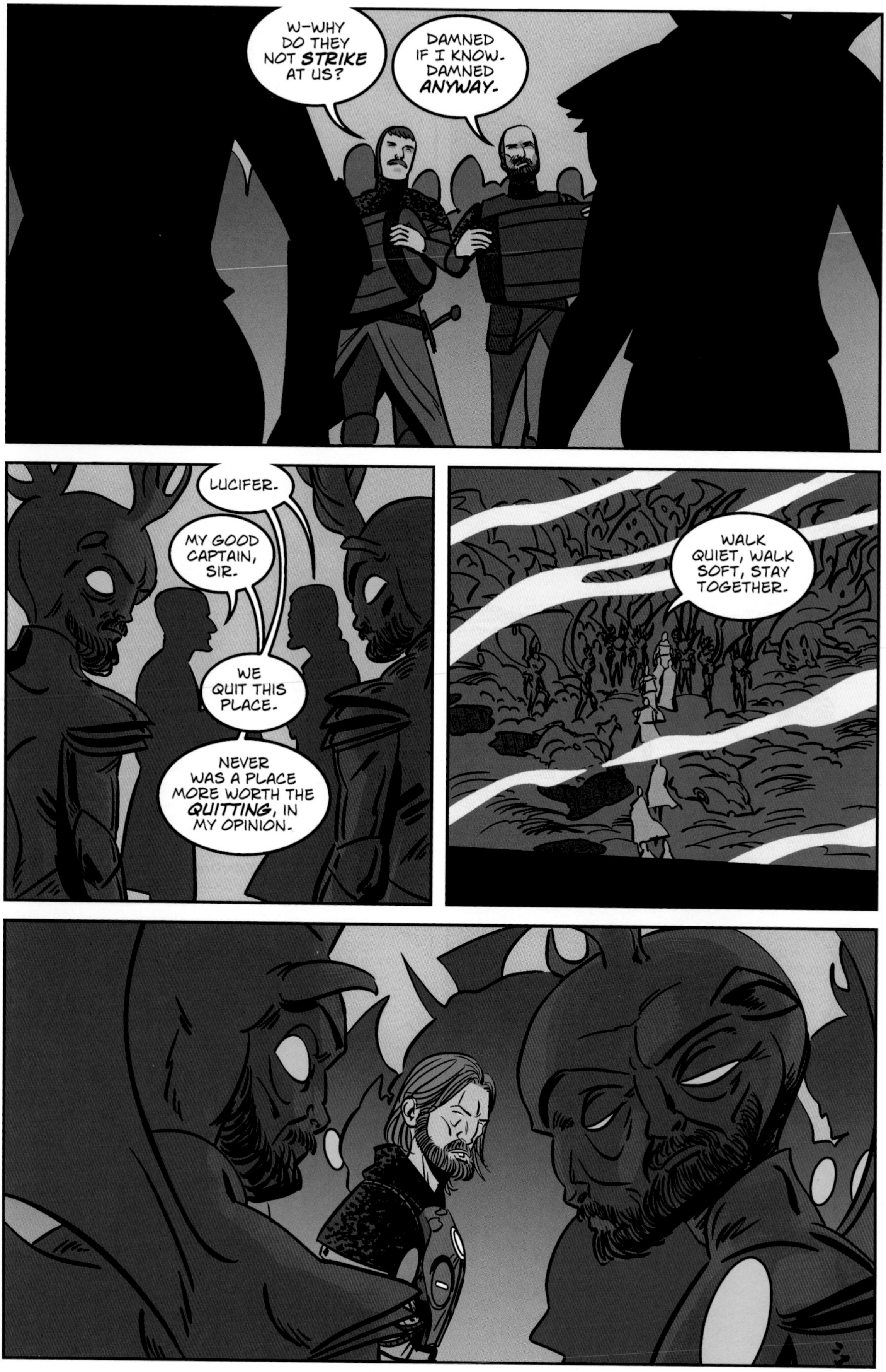
W-WHY DO THEY NOT STRIKE AT US?
DAMNED IF I KNOW. DAMNED ANYWAY.
LUCIFER.
MY GOOD CAPTAIN, SIR.
WE QUIT THIS PLACE.
NEVER WAS A PLACE MORE WORTH THE QUITTING, IN MY OPINION.
WALK QUIET, WALK SOFT, STAY TOGETHER.

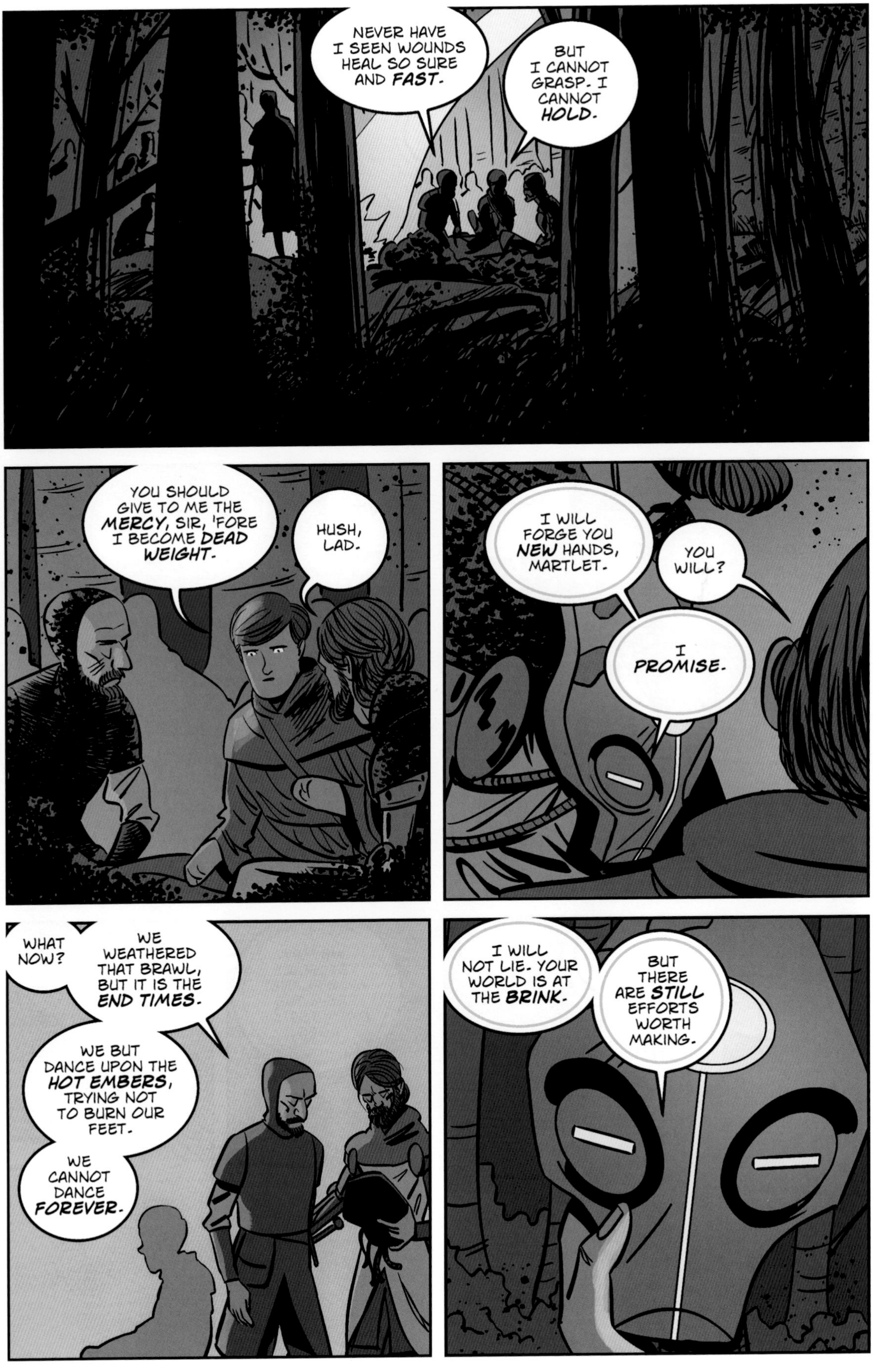
NEVER HAVE I SEEN WOUNDS HEAL SO SURE AND FAST.
BUT I CANNOT GRASP. I CANNOT HOLD.
YOU SHOULD GIVE TO ME THE MERCY, SIR, 'FORE I BECOME DEAD WEIGHT.
HUSH, LAD.
I WILL FORGE YOU NEW HANDS, MARTLET.
YOU WILL?
I PROMISE.
WHAT NOW?
WE WEATHERED THAT BRAWL, BUT IT IS THE END TIMES.
WE BUT DANCE UPON THE HOT EMBERS, TRYING NOT TO BURN OUR FEET.
WE CANNOT DANCE FOREVER.
I WILL NOT LIE. YOUR WORLD IS AT THE BRINK.
BUT THERE ARE STILL EFFORTS WORTH MAKING.

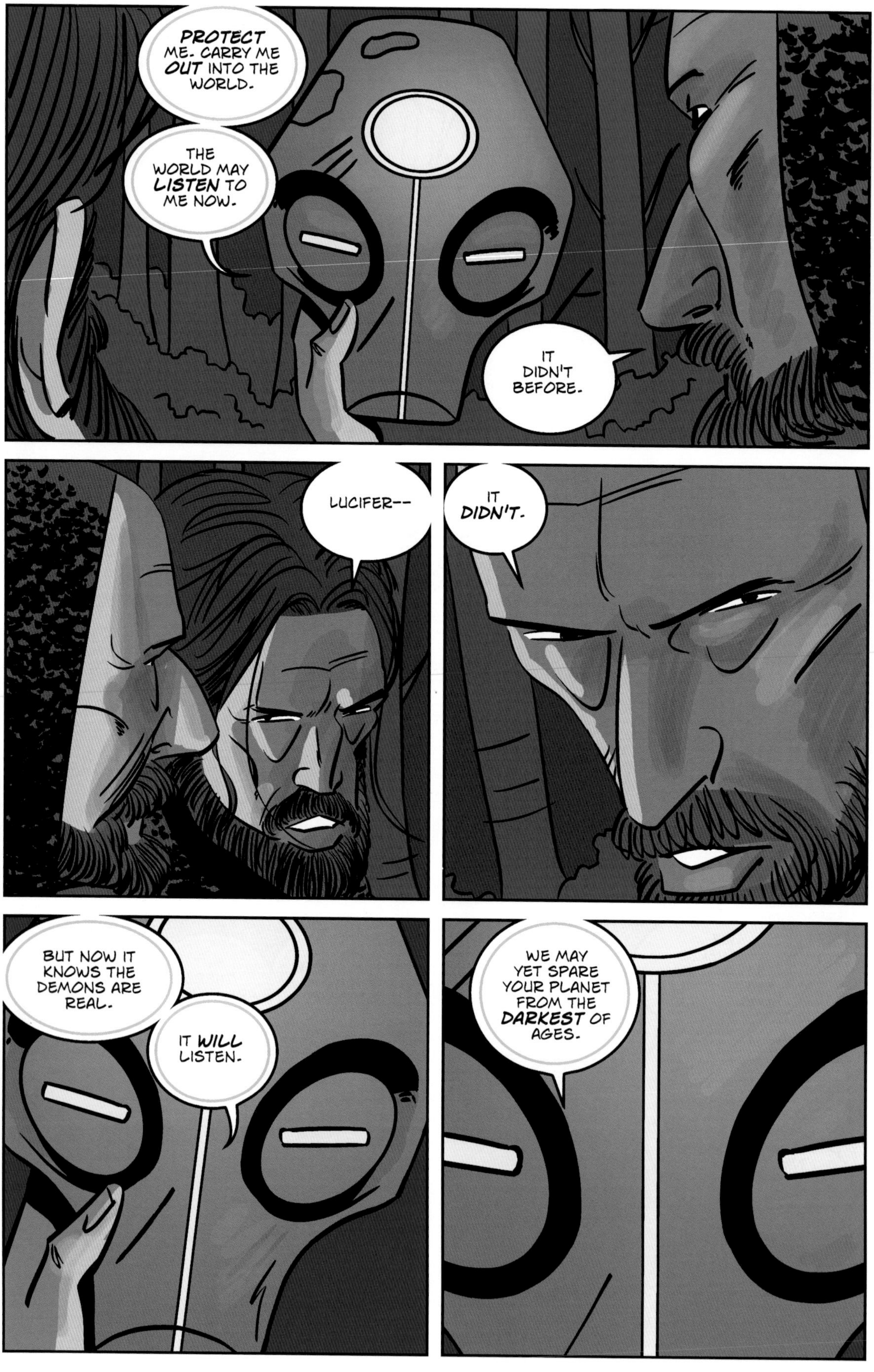
PROTECT ME. CARRY ME OUT INTO THE WORLD.
THE WORLD MAY LISTEN TO ME NOW.
IT DIDN'T BEFORE.
LUCIFER--
IT DIDN'T.
BUT NOW IT KNOWS THE DEMONS ARE REAL.
IT WILL LISTEN.
WE MAY YET SPARE YOUR PLANET FROM THE DARKEST OF AGES.

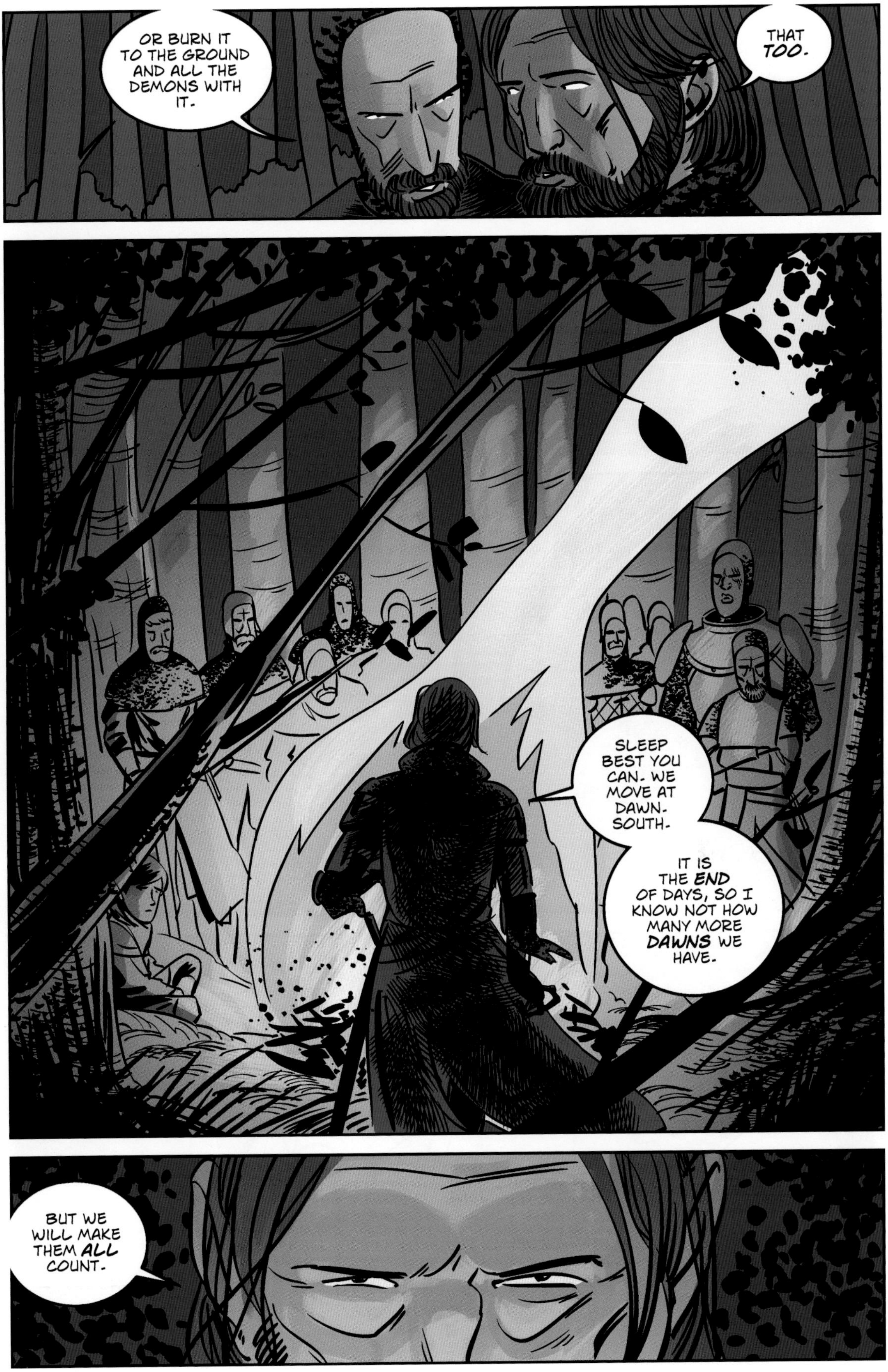
OR BURN IT TO THE GROUND AND ALL THE DEMONS WITH IT.
THAT TOO.
SLEEP BEST YOU CAN. WE MOVE AT DAWN. SOUTH.
IT IS THE END OF DAYS, SO I KNOW NOT HOW MANY MORE DAWNS WE HAVE.
BUT WE WILL MAKE THEM ALL COUNT.

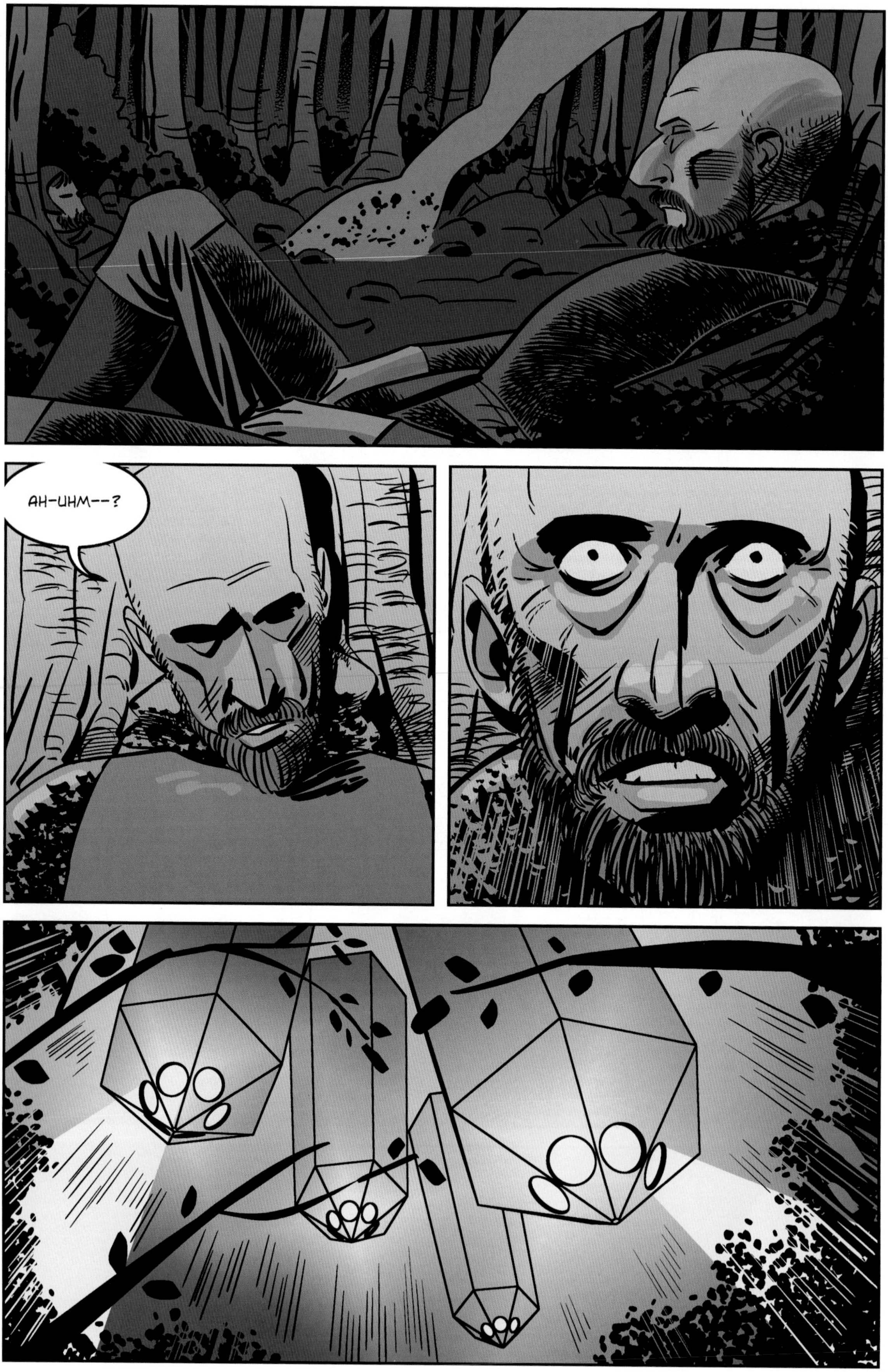
AH-UHM--?

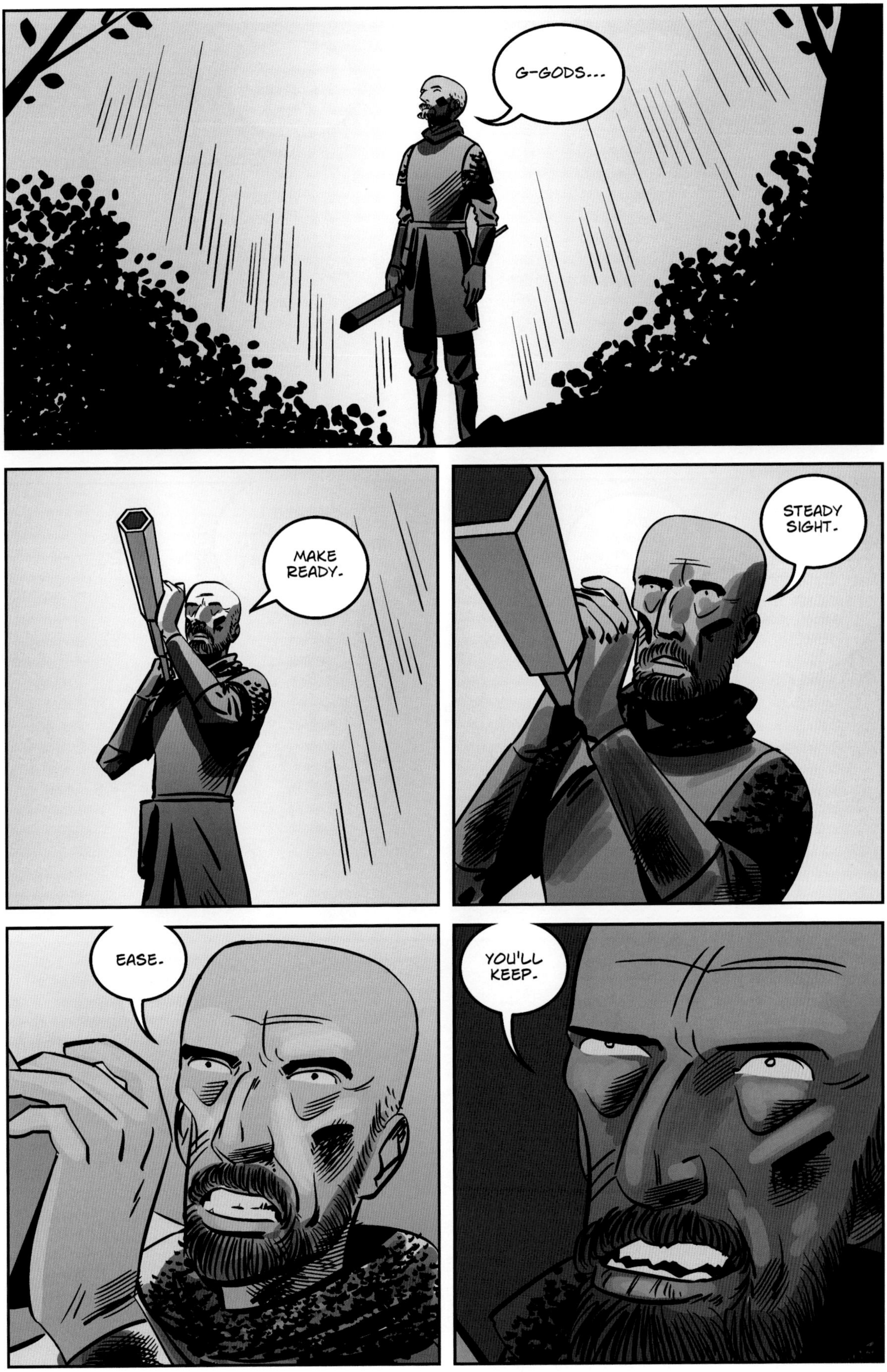
G-GODS...
MAKE READY.
STEADY SIGHT.
EASE.
YOU'LL KEEP.

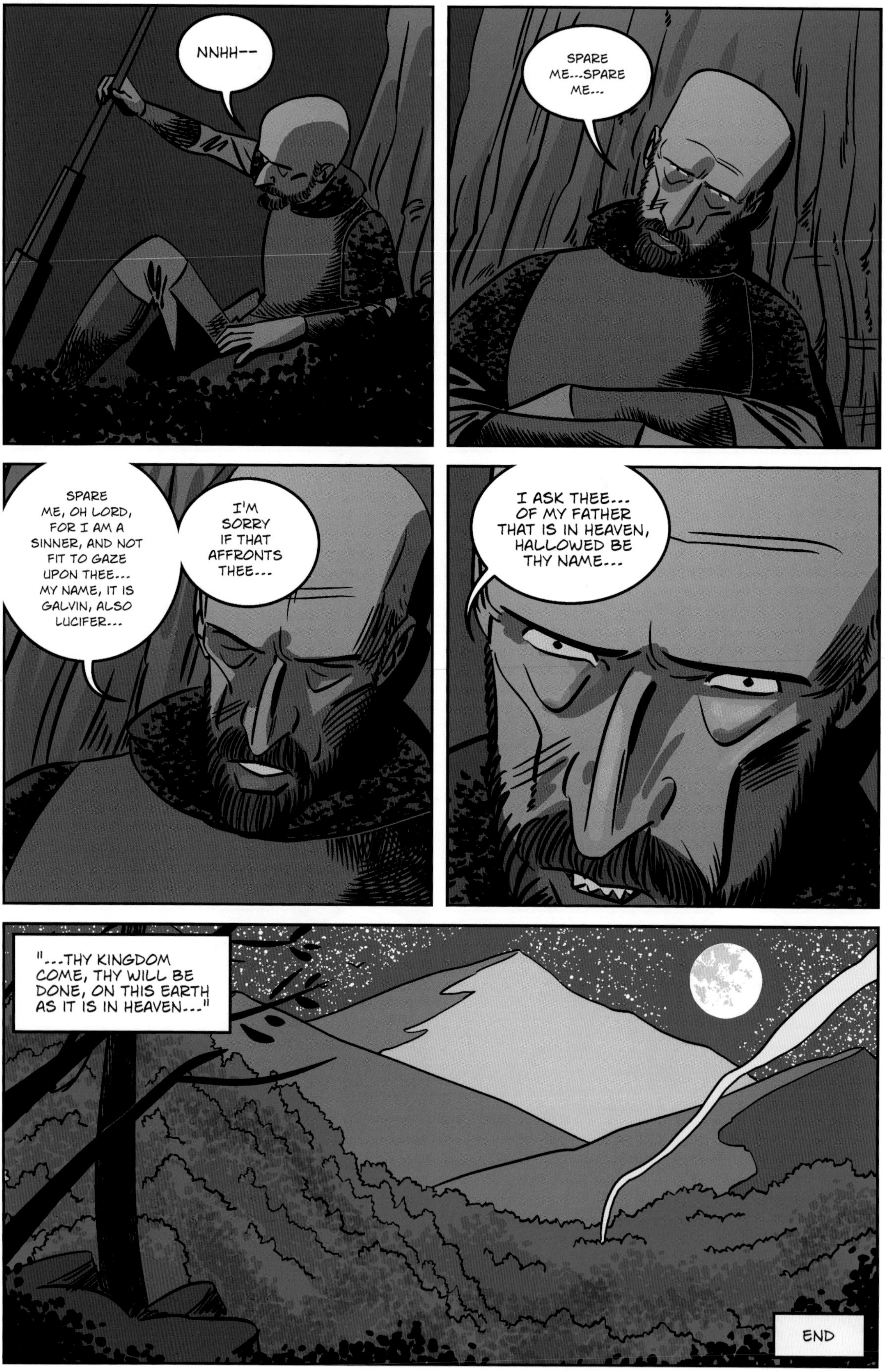
NNHH--
SPARE ME...SPARE ME...
SPARE ME, OH LORD, FOR I AM A SINNER, AND NOT FIT TO GAZE UPON THEE... MY NAME, IT IS GALVIN, ALSO LUCIFER...
I'M SORRY IF THAT AFFRONTS THEE...
I ASK THEE... OF MY FATHER THAT IS IN HEAVEN, HALLOWED BE THY NAME...
"...THY KINGDOM COME, THY WILL BE DONE, ON THIS EARTH AS IT IS IN HEAVEN..."
END

I. N. J. CULBARD'S SKETCHBOOK

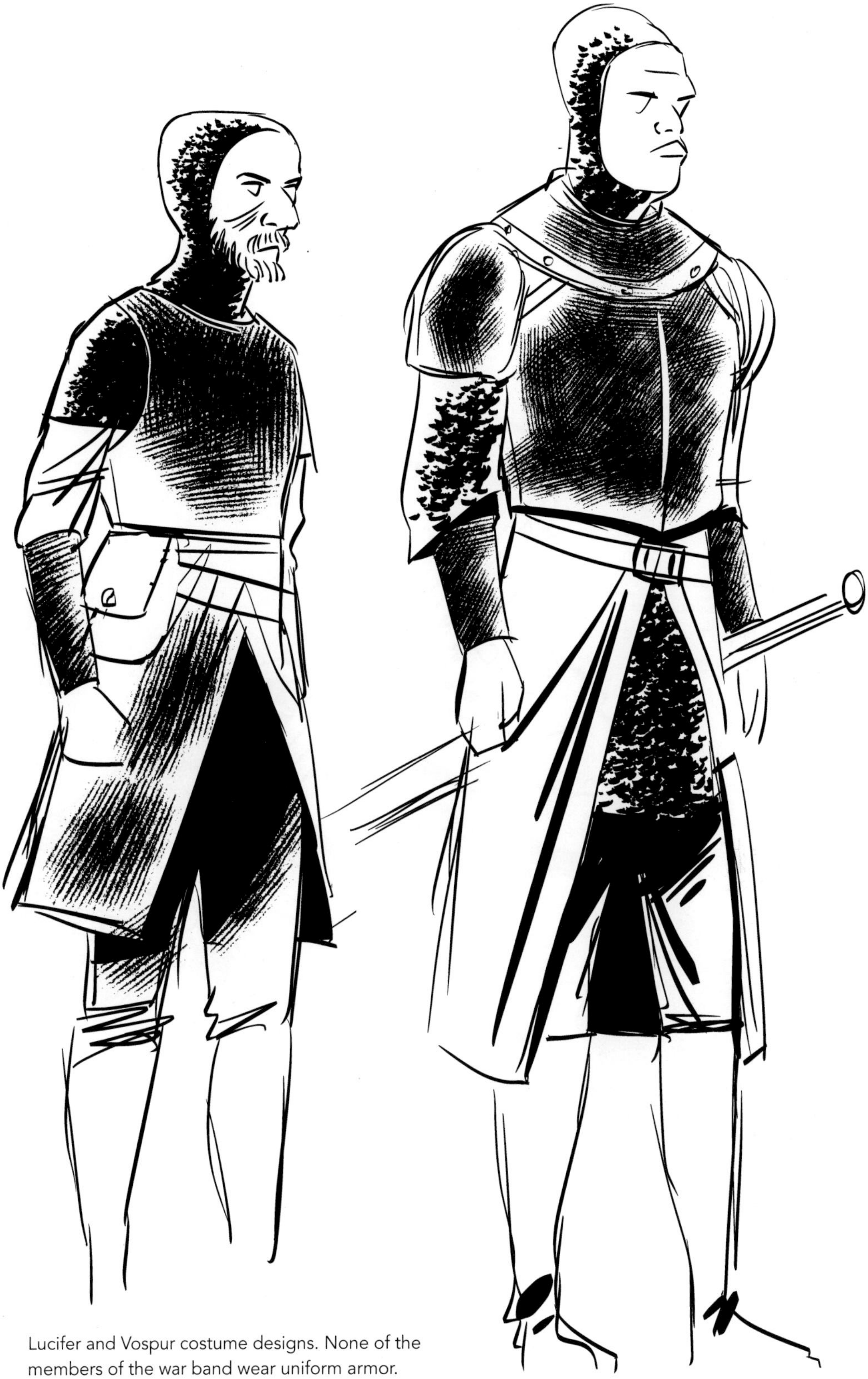

Lucifer and Vospur costume designs. None of the members of the war band wear uniform armor. The differences in costume give the overall sense that it is an army made up of different men from different regions and battles, all unified by coin.

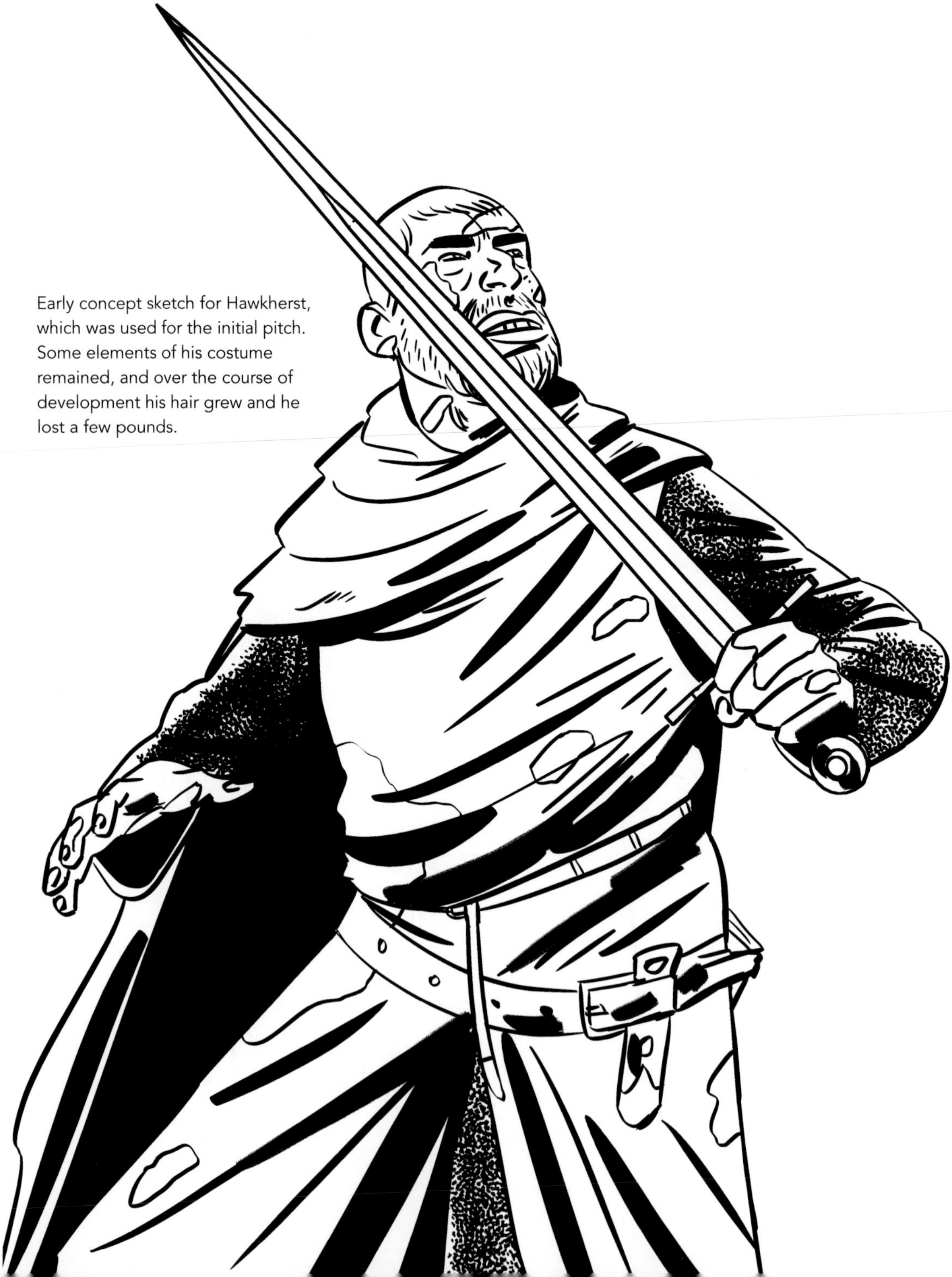

Early concept sketch for Hawkherst, which was used for the initial pitch. Some elements of his costume remained, and over the course of development his hair grew and he lost a few pounds.

Early concept sketch for the aliens as baboon-like creatures. The initial approach was to go the way of medieval interpretation. That was something that was there with the very first pitch, but I did explore other avenues and felt that while this route was indeed odd, it didn't really have quite enough power, certainly not nearly as much power as the Reindeer Men.

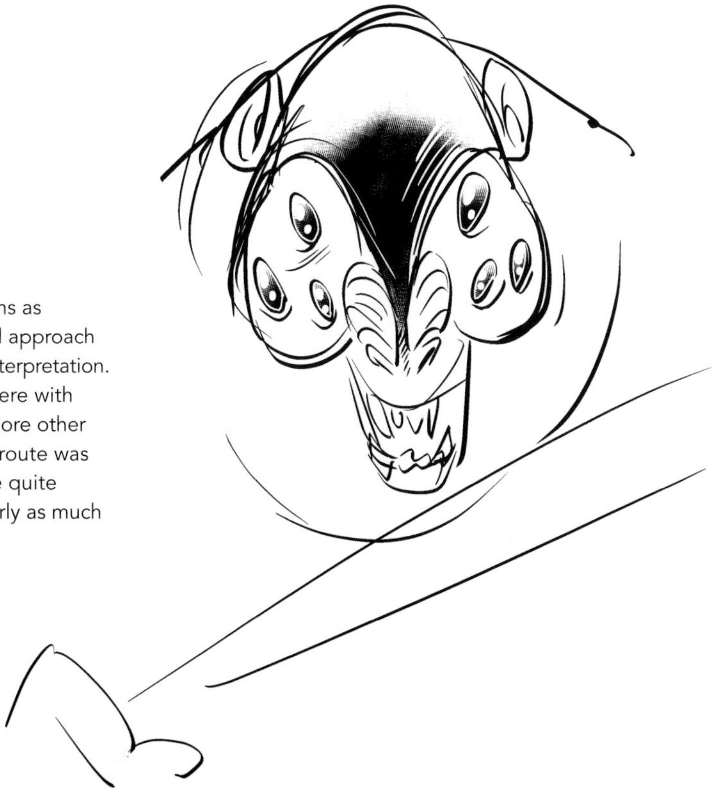

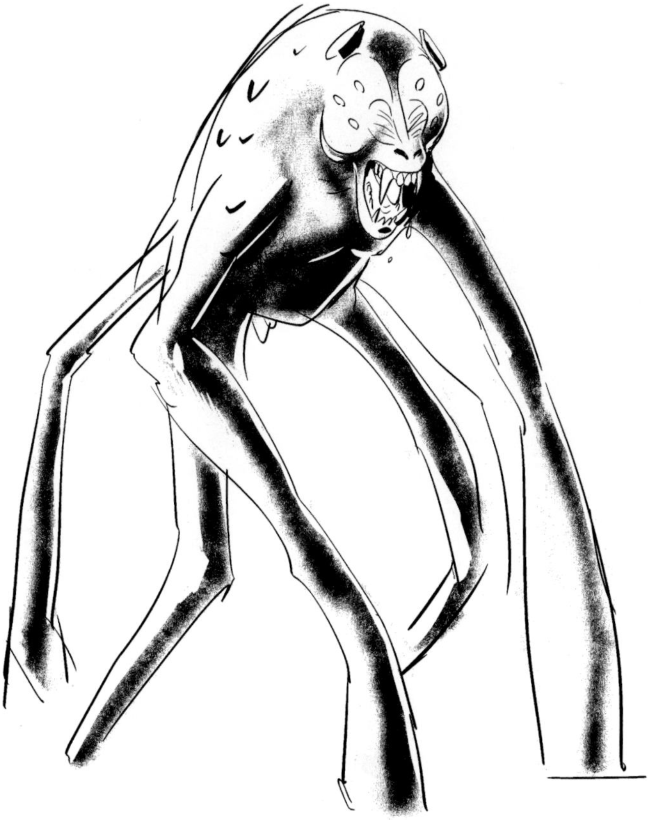

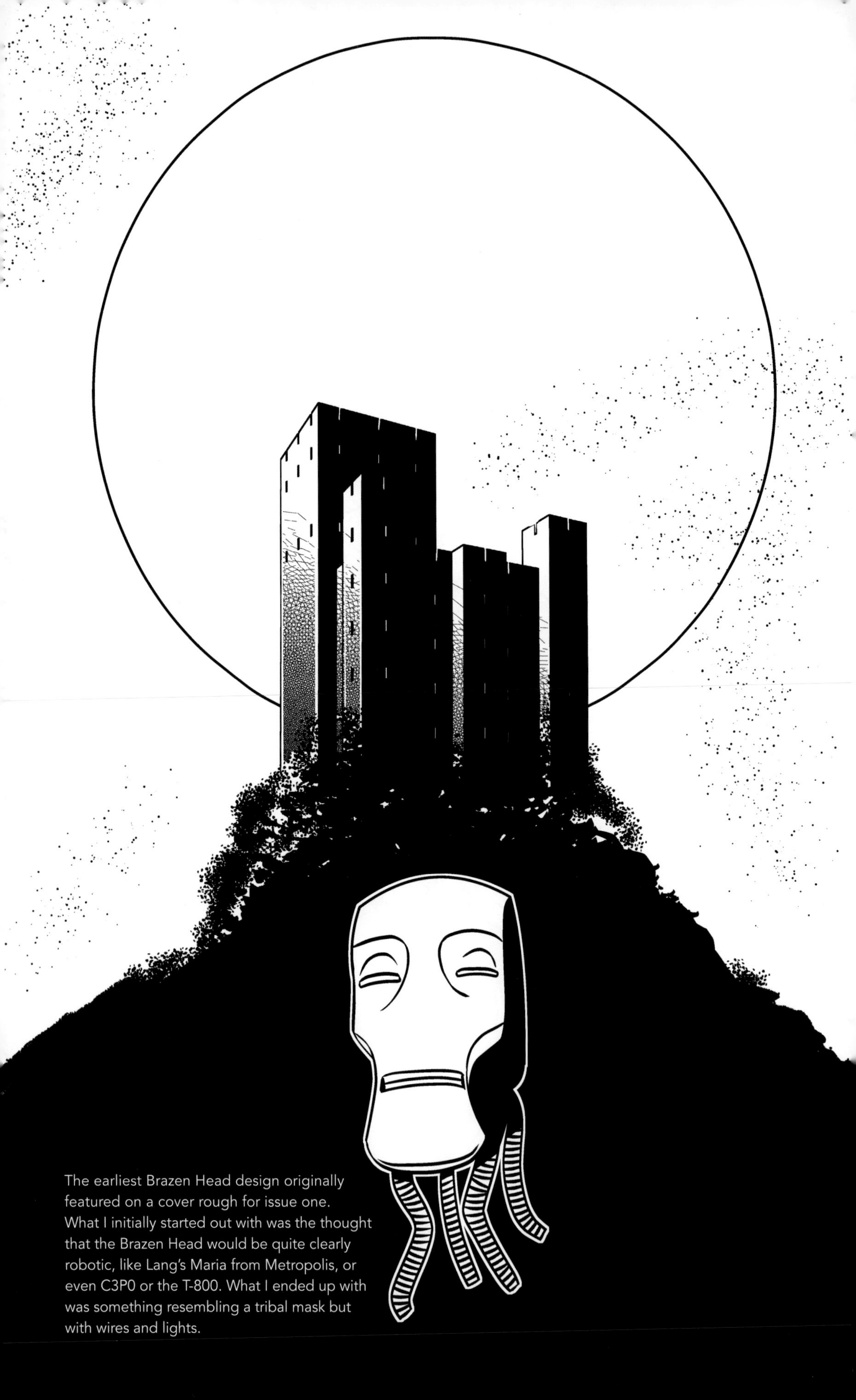

The earliest Brazen Head design originally featured on a cover rough for issue one. What I initially started out with was the thought that the Brazen Head would be quite clearly robotic, like Lang's Maria from Metropolis, or even C3P0 or the T-800. What I ended up with was something resembling a tribal mask but with wires and lights.

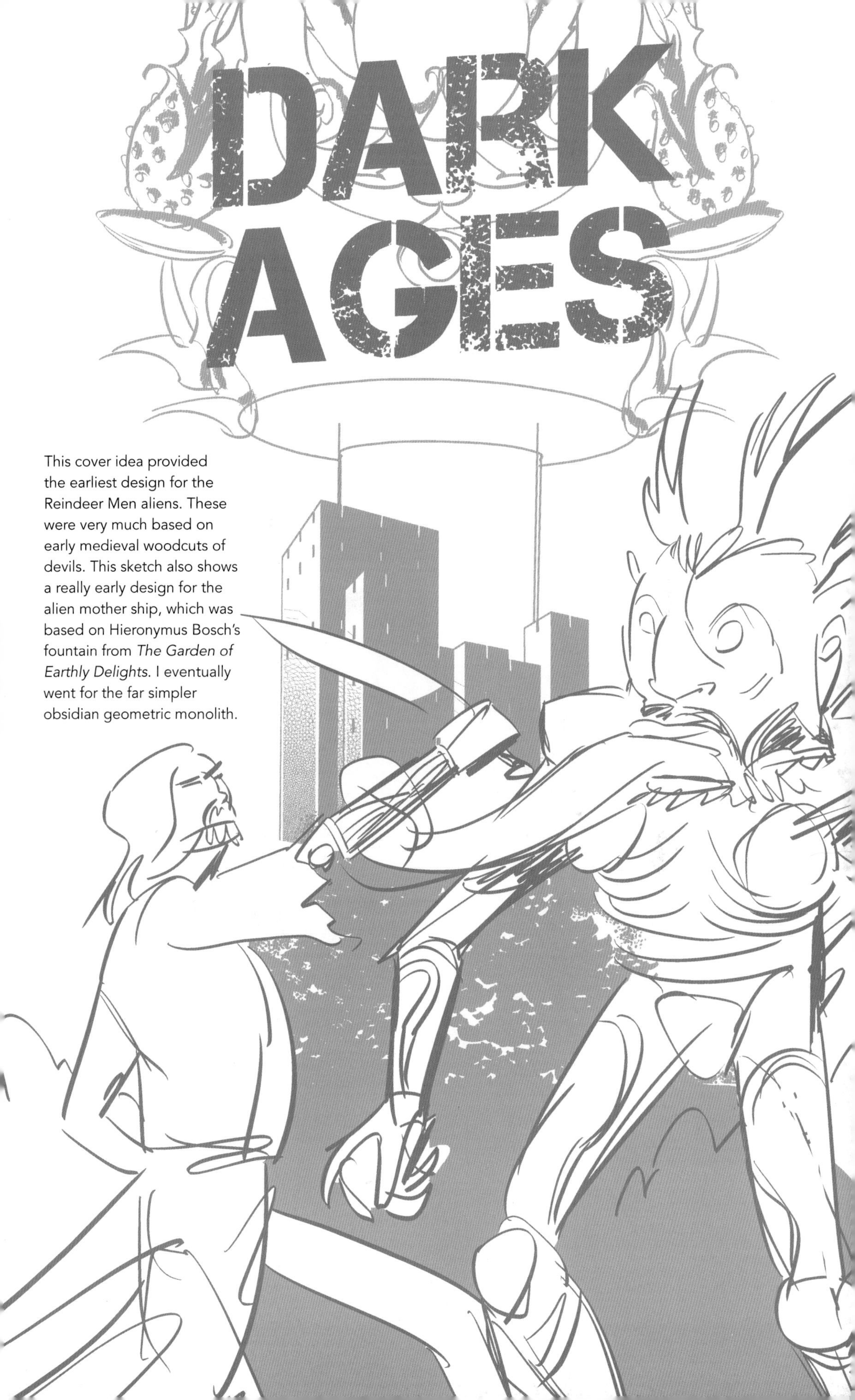
DARK
AGES

This cover idea provided the earliest design for the Reindeer Men aliens. These were very much based on early medieval woodcuts of devils. This sketch also shows a really early design for the alien mother ship, which was based on Hieronymus Bosch's fountain from *The Garden of Earthly Delights*. I eventually went for the far simpler obsidian geometric monolith.

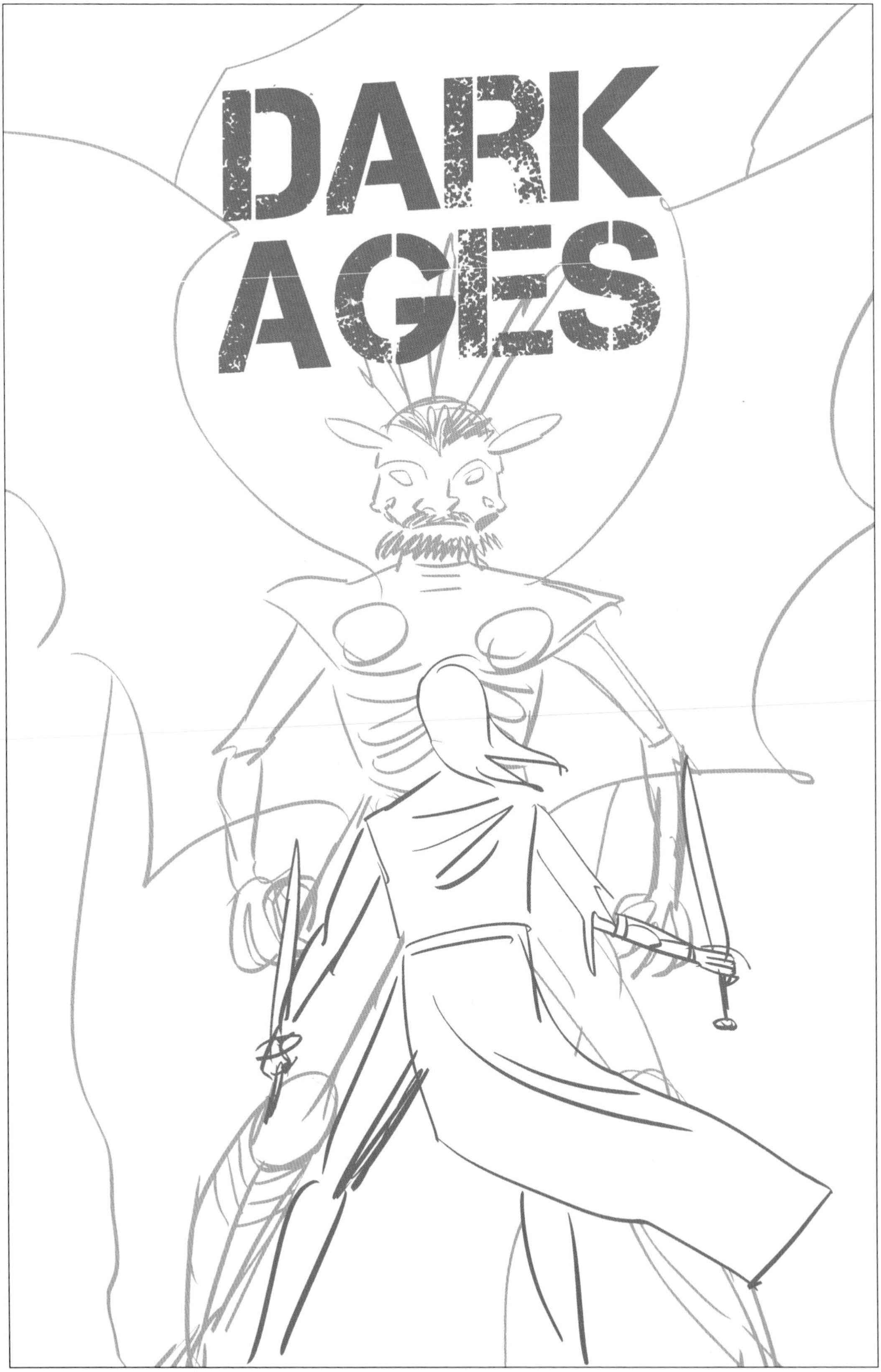
DARK
AGES

More rough cover designs.

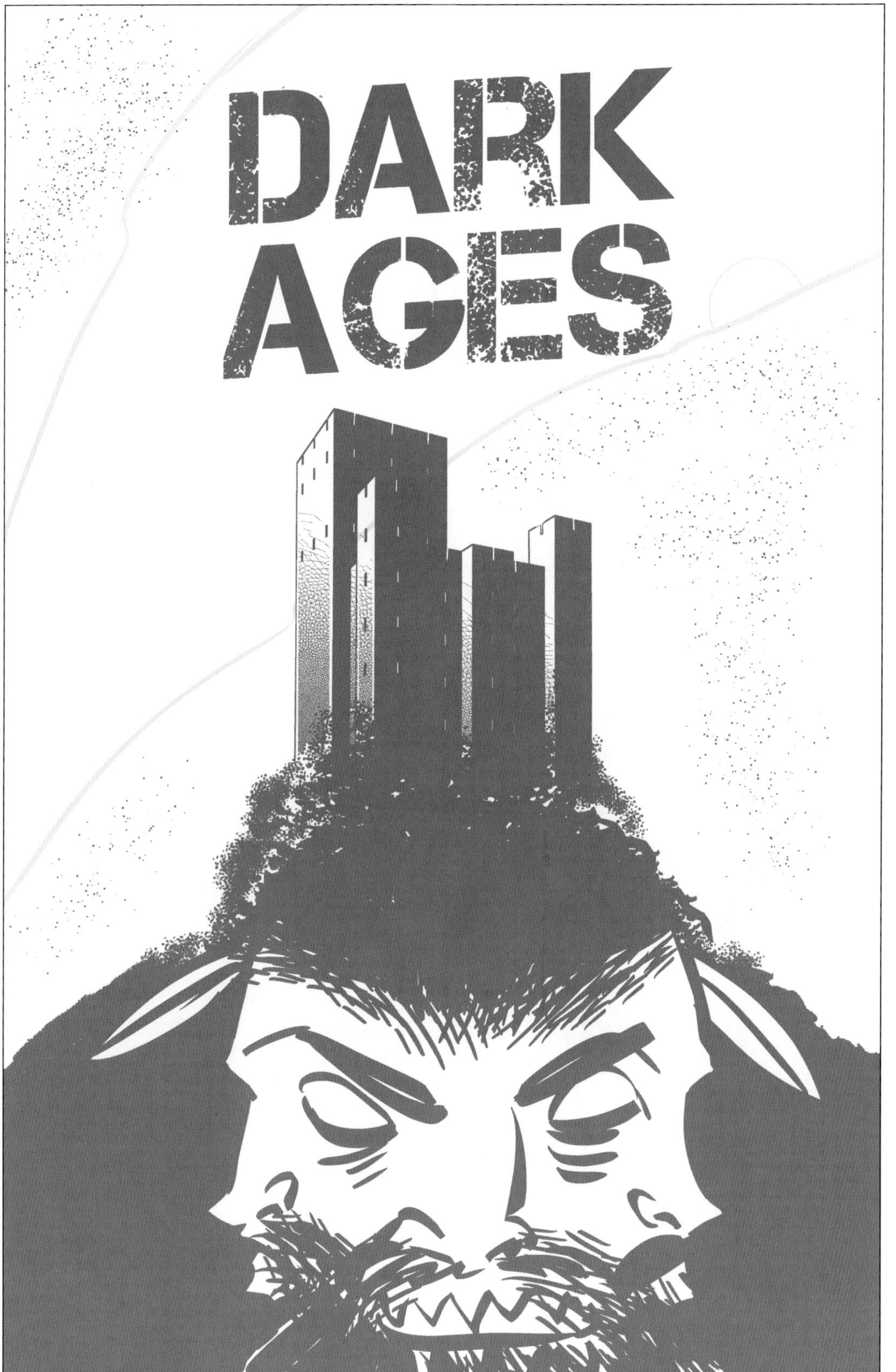
DARK
AGES

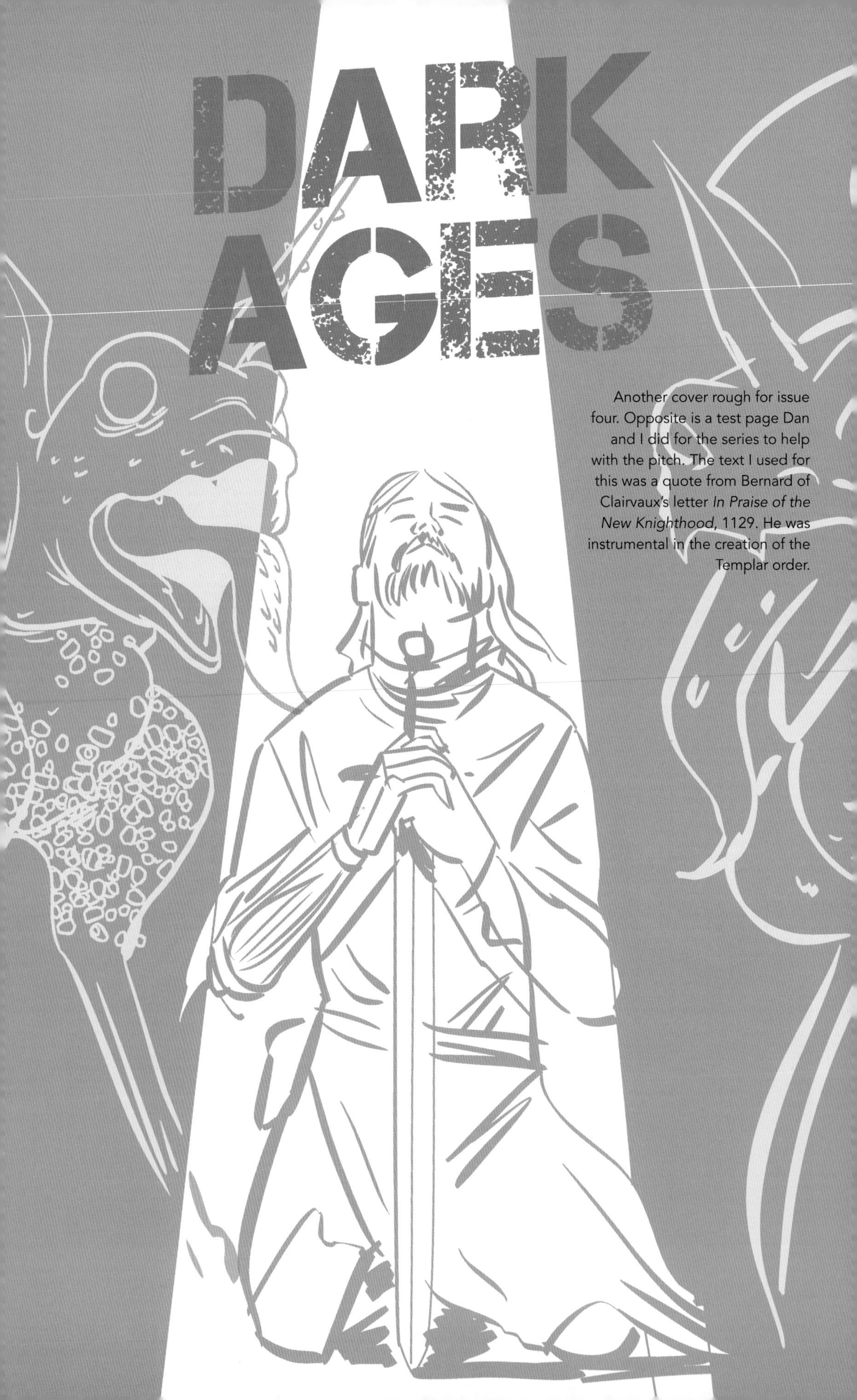
DARK
AGES

Another cover rough for issue four. Opposite is a test page Dan and I did for the series to help with the pitch. The text I used for this was a quote from Bernard of Clairvaux's letter *In Praise of the New Knighthood*, 1129. He was instrumental in the creation of the Templar order.

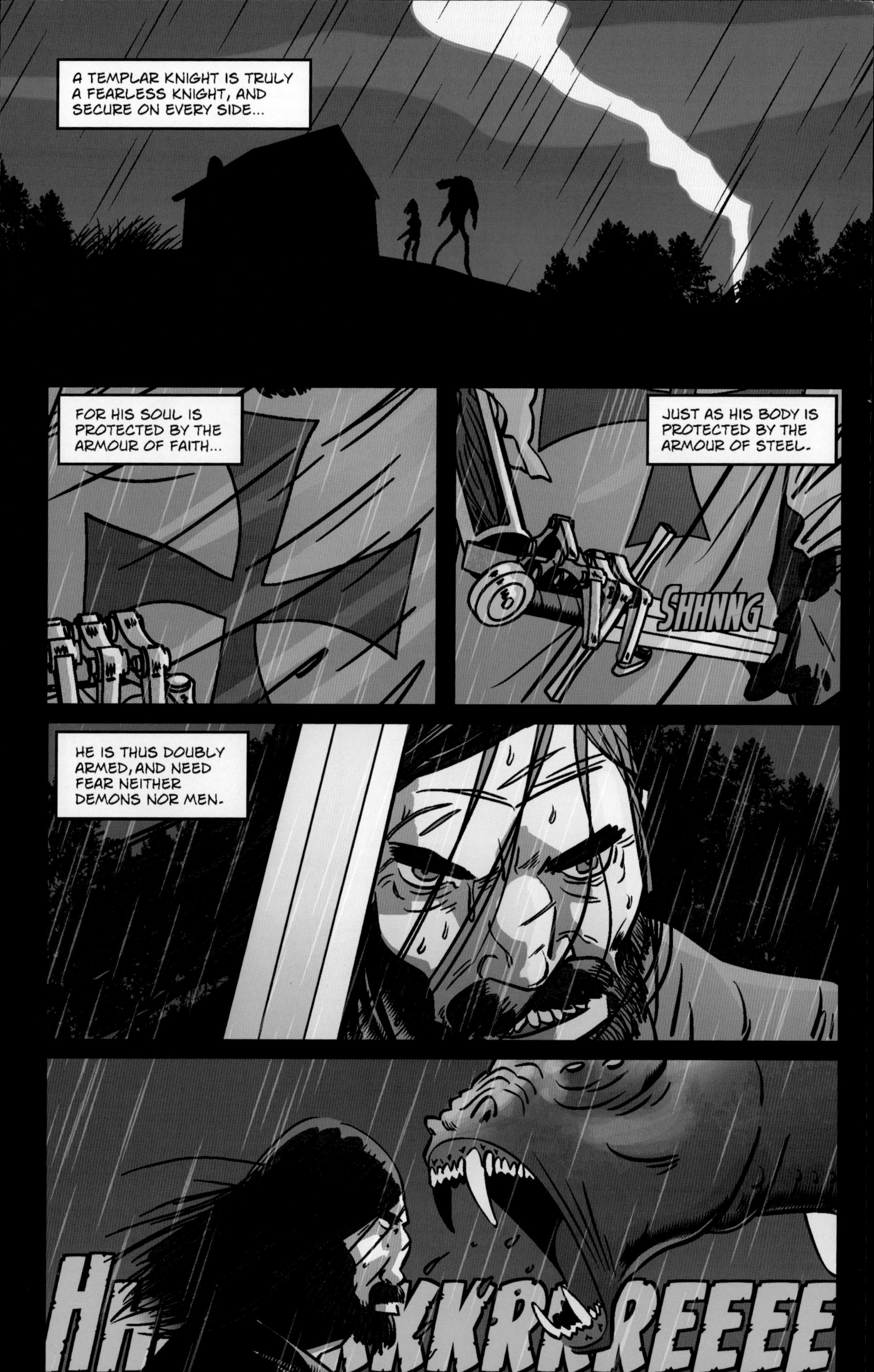
A TEMPLAR KNIGHT IS TRULY A FEARLESS KNIGHT, AND SECURE ON EVERY SIDE...
FOR HIS SOUL IS PROTECTED BY THE ARMOUR OF FAITH...
JUST AS HIS BODY IS PROTECTED BY THE ARMOUR OF STEEL.
SHHNNG
HE IS THUS DOUBLY ARMED, AND NEED FEAR NEITHER DEMONS NOR MEN.

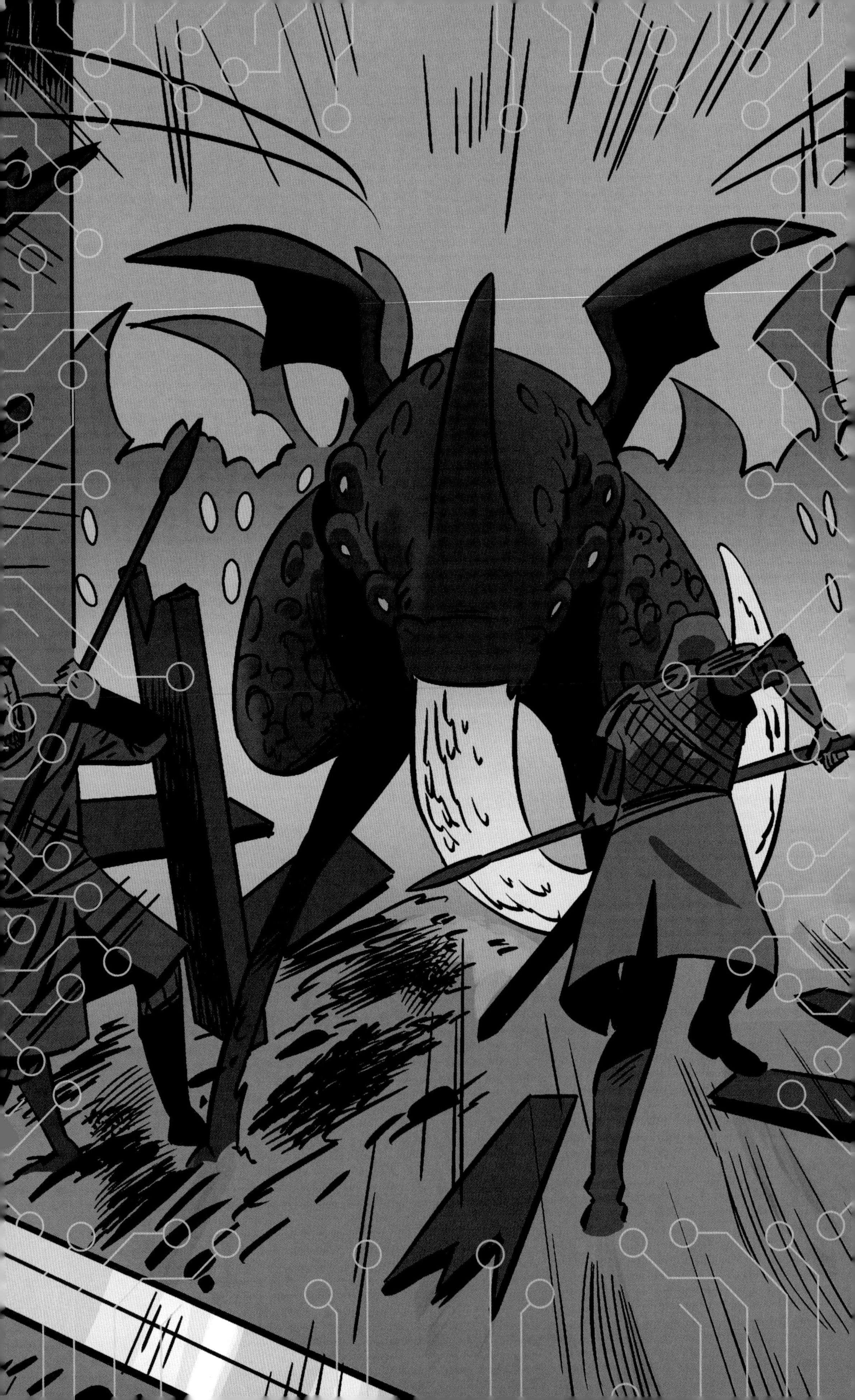

darkhorse originals

"unique creators with unique visions"
—MIKE RICHARDSON, PUBLISHER

BLACKSAD
978-1-59582-393-9 | $29.99

BLACKSAD: A SILENT HELL
978-1-59582-931-3 | $19.99

MIND MGMT
Volume 1: The Manager
978-1-59582-797-5 | $19.99
Volume 2: The Futurist
978-1-61655-198-8 | $19.99

RESET
978-1-61655-003-5 | $15.99

CHERUBS
978-1-59582-984-9 | $19.99

BRODY'S GHOST
Book 1: 978-1-59582-521-6 | $6.99
Book 2: 978-1-59582-665-7 | $6.99
Book 3: 978-1-59582-862-0 | $6.99
Book 4: 978-1-61655-129-2 | $6.99

NINGEN'S NIGHTMARES
978-1-59582-859-0 | $12.99

EVERYBODY GETS IT WRONG! AND OTHER STORIES: DAVID CHELSEA'S 24-HOUR COMICS
978-1-61655-155-1 | $19.99

3 STORY: THE SECRET HISTORY OF THE GIANT MAN
978-1-59582-356-4 | $19.99

365 SAMURAI AND A FEW BOWLS OF RICE
978-1-59582-412-7 | $16.99

THE ADVENTURES OF BLANCHE
978-1-59582-258-1 | $15.99

BEANWORLD
Volume 1: Wahoolazuma!
978-1-59582-240-6 | $19.99
Volume 2: A Gift Comes!
978-1-59582-299-4 | $19.99
Volume 3: Remember Here When You Are There!
978-1-59582-355-7 | $19.99
Volume 3.5: Tales of the Beanworld
978-1-59582-897-2 | $14.99

BLOOD SONG: A SILENT BALLAD
978-1-59582-389-2 | $19.99

THE BOOK OF GRICKLE
978-1-59582-430-1 | $17.99

BUCKO
978-1-59582-973-3 | $19.99

CHANNEL ZERO
978-1-59582-936-8 | $19.99

CHIMICHANGA
978-1-59582-755-5 | $14.99

CITIZEN REX
978-1-59582-556-8 | $19.99

CROSSING THE EMPTY QUARTER AND OTHER STORIES
978-1-59582-388-5 | $24.99

DE:TALES
HC: 978-1-59582-557-5 | $19.99
TPB: 978-1-59307-485-2 | $14.99

EXURBIA
978-1-59582-339-7 | $9.99

FLUFFY
978-1-59307-972-7 | $19.99

GREEN RIVER KILLER
978-1-59582-560-5 | $24.99

INSOMNIA CAFÉ
978-1-59582-357-1 | $14.99

THE MIGHTY SKULLBOY ARMY
Volume 2
978-1-59582-872-9 | $14.99

MILK AND CHEESE: DAIRY PRODUCTS GONE BAD
978-1-59582-805-7 | $19.99

MOTEL ART IMPROVEMENT SERVICE
978-1-59582-550-6 | $19.99

THE NIGHT OF YOUR LIFE
978-1-59582-183-6 | $15.99

NOIR
978-1-59582-358-8 | $12.99

PIXU: THE MARK OF EVIL
978-1-59582-340-3 | $17.99

SACRIFICE
978-1-59582-985-6 | $19.99

SINFEST: VIVA LA RESISTANCE
978-1-59582-424-0 | $14.99

SPEAK OF THE DEVIL
978-1-59582-193-5 | $19.99

UNCLE SILAS
978-1-59582-566-7 | $9.99

DARK HORSE BOOKS

AVAILABLE AT YOUR LOCAL COMICS SHOP OR BOOKSTORE!
To find a comics shop in your area, call 1-888-266-4226

For more information or to order direct:
On the web: DarkHorse.com
E-mail: mailorder@darkhorse.com
Phone: 1-800-862-0052 Mon.–Fri. 9 AM to 5 PM Pacific Time.

Dark Horse Books® and the Dark Horse logo are registered trademarks of Dark Horse Comics, Inc. All rights reserved. (BL 5032)

SCIENCE FICTION
FROM DARK HORSE BOOKS

NEXUS OMNIBUS VOLUME 1

Steve Rude and Mike Baron

A multiple Eisner Award–winning series that defined the careers of acclaimed creators Steve Rude and Mike Baron, *Nexus* is a modern classic. In 2841 Nexus, a godlike figure, acts as judge, jury, and executioner for the vile criminals who appear in his dreams. He claims to kill in self-defense, but why? Where do the visions come from, and where did he get his powers?

ISBN 978-1-61655-034-9 | $24.99

DARK AGES

Dan Abnett and I. N. J. Culbard

1333: The known world is locked in a holy war. As a godless mercenary company slogs across Europe in search of sustenance and coin, they encounter a demonic force born not of hell, but from beyond the stars!

ISBN 978-1-61655-602-0 | $14.99

MASS EFFECT VOLUME 1: REDEMPTION

Mac Walters, John Jackson Miller, and Omar Francia

Collecting the four-issue miniseries, *Mass Effect* Volume 1 features essential developments in the *Mass Effect* gaming saga, plus a special behind-the-scenes section with sketches and more.

ISBN 978-1-59582-481-3 | $16.99

DARK MATTER VOLUME 1: REBIRTH

Joseph Mallozzi, Paul Mullie, and Garry Brown

Sci-fi action from the writers of *Stargate SG-1*! The crew of a derelict spaceship awakens from stasis in the farthest reaches of space. With no recollection of who they are or how they got on board, their only clue is a cargo bay full of weaponry and a destination that is about to become a war zone!

ISBN 978-1-59582-998-6 | $14.99

PARIAH

Aron Warner, Philip Gelatt, and Brett Weldele

Genetically engineered teenage geniuses known as Vitros are labeled a terrorist cell after an explosion at a military weapons lab. The Vitros are rounded up and left on a decrepit satellite orbiting Earth. Now they must band together and use their supergenius abilities to get back to Earth safely.

Volume 1 ISBN 978-1-61655-274-9 | $14.99
Volume 2 ISBN 978-1-61655-275-6 | $14.99

AVAILABLE AT YOUR LOCAL COMICS SHOP OR BOOKSTORE! • To find a comics shop in your area, call **1-888-266-4226.**
For more information or to order direct visit DarkHorse.com or call 1-800-862-0052 Mon.–Fri. 9 AM to 5 PM Pacific Time. Prices and availability subject to change without notice.

DarkHorse.com   Nexus © Mike Baron and Steve Rude. Dark Ages ™ © Dan Abnett and I.N.J. Culbard. Mass Effect © EA International (Studio and Publishing) Ltd. Dark Matter ™ © Dark Horse Comics, Inc. Pariah ™
© Aron Warner. Dark Horse Books® and the Dark Horse logo are registered trademarks of Dark Horse Comics, Inc. All rights reserved. (BL 5041)